WHY POLITICS NEEDS RELIGION

The Place of
Religious Arguments
in the Public Square

Brendan
Sweetman

IVP Academic
An imprint of InterVarsity Press
Downers Grove, Illinois

InterVarsity Press
P.O. Box 1400, Downers Grove, IL 60515-1426
World Wide Web: www.ivpress.com
E-mail: mail@ivpress.com

InterVarsity Press® is the book-publishing division of InterVarsity Christian Fellowship/USA®, a student movement active on campus at hundreds of universities, colleges and schools of nursing in the United States of America, and a member movement of the International Fellowship of Evangelical Students. For information about local and regional activities, write Public Relations Dept., InterVarsity Christian Fellowship/USA, 6400 Schroeder Rd., P.O. Box 7895, Madison, WI 53707-7895, or visit the IVCF website at <www.intervarsity.org>.

Design: Cindy Kiple
Images: Julie Nicholls/CORBIS

ISBN-10: 0-8308-2842-7
ISBN-13: 978-0-8308-2842-5

Printed in the United States of America ∞

Library of Congress Cataloging-in-Publication Data

Sweetman, Brendan.
  Why politics needs religion: the place of religious arguments in
  the public square/Brendan Sweetman
      p. cm
  Includes bibliographical references and index.
  ISBN-13: 978-0-8308-2842-5 (pbk.: alk paper)
  ISBN-10: 0-8308-2842-7 (pbk.: alk paper)
  1. Religion and politics. I. Title.
  BL65.P7S94 2006
  201'.72—dc22
                                                                    2006013030

| P | 18 | 17 | 16 | 15 | 14 | 13 | 12 | 11 | 10 | 9 | 8 | 7 | 6 | 5 | 4 | 3 | 2 | 1 |
| Y | 21 | 20 | 19 | 18 | 17 | 16 | 15 | 14 | 13 | 12 | 11 | 10 | 09 | 08 | 07 | 06 |

For Margaret

Contents

Acknowledgments

I am indebted to many people for their generous assistance and support during my work on this book. I would like especially to thank Edward Furton, who read the whole manuscript in different drafts and offered numerous valuable suggestions, constructive criticism and support for the project. I have had many stimulating discussions about matters concerning religion and politics over the years with my colleague at Rockhurst University, Curtis Hancock. His advice and encouragement on this project have been indispensable. Fr. Bill LaCroix and Bill Stancil, also my colleagues at Rockhurst, read the manuscript and offered valuable suggestions and improvements. James Boettcher, Doug Geivett, Robert Kraynak, Timothy McDonald, Margaret Sweetman, Paul Weithman and Dallas Willard all offered insightful critical commentary on various parts of the argument. I am grateful also to Rockhurst University for a presidential summer grant to support work on parts of the book.

I have presented several of the themes of the book at various universities and conferences in the last few years, including at the Society of Christian Philosophers, the American Maritain Association, the Evangelical Philosophical Society, and the Lilly Fellows National Research Conference. I am grateful to all who took part in these sessions for broadening my knowledge of the subject with their incisive comments and questions. Any errors that remain are, of course, my own.

I have occasionally used a phrase or two, sometimes a few paragraphs, from material I have published previously. I am grateful to the editors of *Philosophia Christi, American Catholic Philosophical Quarterly* and Rockhurst University Press for granting permission.

I wish to thank Dr. Gary Deddo and his excellent staff at InterVarsity Press for their patience and encouragement and for making the publishing process as smooth as possible.

I am indebted to my agent, Steve Laube, for his support of the project and for his mix of business acumen tempered by Christian spirit!

Finally, my greatest thanks goes to my wife, Margaret, and to my sons, Brendan, John and Ciaran, without whose unfailing support and encouragement this book would not have been possible.

Introduction

A New Perspective on Religion and Politics

One day in the late 1980s, as a young graduate student coming home from the university campus, I was waiting for the bus in downtown Los Angeles when I was approached by two homeless women who were begging beside the bus stop on what was a bitterly cold night. They also looked as if they were bedding down for the night on the footpath. I was much moved by their plight, and gave them all I had in my wallet at the time, which was only about $20.00. But as I traveled home on the bus, I thought to myself, *there is something sadly wrong with the way we have structured society, for it is morally wrong that people should have to live like that. It is not consistent with God's plan for humanity.* This was not a sudden realization for me, but was a view I had held for some time about the homeless. It kept coming back to me the next morning, prompting me to write to the mayor of Los Angeles to urge him to more aggressively promote local programs aimed at helping the homeless. It was not the first time that I had written to government officials on this matter, and so I had my argument ready. My main point in my letter was that each person has a basic dignity and integrity by virtue of the fact that he or she is a child of God, and being homeless compromises one's dignity on a number of levels. My letter also implied a further argument: that God created the universe and all life, and has a moral plan for humanity.

I showed my letter to a group of college friends before mailing it. Several of them cautioned me not to try to convince the mayor with this particular argument in favor of helping the homeless because it was a "religious" argument. And religious arguments were simply not appropriate in politics, some of my friends held; others thought that while they might be appropriate there was a cultural bias against them, and the mayor would find it politically easy to dismiss any such argument. I was young and somewhat intellectually naive in those days and did not know what to make of this. I did not know quite how to argue my view, how to proceed with my public argument, for I also wanted to send my letter to the newspapers. (In the end I sent it only to the mayor.)

On another occasion, a friend of mine, then a young assistant professor of theology at a small college, was taking part in a panel discussion on the topic of abortion at a nearby large secular university, but before a largely religious audience. He was asked by an audience member about a recent case where a woman, through fertility drugs, had become pregnant with multiple embryos. There was discussion at the time about whether it would be right for her to abort some of them (which she later did). The person in the audience asked my friend if it would be moral to do so. He replied that it would not be because each embryo has a soul, and is therefore a human being, and has a right to life. This was a nice, succinct religious argument against abortion, and many present, probably a large majority, agreed with it. Immediately, though, he was shot down by two of his fellow panelists, one of whom was an atheist, but the other was a theologian. Why? Because he had given a "religious" argument against abortion. Their view was that while one could hold this kind of argument privately, could advocate it in one's private life and circle of family and friends perhaps, one should not offer this "religious" argument as a contribution to public policy debates. My friend inquired as to what exactly was wrong with presenting a "religious" argument in public political discussions and wondered also if it would be okay to present a secular argument in these discussions. Listening from the audience, I found the view of one of the panelists especially irritating because he went on to say that since the main argument against abortion is a religious argument, and since we should not introduce religious arguments into politics, then there is no good argument against legalizing abortion in a secular society! This is a view we hear all the time now, not just on the topic of abortion, but on many other moral and social issues as well.

I well remember the discussion that followed. It was often heated, and quite confusing, yet it left what I call the secularist position on this matter not looking quite as obviously true as some panel members had initially thought. In fact, the panelists who were against using religious arguments in public made two moves that I would later come to recognize as unsatisfactory ways of excluding religious belief from politics: they offered what I thought were rather smug, rather emotional rejections of religion, rather than actual substantive reasons that might give the audience pause; and anytime anyone pressed them for these reasons, they hid behind the "no-establishment clause" of the First Amendment to the U.S. Constitution rather than addressing the general *moral* question as to whether religious arguments should have a role in political debates. But those present that day who thought that religion *had* a place in public life were also confused, and worried. This was because they realized that although they believed their religious views to be true, and also, on some topics at least, regarded them as very important, they did not quite know how to deal with somebody who came from a different religion or a different worldview, especially since they were acutely conscious of living in a pluralist society. So overall the discussion did not achieve much, other than to make everyone realize that this is not only a vitally important but also a quite complex matter.

This book is an attempt to show that the project to remove or restrict religion from politics, while very strongly supported by many in our society, is in fact based on a misunderstanding of and confusion over some basic ideas concerning modern pluralism. I argue that it is quite appropriate to introduce religious arguments into politics in a liberal democratic society. My approach to this question will be through the concept of a worldview, which I will examine in detail. I argue that everyone has a worldview, that secularism is a major worldview in contemporary America, and that religious belief is a more reasonable worldview than secularism. Once one comes to appreciate these points, the debate about excluding religious arguments from politics is completely changed. Many of the arguments offered for excluding religion from politics will be seen to be flawed arguments. I also hold that democratic politics needs religion if it is to be truly democratic, concerned with fairness among worldviews, equality and a vigorous public discussion. No democratic society, I contend, can seek to exclude from the public debate over the momentous issues of the day any worldview that is a major player in the lives of many who live in that society.

The examples referred to above, and many others that many readers could probably supply from their own experiences, highlight a problem in our culture—that it is regarded as bad form or somehow in bad taste to refer to one's religious beliefs or to offer arguments that appeal to religion in some way in the public square. This is true even when we are talking about momentous issues that are the subject of national debate and that would have a significant effect on society, such as abortion, euthanasia, health care policy, the plight of the homeless, capital punishment, gay marriage and the morality of war. It is now almost the default view in modern Western culture, the culture of democratic pluralism, that one's religion should be a private matter and should make no contribution to public debates on political, moral or social questions. Many readers will likely identify with the experiences mentioned above, and some will have had similar experiences themselves. Faced with this "official," establishment reaction to any appeal to one's religious beliefs in politics, some religious believers may feel a little bit marginalized from the political discussion, especially in contemporary American society, feeling perhaps as if they do not quite belong in that discussion, as if there is something "wrong" with their views. This is especially true in certain areas of life, such as in debates that take place in political parties, the universities, the courts and the media. It is not easy to see what is supposed to be wrong with an appeal to religious arguments, but there is an unmistakable presumption that there is *something* wrong with them, that one should in general keep quiet about one's religious views in political discussions.

Some people might object that it is a bit far-fetched to say that religion is becoming marginalized in modern societies—we are not just talking about America here, for this phenomenon is now widespread in western Europe as well. Religion, they will claim, still has a huge influence, perhaps too much of an influence, on many aspects of our culture. Some may point to the election results of 2004 as evidence that the religious worldview is becoming dominant politically, and is therefore actually strengthening its grip on our culture for the foreseeable future. From one point of view this is true, simply because, given that such a large percentage of the population is religious, the religious worldview is bound to have *some* influence in many areas of society. Yet despite the fact that the vast majority of people are religious believers in this country, it is still the default view that religion should have no place in public life. This default view has been promoted widely in our culture, and I think there can be no doubt that it has curbed the influence of religion quite significantly and will continue to do so in the future. In addition, as I have already mentioned, this is a trend in most Western societies: witness the decision of the leaders of the European Union to propose a new European constitution in 2003 that contained no reference to God or the Christian heritage in shaping the values embodied in that constitution.

I need to underscore an important distinction at the outset. Our concern in this book is not with constitutional or legal matters in the United States regarding religion and politics, but with the *moral* (or philosophical) question of what role one's worldview (religious or secularist) can legitimately play in politics in a democratic, pluralist society. In other words, given that we accept the basic principles of the democratic system of government, I am interested in asking if it is morally acceptable for the religious worldview to have a role in politics. If, say, an individual wished to argue against euthanasia at a public meeting, would she be doing something wrong if she were to refer to her religious beliefs as part of her case against euthanasia? If an individual wanted to write to the newspapers to protest against capital punishment, would it be wrong for him to appeal to his religious beliefs in his argument? More generally, is it somehow immoral to introduce one's religious ideas, beliefs and values into public debates about momentous issues, debates that normally take place in public media (newspapers and TV), political parties, universities, town hall meetings, advocacy groups, churches, books and magazines, public lectures and so on? And, perhaps most important of all, is it wrong to vote based on one's religious beliefs? (Or based on one's secularist beliefs?)

I am only secondarily interested in the *legal* question of what role religious beliefs can have in a particular society, say U.S. society, according to that country's constitution and laws. The moral question is obviously the main question, the question one needs to look at first before one deals with the legal question, just as one must first identify the moral issues surrounding stealing before one passes laws about stealing. Ideally, the answer to the legal question depends upon the answer to the moral question. If one wishes to argue rationally and morally that religion should have no place in public life, one cannot simply appeal to the authority of a particular document (the U.S. Constitution, say) to support this controversial and far-reaching claim. This would be a kind of constitutional fundamentalism, where one appeals to the authority of a text, but gives no thought to whether the values embodied in the text are actually true or how they are justified or whether they are still appropriate for our changing society. Unfortunately, in U.S. society many often seem willing to allow the debate over the meaning of the Constitution to serve as a substitute for the moral debate, to be willing to just settle for the constitutional debate, and to ignore the moral issues altogether.

There are many different ways of characterizing the contemporary world: as a global village, as a cosmopolitan society, as a world pursuing democratic values, as being in thrall to consumerism and mass communications, as the triumph of individualism and so forth. But one of the most interesting ways to describe it is as *a world of ideas*. Today, more than ever before in history, in part due to mass communications, but also due to the spread of democracy and the rise of pluralism, we are awash in a sea of ideas, images, political claims, fashion statements, moral arguments and ideologies. They come to us from every place: religion, secularism, political parties, movies, television news programs, radio talk shows, books, magazines, pop music, interest groups, bumper stickers, mass culture and the Internet. Sometimes ideas from these different sources clash with each other; sometimes they overlap; often they introduce some new fashion, or start some new trend that influences people's thinking and behavior. Yet many people find so many diverse, complex and often ideologically inspired views from so many different sources very difficult to handle; further, the plethora of ideas coming at us from all angles has contributed to much intellectual, moral and political confusion in modern society.

That is why it is essential to begin our discussion in this book with an introduction to the concept and definition of a *worldview*, in which we consider the overall structure of a worldview, the rationality of worldviews, the relationship of worldviews to religion, and how all worldviews have similar structures, including the worldviews of religious belief and of secularism. An analysis of the concept of a worldview is necessary in the debate about whether religious arguments should have a role in politics because all of our ideas, beliefs and values represent different and often conflicting worldviews, something that is often overlooked in the confusion of modern discourse. I want to encourage every reader interested in the questions raised by this book to recognize that your beliefs and values, and the outlook and lifestyles these beliefs and values support, are all fundamentally part of your worldview. This point might seem so obvious that it almost goes without saying, but recent polls on this matter have shown that while the vast majority of American adults agree that they have a philosophy of life or rules that guide their daily lives, nevertheless most religious and lay leaders in America's churches have little or no understanding of the nature, structure and defense of their worldview.[1] The same is true, I contend, for many of our political and civic leaders, and across the population as a whole.

Every time we make a moral judgment, or make a claim about the nature of reality, or about what sort of beings human beings are, or about whether God exists, or about the nature of the good life, or about which political system is the best, or about whether a law should be passed regarding such and such, we are appealing to our worldview. We may not be aware that this is what we are doing, of course; nor may we be making a rationally defensible appeal to a worldview. Indeed, our worldview might not even be rational. Also, we might not even appreciate that we hold a worldview! Nevertheless, whenever we make a claim relating to these kinds of topics, we are committing to a worldview, are involved in a worldview, are living according to a worldview. And so an overall grasp of the concept of a worldview is essential to understand the political dynamics of modern pluralism. I contend that we cannot understand the philosophical and political issues concerning religion and politics unless we understand the concept of a worldview, and so our first chapter will take up this topic.

Two of the main categories of worldviews are religious worldviews and secularist worldviews. After our discussion of the concept of a worldview in general, I will show that secularism is a serious and influential worldview in the modern world and that it plays a significant role in the debate in the public square. This is not as controversial a claim to make today as it once was. We see many references today to secularism as a worldview, many individuals now identify themselves as secularists (rather than atheists), and there are even various groups established to promote secularism politically. Secularism, broadly understood, is the view that all of reality is physical, consisting of some configuration of matter and energy, and that everything that exists either currently has a scientific explanation or will have a scientific explanation in the future. The universe is regarded as a random occurrence, as is the appearance and nature of life on earth. Thus, secularism is not simply the negative claim that there is no God or that there is no soul; rather, these claims are supposed to follow from its positive theses. Like other worldviews, especially religious ones, secularism contains beliefs about the

---

[1]The results of recent surveys on people's religious beliefs are reported and analyzed in George Gallup Jr. and D. Michael Lindsay, *The Gallup Guide: Reality Check for 21st Century Churches* (Loveland, Colo.: Group Publishing, 2002). See also the various polls relating to religious belief carried out by George Barna at <http://www.barna.org>. These polls show that people have little understanding of the notion of a worldview.

nature of reality, the nature of the human person and the nature of morality. And many of these beliefs have political implications.

This view is contrasted with the religious worldview, which I wish to understand in this book only in a quite general sense. I am talking about that view of the world that is based around some or all of the following types of beliefs: belief in a transcendent, unseen, sacred realm; belief in God (or a Supreme Reality or Realities); belief that God (or the Supreme Reality or Realities) created the universe and all life; that human beings consist of body and soul; that the soul can exist after death; that human beings differ in kind from other animals; that human beings have free will; that there is an objective moral order and so forth. The religious view of the world, understood in this general sense, is quite familiar to us. But the secularist worldview is not quite so familiar, with the consequence that sometimes we do not sufficiently appreciate that secularism *is* a worldview, and that it is clearly operating in the moral and political arena.

One of the confusions that has gotten us into our present state is that, because we do not appreciate the significance of the concept of a worldview for understanding the modern pluralist state, we have been slow to acknowledge that secularism is a worldview in itself, and this has hampered us from analyzing fairly the various moral arguments for excluding religious belief from politics. Indeed most of the discussion of religion and politics in recent years, especially in the United States, suffers from a failure to appreciate the significance of the fact that secularism too is a worldview. When we appreciate that secularism is a worldview we are less likely to confuse secularism with "neutral reason" and to mistakenly think that it is possible for the public square to be neutral toward competing worldviews. In short, once we understand what is involved in holding a worldview and we begin to look upon secularism as a worldview in itself, it changes everything, especially our understanding of the role of religion in politics.

One of the other main arguments of the book is that all worldviews are *faiths* (in the sense that they hold some beliefs for which they do not have conclusive evidence or proof), that a faith must be *rational* in order to be taken seriously, especially in politics, and that the religious view of the world in general is a rational faith, and more rational than secularism. I develop this argument to show that eight of the major arguments proposed by liberal political philosophers for excluding (or seriously restricting) religious beliefs from politics must all be rejected. I argue that in a modern pluralist state religious arguments have a legitimate role in politics, though I do support some restrictions on the types of religious beliefs one can appropriately introduce into the political arena (these restrictions will also apply to secularist beliefs). So I will not be arguing that my own worldview, which is that of Christianity (specifically Catholic Christianity), should be the official worldview of the state or that the laws of the land should be based on beliefs and values specific to Christianity. Secularists too, I argue, cannot call for a secularist state for a secularist society. Nevertheless, I will propose that some significant religious beliefs have a legitimate place in public political discussion and that politics needs religion because the religious view of the world can make valuable, indeed profound, contributions to modern debates concerning a host of issues. I will try to illustrate that religion can enrich discussion, guide public policy and even be the basis for some laws. The overall argument I present is compatible, I believe, with a variety of different worldviews, religious and secularist, as long as they accept some version of the basic principles of democracy (which I understand as a political theory based on popular sovereignty and a commitment to some account of democratic values, such as freedom, equality and justice). Nevertheless, my position in this book goes against the standard view of most liberal political theorists today (e.g., John Rawls, Robert Audi, Thomas Nagel, Kent Greenawalt, among many others), who hold that religious beliefs should have little or no role in politics.

Some readers, especially American readers, might be surprised that I am emphasizing the rationality of religious belief and that I will be drawing significant attention to the rationality of religious belief throughout the book. This is unfortunate but is the result of a long history in the United States, perhaps due initially to the influence of various forms of Protestantism, of over-emphasizing the view that religious belief is a matter of faith, not in the sense identified above, but in the sense that religious beliefs are nonrational, or are outside of reason, or are private beliefs, or something along these lines. Yet this way of talking about one's religion, which is common to all religious denominations, is misleading, and it can lead to the conclusion that religion cannot be taken seriously when it comes to dealing with substantive matters of legal, social and public policy. This has become a mainstream view in the United States, especially among the intelligentsia, the educated elites and the media, and it is now a view in which many young people are indoctrinated. Indeed, many religious believers themselves in all denominations have been thoroughly seduced by the view that religion is a matter of faith, and so has no role in politics, should not interfere in politics, cannot contribute anything valuable to politics. In the United States in particular, we need to get away from the culture of thinking of religious belief purely as a nonrational, even irrational, faith, based mostly on appeals to authority. I will try to show that the religious view of the world in general has nothing to fear from rational debate and scrutiny (although some specific religious beliefs in various religions might not survive rational scrutiny, just as many secularist beliefs surely would not). In fact, religious believers should positively welcome rational scrutiny as reasonable people seeking the truth and trying to build a better society.

I will not, of course, be arguing that all religious beliefs are rational, just as we would not think that all secularist beliefs are rational. Nor do I think that all religious beliefs have a legitimate role to play in the public square. But I will argue that a general set of religious beliefs are rational and so do have a role to play. These beliefs will pertain in particular to political discussions in our culture today about many issues, for example, on abortion, euthanasia, social welfare policy, workers rights, certain business practices, exploitation, the nature of the family and the morality of war. Many of our moral conflicts today concern these and related topics. And I will argue that often disputes over these matters come down to a difference of worldview—usually religious versus secularist—and that the religious worldview has a quite legitimate role in the public discussion. I will not be arguing that arguments based on appeal to any kind of religious authority have a place in public political debate, but this restriction will not be sufficient to rule all religious arguments out of politics. In short, my arguments will appeal to reason and evidence, and not to revealed faith or religious authority.

I would like to ask each reader of this book, especially if you are a religious believer, but even if you are a secularist, to think about whether you would consider yourself to be a reasonable person! And do you think that the worldview to which you subscribe and by which you largely regulate your life (and perhaps your family's life) is reasonable? And if it is, what role can it legitimately play in political debates? I believe that most people interested in the debate between worldviews in a pluralist democracy (and of course those who are reading this book!) are reasonable people and that significant parts of their worldviews are reasonable. Therefore, the question of what role one's worldview should play in politics is a very live issue. The book is aimed at encouraging reasonable people to look at the role of religion in politics in a new way—through the concept of a worldview—a way that may seem quite foreign initially, especially when contrasted with the current approach in our society, where the discussion is usually dominated by the much narrower question of what the First Amendment to the U.S. Constitution says about religion and how this amendment should be interpreted and implemented.

The arguments of this book will appear to some readers as unusual, even bold and probably controversial. There seems little doubt that they will be provocative! They go against what has been called the standard approach[2] in contemporary intellectual life (especially in contemporary philosophy), which is very sure of its attempt to exclude religious beliefs from the political arena. Because of its initial strangeness my position may be challenged by some religious believers, as well as by secularists and atheists, though I suspect that average Americans will be much more amenable to my thesis than perhaps the educated, liberal, largely secular class. Nevertheless, I believe my arguments are reasonable, and I have tried to explain them clearly and to defend them. I believe that my overall thesis has profound implications for the role of religious belief in politics; it can be used to lessen the confusion surrounding this complex topic and, hopefully, to deepen our understanding of some of the controversies surrounding these matters in Western societies, especially U.S. society. My hope is that the book will encourage readers to think "outside the box" on the importance of the concept of a worldview for clarifying the relationship between religion and secularism, and so for the role of religion in politics. Thinking from this new perspective is rare today, and also quite difficult given the general confusion generated by the constitutional and legal position in U.S. society. Moreover, nobody denies that the questions and difficulties we are discussing in this book are very complex and have no obvious, quick answers. But thinking outside the box on these matters may help us navigate our way more clearly through the myriad arguments and issues involved. It might even possibly change the way we think about religion and politics in the future.

Most of the current philosophical work on religion and politics argues that religious beliefs should either have no role in politics or that they should be seriously restricted in politics. More worrying is the fact that there is little

---

[2]See Paul Weithman, *Religion and the Obligations of Citizenship* (New York: Cambridge University Press, 2002), pp. 6-9.

discussion actually devoted to a careful analysis of the moral question; there are only a handful of books on this topic, usually in the disciplines of philosophy and legal theory, hardly any in theology or political science. Perhaps understandably, there is a plethora of interesting books on the constitutional or legal question and its application to U.S. society. I hope to show, however, that the constitutional question, though important, is ultimately secondary, and that it cannot be properly answered until the moral question has been addressed. Unfortunately, many people writing on this topic today seem to have a quite superficial view of religious belief in general, often accompanied by a lack of knowledge about the history of religious thinking, and this may be responsible for a more general failure to appreciate the fundamental questions concerning religion and politics. Sadly, there is sometimes an animus on the part of some toward religious arguments, especially on moral issues, as well as toward particular religious figures and groups. This animus may sometimes blind people and make it harder for them to move outside the box, and look at the deeper issues: that the concept of a worldview is essential to an understanding of democratic pluralism; the moral question, instead of the legal question; the significance of secularism as a worldview in itself; what it means to hold a "reasonable" position; the difficulties of handling competing worldviews in the same state; and how democracy itself must be justified.

After briefly describing two major worldviews in contemporary U.S. society as examples to work with—Christianity and secularism—the first chapter describes the overall structure of a worldview, the features that are common to all those worldviews with which we are concerned, especially those at the center of the contemporary debate in America concerning matters of religion, secularism and politics. Here I give special attention to the notion of "faith" and the role it plays in a worldview. This discussion then serves as the foundation for the argument in chapter two that secularism is an influential worldview in itself and that it has a similar structure to the religious worldview. Chapter three explains the religious worldview in detail and also takes up the issue of what we mean when we describe a belief as "religious"; I also consider the question of whether the religious worldview is a *reasonable* worldview and argue that reasonable religious beliefs can be introduced into politics.

In chapters four and five I turn to some specific arguments for excluding or seriously restricting religious arguments in politics. I critically analyze eight main arguments, including the arguments that religious beliefs are not fully rational, that "secular reason" is neutral toward religion, that religious beliefs are dangerous (but secularism is benign), that religious beliefs should not be forced by law on those who do not think they are true, and that religious beliefs must be excluded according to the Constitution, among other arguments. These arguments are offered by a variety of people, including philosophers and legal thinkers. They are also extremely popular among the establishment and intelligentsia, and also among the media; consequently they have become more influential in popular culture.

In chapters six and seven I present my own views on what kinds of religious beliefs we might actually bring into the public square in a modern, democratic state. These chapters discuss the views of influential political philosopher John Rawls, the relationship between religion and democracy, and they examine what role religion can play in political issues relating to minority rights, pastors and churches, voting, hiring, judicial decisions and decisions made by politicians. In chapter seven, I also take time to consider a fictional example as a means of illustrating some of my arguments and responding to objections. I also look at the very intriguing implications of my view for the terminology of the religion-politics debate.

Finally, in the last chapter, I turn to reflect on American society in the light of my earlier arguments. After a brief critical overview of the particular form of pluralism prevalent in U.S. society, which is conceived of as secular, liberal and democratic, I then apply my arguments to several controversial issues in American life, including school prayer, euthanasia and other moral issues, the display of traditional religious symbols in public places, and the pervasive presence of moral relativism in American life. I try to illustrate how what I call the "rhetoric of relativism" serves as a substitute for moral argument in our current moral discourse, which is nowadays more about style than substance. The rhetoric of relativism further prevents us from seeing the proper relationship between religion and politics in a democratic state.

The book is aimed at the general reader and not at philosophers, scholars or specialists on the topic. It should be of interest both to those who believe that religious arguments have a legitimate role in politics and to those who think that religion should be restricted in political life, as well as to those who are unsure or undecided on the topic. It may have special interest for pastors, theologians and students of theology, politicians, teachers, social workers, judges, lawyers, for those who work in public life, as well as for all those with a general interest in the subject. Although I have engaged the most important views and thinkers on this topic, I have tried hard not to overburden the discussion with overly technical debates or terminology, and I have kept many of the scholarly references to the footnotes. I have tried to avoid distracting readers with the fine points of scholarly detail, yet at the same time making sure that I have fully discussed the substantive issues in a responsible way, while being fair to those who disagree with my views. I have tried to produce a readable, interesting book, rather than a highly specialized, heavily nuanced tome. My general aim is to present a new perspective on the issue of religion in politics, one that is, I believe, interesting, provocative and original. If I can stimulate further informed reflection in those who, like me, find this topic fascinating and vitally important in the modern world, then I will feel that I have succeeded.

For on at least one issue there *is* general agreement: the topic of religion and politics is one of the topics of our times.

1

Understanding Worldviews

We saw in the introduction that one of the defining but often overlooked features of modern society, especially when we are dealing with matters of culture, morality, politics and law, is that it is a *world of ideas*. Of course, there are many different ways to try to understand modern society, but one of the more interesting ways from the point of view of pluralism is to see it as a society that is constantly being shaped by competing ideas, beliefs and values. This is a point to which we often don't pay enough attention, although it is before our eyes now more than ever before. We are often inclined to tune out the many ideas and value judgments that are coming at us from all angles. This is a natural reaction in all of us. Perhaps it is also an attractive option because it helps us avoid dealing with the challenge of pluralism. It is not just that we find different worldviews and beliefs confusing and often hard to understand and keep distinct from each other, we also may find them upsetting because they highlight the fact that there are many people out there who do not agree with us on so many of the matters we find most important. Yet we must face this challenge very directly if we are to deal with the relationship of religion to politics in a democratic society, and if we are to appreciate the debate between religion and secularism.

What I want to encourage us to do from the point of view of understanding the role of religion in democratic politics is to start thinking of cultural, political and social debates in terms of worldviews. It is very helpful to realize that all of the varied and often competing ideas with which we are constantly being bombarded are best organized and understood from the standpoint of the *worldviews* the ideas express, and within which these ideas are supposed to get their rational support. If we simply consider an idea itself, or perhaps a moral claim, or maybe a political argument in isolation from the worldview of which it is a part, one is almost always ignoring the significant underlying assumptions and beliefs that generate that idea and on which its legitimacy rests. And an understanding of these assumptions is essential in order to grasp the complete moral, religious and political story in our society. I would like to try to bring some order and clarity to the widespread confusion over these matters by proposing a strategy for understanding worldviews, a strategy that we can then employ to help clarify how the debate between worldviews in a pluralist democracy should be conducted, especially as that debate concerns religion and secularism.

In our discussion of worldviews, we will be mostly concerned with the worldviews of the main world religions (especially Christianity) and of secularism, since these are the main competing philosophies of life in modern culture. But what we have to say will apply to all worldviews. In this chapter, I will show that all worldviews have a similar structure, a set of features in common that allow us to describe them as worldviews. I will concentrate on describing this *formal structure* of a worldview, a structure that is common to all those worldviews with which we are concerned, especially those at the center of the contemporary debate in America, and most Western societies, concerning matters of religion, secularism and politics. We are not as interested for the moment in the actual *content* (the beliefs, principles, values, practices and so on) of any particular worldview, except insofar as appeal to these will help us illustrate the points we are making about the formal structure of worldviews. (I will occasionally use the phrases "philosophy of life" and "view of the world" as synonyms for "worldview" for the purposes of literary variety.[1])

Worldviews: The Center and the Outer Edges

Worldviews can be quite complicated to break down into their component parts, and so I would like to begin by first distinguishing between what we might call the outer edges of a worldview (where we would look at its theoretical justification and structure) and the center of a worldview (where we would look at its practice). This is mostly a formal distinction, but an important one. The center of the worldview might be said to contain those beliefs

---

[1]The German word *Weltanschauung* is sometimes used to refer to a worldview; this term is usually intended to emphasize the practical rather than the theoretical beliefs and attitudes of the holder of the worldview. The philosopher Immanuel Kant appears to have been the first to use the German term, in his *Critique of Judgment* (1790).

that are closest to the actions of the holder of the worldview, that immediately motivate his behavior. One could say that this is where he is closest to his worldview. This is where he would immediately recognize his worldview when it is being talked about, notice that its features apply to him, that this is the worldview he lives by and so forth. The outer edges of the worldview refer to the philosophical justification, theoretical development and overall structure of the worldview. This area will often be more abstract and remote than the center where the beliefs are more practically orientated and relate directly to one's behavior.

For example, a Christian might not immediately appreciate the fact that her religion teaches that human beings are not completely physical beings and that human beings differ in kind, not just in degree, from other species, although these are key foundational beliefs of her philosophy of life. But suppose she fasts every year for a few days to raise money for a local church charity. She would probably recognize immediately that the belief that personal sacrifice is edifying is part of her philosophy of life. The first belief is more at the outer edges, whereas the second belief is more toward the center of her worldview, more in the area where she lives and practices her worldview. Similarly, a secularist might not immediately acknowledge the claim that science can explain all of reality, even though it is a key foundational belief of his view of the world, but say he believes that, when it comes to moral values, human beings are really on their own and must choose values without any guide from God or religion. He struggles with moral values at the center of his worldview, where he lives and practices it. Some people might not even recognize their worldview when presented with a detailed discussion of its theoretical structure! Of course, some worldviews have large, complex structures (e.g., Judaism) and some do not (e.g., Ethical Culture). And some followers of a worldview know little or nothing about the structure of the worldview, but mainly follow those who do know about its structure! Some followers of a worldview are on its periphery in terms of understanding its main beliefs, in terms of keeping close attention to those who promote it and in terms of being concerned about its rationality and consistency; others are close adherents to their worldview in terms of all of these matters.

This distinction is important, however, because it will no doubt be the case that many members of a worldview (perhaps the majority) will have little or no knowledge of the outer edges of their worldviews. This means they will be unable to justify their philosophy of life in any substantive or convincing way, or would be unable to identity some of its key abstract beliefs. They will not be able to distinguish between the foundational and non-foundational beliefs (of which more later), will not be able to discuss the rationality, the evidence and perhaps the degree of faith involved in holding these beliefs. They will simply live the worldview, if we might put it like that, paying little or no attention to the coherence or justification of their view, or even to the fact that it *is* a worldview. There will also be many people who will be just the opposite: they will have a deep knowledge of their view of the world, both the outer edges and the center, and the relationship between them. They will be very concerned with the justification of their position and with how it compares and contrasts with other positions. (Indeed, some people may be obsessed with their worldview; I run into many of these people at academic conferences!) Each person will have to decide for himself or herself where he or she stands on this continuum with regard to an appreciation of the outer edges and the center of their worldview.

I wish to highlight this distinction, however, between the center of a worldview and its outer edges because it will not do for some to claim that they really do not hold a philosophy of life, that they just simply live and do not pay any attention to theoretical matters. My point is that even if one is not concerned with the outer edges of one's worldview and lives as if there are no outer edges, there *still are* outer edges, and their relationship to one's behavior is of the utmost importance for the justification of one's worldview. The philosophical defense of one's view is also essential for the important question of its role and place in a pluralist society consisting of many worldviews. In short, all worldviews have outer edges whose relationship to the center of the worldview is crucial, even if the adherent of the worldview might only be close to the worldview at the center. Looking at the issue from the other way round, a person's beliefs and behavior can always be explained and justified (either more or less) in terms of the outer edges of a worldview, whether that person explicitly acknowledges that particular worldview or not, or is concerned with its justification. If this were not true, it would mean that we had simply abandoned rationality altogether in the analysis of worldviews. To deny this would be tantamount to saying that people simply live at the center of their worldview and that the question of the rationality of these worldviews is not important. This would be to eschew rational appraisals of worldviews, to abandon the debate in a pluralist society over justification, consensus, legislation and so on to a kind of irrationalism.

So having argued that everybody has a worldview whether they realize it or not and that the justification of the worldview is a very important matter, let us now move on to offer a general description of two major worldviews in contemporary America. These are worldviews that are prominent in American society; they will serve nicely as models with which to illustrate the various points in our subsequent analysis of the formal structure of a worldview.

Two Major Worldviews in Contemporary America

Let us briefly overview two influential worldviews under those headings most relevant for our analysis. I will describe the worldviews in terms of what beliefs they hold about the nature of reality—what they believe is objectively true or really obtains about reality—about our universe, about human beings (our place in the universe) and about morality. (Beliefs on these subjects are often called metaphysical beliefs by philosophers.) We will also describe the position of each worldview on the role of the church, on their attitude to other worldviews, on church and state, faith and reason, and on democracy. This overview of the important areas is not meant to be exhaustive, but nevertheless it does cover the main categories of beliefs within a worldview, and it will be helpful for our analysis later. The worldviews I have chosen for the purposes of illustration are Christianity and secular naturalistic humanism (hereinafter called "secularism").

Christianity.

Metaphysical beliefs. God exists, and he possesses the qualities identified in traditional Western theology and philosophy. He is eternal, omnipotent, omniscient, all-good, all merciful and so forth. God created the world and all that exists, including all life, according to a particular design. Human beings occupy a special place in God's creation. God is three persons in one Being: Father, Son and Holy Spirit. Jesus Christ was God incarnate.

Human life. Our purpose in life is to serve God and to love one another. The "golden rule" is central to Judeo-Christian ethics: do unto others as you would have them do unto you (Matthew 7:12). Though sinful, human beings are basically good. There is an objective moral law (human nature), grounded in God's law and God's plan for humanity. This is discoverable in part by reason. As a result of being created in God's image, each human being is unique and has a special dignity and integrity that ought not to be violated. Human beings are by nature social beings. Human fulfillment is promoted by marriage and the family in particular; divorce, abortion and euthanasia are morally wrong. Human beings are made up of body and soul. Human beings may, through God's grace, enjoy happiness and eternal life with God, resurrected as body and soul.

On the church. The main guiding text for this view is the Bible, which is God's revealed word to humanity. While the principal understanding of the church is the whole community of believers, this view includes official institutions and spokespersons who often represent and speak for the worldview in certain contexts. The church as an institution helps to model, explain and promote the worldview in a public way.[2]

On church and state. Proponents hold that their worldview has a role to play in politics, that is, appeal to religious truths and values is appropriate in public political and moral debates, and also can be an appropriate guide when passing legislation on some matters. The church, and those who hold this worldview, has the authority and the moral right to engage in public debate. Nevertheless, in general the various branches of Christianity are committed to the separation of church and state in the sense that no particular branch seeks to establish its view as the official worldview of the state.

On other worldviews. Other worldviews are more or less right insofar as they share this view of the world. Missionary work is important, as is dialogue.

On faith and reason. This view has a high regard for reason, but at the same time recognizes the important role of faith in trusting God and in committing to one's beliefs.

On democracy. Most Christian churches accept the basic principles of democracy, such as popular sovereignty, freedom, equality and justice, though what each of these values means may need to be defined by reference to some of the main beliefs of the specific worldview in question. Nevertheless, a prominent place is given to these values in this worldview.[3]

Secular naturalistic humanism (secularism).

Metaphysical beliefs. All of reality is physical, consisting of some configuration of matter and energy. Everything that exists either has a scientific explanation currently or will have a scientific explanation in the future. Con-

---

[2]See John 3:16-17; Matthew 3:16-17; John 8:58; 1 Corinthians 15:14-17; Matthew 28:18-20; 1 Peter 3:14-17.
[3]See my discussion of religion and democracy in chap. 6 for more on this topic.

sequently, there is no God. The universe is a random occurrence. All life on earth, including human life, is the purely random outcome of a purely physical process called evolution. Human beings occupy no special place on the evolutionary tree from an objective point of view, although they currently do from the point of view of being the most evolved, advanced species.

Human life. Despite the random nature of the universe and of the process of evolution, there is still meaning in life, even if there is no ultimate purpose to life. There is no human nature, only biological nature. There is no soul, since everything that exists is physical. Human beings are basically individual beings first and social beings second. Human beings are autonomous centers of rationality who must regulate their lives through their own free choices. The meaning of life is to maximize happiness and to minimize pain. Happiness is to be understood, with certain qualifications and limits, as the fulfillment of one's desires. One main moral principle must be obeyed when fulfilling one's desires: one can exercise one's rationality and one's freedom in making any choice so long as the choice does not harm others. There is no afterlife.

On the church. This view does not have as well established a history as traditional religion, but some of its famous spokesmen in the past would include (perhaps) David Hume (1711-1776), Julien Offray de La Mettrie (1709-1751); Voltaire (1694-1778), John Stuart Mill (1806-1873), Karl Marx (1818-1883), Oliver Wendell Holmes (1841-1935), Friedrich Nietzsche (1844-1900) and B. F. Skinner (1904-1990). Contemporary spokespersons for secularism (of which much more is written in chapter two) might include Steven Pinker, Thomas Nagel, John Searle, Frederick Crews, Carl Sagan, Ann Druyan, Ayn Rand, Richard Dawkins, Maxine Greene, Kai Nielsen, Simon Blackburn, Francis Crick, Paul Kurtz and many others.

On church and state. Members of this view believe that secularism has a role to play in the public square, that is, appeal to its truths and values is appropriate in public debates, and also can be an appropriate guide when passing legislation on some matters. Traditional religious belief, however, has no role to play in the public square either because it is false or because religion and the state should be kept completely separate.

On other worldviews. Other worldviews are more or less right insofar as they share this view of the world, wrong if they do not. "Missionary" work—promoting one's worldview—is important.

On faith and reason. This view relies heavily on reason and is generally critical of traditional religious worldviews, regarding most of them as forms of superstition. It holds that the main justification for any belief should be based on reason and evidence.

On democracy. This view usually places a high priority on democratic values, such as popular sovereignty, freedom, equality and justice (especially in our society), though it is not *necessarily* committed to the democratic form of government (for example, some secularists might be committed to Marxist political theory).

Some clarifications.

I have been deliberately very general and selective in my description of these two worldviews because our concern is only to capture the central beliefs of each view. These are by no means the only views of the world in contemporary America; there are many others, for example, Judaism, Buddhism, Islam, Hinduism, Taoism, astrology, New Age religions, Ethical Culture, White Supremacy and of course the *specific* versions of Christianity and secularism (which do not always agree among themselves).[4] Many of these other worldviews will have much in common with Christianity in particular, given that the Judeo-Christian worldview has been such a big influence on Western culture. But I have selected these two because they are major views, and because they are examples with which to illustrate the theoretical points that follow in this and subsequent chapters. I have selected the worldview of Christianity to represent religion in the debate with secularism in a democratic society because, as I noted in the introduction, it is my own worldview, and hence the religion I am most familiar with, but also because it has been such an influential worldview in Western history. But I do want to emphasize that the arguments I will make in this and subsequent chapters can be applied to *all* religious worldviews (and indeed all secularist worldviews as well). These examples of major worldviews will, in short, help us make explicit the logic of the contemporary debate, and the theoretical points I discuss will apply to *any* worldview one cares to take. I am also not as con-

---

[4]For an excellent introduction to the idea of a worldview, both in terms of describing different worldviews and in terms of analyzing the theoretical structure of worldviews, see David K. Naugle, *Worldview: The History of a Concept* (Grand Rapids: Eerdmans, 2002). For an informative descriptive overview of the various religions in the contemporary United States, see R. Fowler, A. Hertzke and L. Olson, *Religion and Politics in America: Faith, Culture and Strategic Choices,* 2nd ed. (Boulder, Colo.: Westview, 1999), chap. 2. For an introductory overview of the various worldviews, religious and secularist, that have shaped human history, see Ninian Smart, *Worldviews: Crosscultural Explorations of Human Beliefs,* 2nd ed. (Englewood Cliffs, N.J.: Prentice Hall, 1995).

cerned with the fine points of detail in my descriptions, nor do I suggest that my descriptions are exhaustive. (I have not mentioned the Eucharist, for example, in my description of Christianity.[5]) I have tried to describe the important beliefs of each view in our main areas of interest. These areas are central to the identity of the worldview, but they are central also in the sense that they are very relevant for the general debate concerning worldviews in a pluralist democracy, such as ours.[6]

I have stuck to general worldviews here, rather than dealing with specific denominations or versions of the worldviews, because more specific descriptions are not necessary and may only confuse matters. I will, however, occasionally use denominational examples for the purposes of illustration when it is appropriate. I acknowledge that while these descriptions will accurately reflect the general worldview of millions of people, it is also true that many will hold some variant of these philosophies of life and may not agree with everything listed in the description of their particular worldview. This is inevitable since I have kept the descriptions at a certain level of generality. Some of these disagreements might be serious, and it is possible that one might reject so many of the beliefs listed that one would not qualify as an adherent of the worldview I have described. Obviously, this is not the place to get into a discussion of precisely what set of beliefs would make one a Christian or a Secularist. We are concerned only with a more general outline of worldviews; although details of the differences in variations are important, they will not usually be relevant for the arguments which follow, and will not affect our conclusions.

In the second worldview described above, secular naturalistic humanism (referred to in what follows as secularism for the sake of simplicity), it is im-

---

[5]When comparing individual worldviews one should be concerned with the fine points of detail, of course, but the fine points are not necessary in order to advance my arguments in this book.

[6]The concept of a worldview has gained prominence in recent times, especially in the context of pluralism, as people try to understand their own worldview and its relationship to other worldviews. Some thinkers who have in one way or another discussed the concept include C. S. Lewis, *The Abolition of Man* (San Francisco: HarperSanFrancisco, 2001); Hannah Arendt, *On Revolution* (Middlesex, U.K.: Penguin, 1991); Francis Schaeffer, *How Should We Then Live?* (Wheaton, Ill.: Crossway, 1983); Thomas Kuhn, *The Structure of Scientific Revolutions* (Chicago: University of Chicago Press, 1970). For two very accessible books on the concept of a worldview, the first providing an overview of seven basic worldviews, and the second more concerned with the definition of a worldview, see James W. Sire, *The Universe Next Door: A Basic Worldview Catalog* (Downers Grove, Ill.: InterVarsity Press, 1976), and *Naming the Elephant: Worldview as a Concept* (Downers Grove, Ill.: InterVarsity Press, 2004).

portant to appreciate that, though related, this is not the same view as secular humanism.[7] Although secularism and secular humanism share a similar way of understanding the world and hold many beliefs in common, they differ in their respective emphases on science. Secularism is a view that places a huge emphasis on science, since it claims that all of reality is physical, and has, in principle, a scientific explanation. (This view is sometimes also called naturalism or philosophical atheism.) While secular humanists, if forced to fully explore those beliefs and values entailed by their major theses, might come out very close to secularism, its proponents nevertheless have not usually stressed either the view that all of reality is physical or that all of reality has a scientific explanation. Their view is based more on the negative proposition that there is no God.

In fact, we might say that in the past secular humanism, and atheism generally, was primarily a *negative* thesis in the sense that one of the beliefs motivating the view and used to defend the view was the negative claim that there is no God. In addition, atheists very often defined themselves in terms of what they did not believe (i.e., they did not believe in God or traditional religious morality), rather than in terms of what they did believe. Further, atheism was primarily defended by attacking religious belief. However, in recent times this view has gradually evolved into a more *positive* position, advancing the claims that all of reality is physical and that science will eventually unravel the mysteries of the universe. These are *positive* claims, and the claim that there is no God is a consequence of these positive claims, rather than a motivating, foundational claim of the position. Thus we have seen in the twentieth century a gradual shift from the negative worldview of atheism to the positive worldview of secularism. *It is this very significant shift that I wish to reflect in my description of the second worldview above.* We will also see as our discussion unfolds that the move from a negative view to primarily a positive view is significant for the de-

---

[7]George Marsden, *The Outrageous Idea of Christian Scholarship* (New York: Oxford University Press, 1997), p. 124, points out that John Courtney Murray, S.J., used this term in the 1950s, and that it was legally recognized in 1961 when Justice Hugo L. Black wrote in a 1961 supreme court decision (*Torcaso* v. *Watkins* 367 U.S. 488, p. 495): "Among religions in this century which do not teach what would generally be considered a belief in the existence of God are Buddhism, Taoism, Ethical Culture, Secular Humanism and others." It is interesting to see secular humanism here being described as a "religion," suggesting some support from recent American legal thinking for the arguments of my second chapter. See also John Courtney Murray, S.J., *We Hold These Truths: Catholic Reflections on the American Proposition* (New York: Sheed & Ward, 1960), pp. 21-24.

bate on the role of religion in politics in a democratic society.

I have also aligned secularism in my example with a utilitarian moral theory (the moral theory of philosophers Jeremy Bentham and John Stuart Mill) and with a Rawlsian political theory (after influential contemporary philosopher John Rawls). But it is not necessarily committed to these theories, even though secularists in U.S. society have tended to be both utilitarians and followers of Rawls's political theory (though Rawls distanced himself from utilitarianism). I also acknowledge that there are different theories of secularism, just as there are more specific religious theories, but these differences will not affect my overall argument.[8] We will look at the worldview of secularism in much more detail in the next chapter.

The Formal Structure of a Worldview

With these examples of major worldviews in place, let us now turn to a definition and analysis of the formal structure of a worldview. I will define a worldview in such a way as to capture the salient features common to the structure of most worldviews. I intend this definition to be a "working definition" in the sense that it is meant to capture those features that seem to be present in most of those worldviews that attract our interest in pluralist societies. The definition is not intended to be exhaustive of every worldview, but it will be adequate for our purposes. It will apply to all of those worldviews that have had a significant number of followers throughout history, and applies to *all worldviews that make claims about the nature of reality as a whole, about the nature of persons, and about the nature of moral and political values.*

A worldview contains the following features:

1. It is a philosophy of life, which is concerned with three primary areas: the nature of reality, the nature of human beings, and the nature of moral and political values (a worldview that revolves primarily around these three areas I will occasionally refer to as a *substantive* worldview).

2. It contains a number of life-regulating beliefs (relating to the three areas mentioned).

3. Not all of the beliefs in a worldview can, even in principle, be fully proven or demonstrated, and so are based on faith, to some extent.

---

[8]For an overview of some of the different approaches to secularism and naturalism, see Kai Nielsen, *Naturalism and Religion* (New York: Prometheus, 2001), chap. 5.

4. A worldview is often exemplified by certain rituals, practices and behaviors.

5. A worldview motivates and promotes certain types of behavior, and it discourages and prohibits other types of behavior (i.e., it motivates and promotes a theory of *morality*).

6. A worldview has organs and outlets and authorities to promote the worldview, such as spokespersons, advocates, publications, organizations, etc. One might collectively describe the institutions, individuals, publications and so on, that promote a worldview as its "church."

7. Worldviews are engaged in "missionary" work. The adherents of a worldview are often engaged not just in practicing their worldview but also in explaining and defending it for the purposes of convincing others to become members of the worldview (in short, members of worldviews raise money for their cause!).[9]

Let us turn first to the point that a worldview is a philosophy of life. This means that it is one's theory or view or position or thesis about life and its nature, purpose, meaning and so forth. This is not to say that a worldview is merely a matter of intellectual beliefs or propositions; it will also contain, in its fullness, emotional (involving the will), narrative (it will have a history) and community aspects, since it is fundamentally a way of living in the world. A worldview is always a philosophy of life in this sense, and any position that looks like a worldview but that does not advocate a particular philosophy of life is not a worldview according to my definition. Judaism, for example, is clearly a philosophy of life—or view of the world—and therefore satisfies the first point of the definition. Supporting the English soccer club Arsenal (while an extremely worthy thing to do!) is not a philosophy of life; normally, this activity does not entail or imply or advocate a view of the world or a philosophy of life. Neither is supporting the Kansas City Chiefs a worldview, though some people seem to think that it is! (As mentioned, I will occasionally call a worldview which satisfies my definition a *substantive* worldview.)

Second, a philosophy of life contains a number of *life-regulating* beliefs. The first point of the definition leads to the second point, although they are not identical, for it would be possible for an individual to subscribe to a number of life-regulating beliefs, but for them not to constitute

---

[9]I am not as concerned in the discussion that follows with how many features of the definition a worldview would have to exhibit before it could be called a worldview. That question would sidetrack us from our current task.

a philosophy of life or worldview. Indeed, some of our life-regulating beliefs are not part of our philosophy of life. But it is not possible to have a philosophy of life that does not contain a number of life-regulating beliefs. To appreciate this point we need to say a little more about what we mean by a "life-regulating" belief. I understand by a life-regulating belief *a belief that one lives according to, or that regulates one's behavior according to, or in the realm of, the three primary areas already mentioned: the nature of reality, the nature of the human person and the nature of moral and political value.* Examples of such beliefs include the golden rule of Christianity, "Do unto others as you would have others do unto you," or one of the main principles of secularism, "All behavior can be permitted as long as it does not harm others,"[10] or one of the key points of Marxism, "From each according to ability, to each according to need." Principles such as these clearly advocate a particular way of living, a particular way of seeing the world, and clearly promote and discourage certain types of behavior. For example, a Christian who believes in the golden rule believes that if you see Mrs. Jones struggling to cross the road at a busy intersection in normal circumstances, you should help her to cross the road. It is morally right to help her and morally wrong not to help her. These are not just beliefs that the Christian holds; rather, the Christian seeks to live according to them and to recommend that others do likewise. In this way the beliefs are clearly "life-regulating."

Various other beliefs could be said to be life-regulating too, and we need to distinguish them from the above-described beliefs and to emphasize that the definition does not refer to them. An example would be the belief "one should always brush one's teeth in the morning and in the evening," or "one should eat bran flakes because they are good for digestion," or "if you read books about the stock market, you will better invest your money." Such beliefs could be said to be life-regulating in the sense that one may very well regulate one's behavior according to them, such as always consulting books about the stock market before investing. However, such beliefs are not normally concerned with regulating one's behavior according to or in the area of the meaning of life, the nature of the human person, with how one should behave toward others and conduct oneself generally toward others. So such beliefs, while regulating in some sense, are not what I mean by "life-

---

[10]This is one of the key principles of modern liberal political theory. It is sometimes called the "harm principle," and has its origins in the work of John Stuart Mill.

regulating." Of course, there could be some dispute over whether a particular belief was a life-regulating belief in my sense. For example, the belief
"if you want to live longer you should not eat foods high in cholesterol" is
currently one such controversial belief. Some people believe that if you do
not monitor daily and try to control your cholesterol level, you are being
irresponsible, while others believe that this is going too far!

Worldviews and Faith

We now turn to the third part of the definition of a worldview, the claim that
not all of the beliefs in a worldview can be fully proven or demonstrated.
This is a crucial claim for the overall arguments of this book. I wish to argue
that in every worldview concerned with or dealing with issues generally in
the area of the nature of reality, the nature of human beings and issues of
moral and political values (i.e., in every *substantive* worldview), that whatever view one adopts is *always* based at least partly on *faith*. Or to put the
issue in the negative: no worldview that is concerned with these questions
can be fully proven to be true.

I need to take a moment here to explain clearly what I mean by faith and
to distinguish my use of the term from other uses. Faith is one of those
words that has many meanings, and it can lead to confusion. It is used both
as a verb and as a noun. The notion of faith has been used in at least five
significant ways:

First, to describe a commitment to a belief or view for which *the evidence
is not certain or conclusive* (this is sometimes called the cognitive or propositional sense of faith because it involves belief in a truth or truths distinct
from the mind); an example would be believing that God exists. This commitment involves *a movement of the will,* as well as of the intellect.

Second, to describe the *strength* of the commitment to a view or belief
(this might be called the "trust" sense of faith because there is sometimes no
clear distinction between the commitment and the truth(s) to which one is
committed); an example of this meaning of the term is reflected in the statement, "Mr. Smith is a person of deep faith."[11]

Third, to describe the *content* of one's worldview, what one's worldview

---

[11]We need to note that Smith *himself* very likely makes the distinction between his commitment
and the truths to which he is committed. Yet when his faith is described in this way by a third
party it is usually the *depth* of his faith that is being referred to, and also that this depth of
faith will be significant in any discussion with him about matters concerning worldviews.

teaches or what one holds as a member of a certain worldview; we can illustrate with the phrase, "my faith tells me that God created the world in six days." This use of the term is common in the United States, but less so in other countries.[12]

Fourth, to describe believing in something *without evidence* (this is sometimes how atheists and some religious believers describe religious belief); for example, in the statement, "faith is not subject to reason."

Fifth, to describe the set of beliefs that make up a worldview (usually a religious worldview); for instance, in the statement, "Hinduism is an interesting faith."

This is not meant to be an exhaustive list of the various meanings of the word *faith,* but simply an attempt to give us some understanding of some of the main ways the term is used (the third and fifth senses above are very similar). It can be a quite revealing exercise to take some popular uses of the term and try to match them with the above descriptions (e.g., "we are looking for a faith-filled person," or "so and so is a person of faith," or "I have faith," or "I am coming at this matter from a faith perspective," etc.). Sometimes more than one meaning might be intended by a particular usage; often, I suspect, the person using the term might have difficulty describing what he or she means by it.

I am using the term *faith* in this book (unless indicated otherwise) in the *first* sense mentioned—to describe holding a belief for which the evidence is less than one hundred percent certain or decisive.

The philosopher C. J. Ducasse once defined faith as "a very firm belief either unsupported by or insufficiently supported by evidence."[13] Ducasse's definition, of course, is a tongue-in-cheek dig at the faith of religious believers, and it refers to the fourth sense above! But Ducasse ignores the other senses, especially the first sense. I describe a *rational* faith as a faith where

---

[12] In an interesting discussion of religion and science matters, Howard Van Till suggests that this is the sense in which influential philosopher of religion Alvin Plantinga often uses the term *faith.* See the special issue "Creation/Evolution and Faith" of the *Christian Scholar's Review* 21, no. 1 (September 1991), for articles by Van Till and Plantinga. Perhaps this is also the primary way in which St. Thomas Aquinas used the term (he spoke of the "articles of faith"); see Brian Davies, *The Thought of Thomas Aquinas* (Oxford: Clarendon, 1992), pp. 274-85. For a discussion of this sense of the term, see Alvin Plantinga and Nicholas Wolterstorff, eds., *Faith and Rationality* (Notre Dame, Ind.: University of Notre Dame Press, 1983), pp. 10-15. This third meaning of faith involves both propositional *and* passional (commitment) elements, but I wish to highlight the identification of the *specific* beliefs one holds on various religious matters.

[13] C. J. Ducasse, *A Philosophical Scrutiny of Religion* (New York: Ronald Press, 1953), p. 74.

one holds a very firm belief in a truth or set of truths, and where the truths are well supported by evidence and argument. An *irrational* faith is one where the evidence and argument do not seem to support the truths to which one is committed.

I will be arguing in this book that all worldviews are faiths (in the first sense identified above), that a faith must be rational in order to be taken seriously, especially in politics, and that the religious view of the world in general is a rational faith, and more rational than secularism.

When I say that a worldview is based on faith, I mean that at least some of the beliefs of the worldview are accepted on evidence that provides less that one hundred percent certainty. These propositions or beliefs must therefore be accepted on faith, which is to say that the person who holds them makes a commitment to hold them. He or she "goes beyond the evidence." It is necessary to make a commitment because the evidence does not definitively establish truth. The propositions in question, that is, cannot be known with certainty to be true; so if one is going to believe them, one must do so on faith (they can only be believed to be true on the basis of evidence that is less than perfect).

There is nothing wrong with accepting propositions and beliefs for which we do not have one hundred percent proof. And I am claiming here that everyone who holds a *substantive* worldview holds at least some propositions that are accepted partly on faith. What matters in evaluating such propositions is the *degree of faith* involved, that is, how much faith it would take to believe the proposition. If too much faith is involved, the belief may well be irrational; if a smaller amount of faith is involved, the belief may well be reasonable. One accepts such propositions on the basis of a mixture of rational argument, evidence and faith. If we are unable to find one hundred percent proof for a particular proposition, then we can still commit to believing the proposition, *if there is reasonable evidence and argument to support the proposition.*

Beliefs based partly on faith constitute a perfectly respectable set of beliefs. Examples of such beliefs would be that the big bang occurred, that eating low-fat food will prevent me from having a heart attack, that adultery is immoral, that God exists, and so on. Many of the beliefs most of us hold are of this kind. With these kinds of belief, we say that a belief is *rational* (rather than *true*). By this we mean that while we do not have enough evidence to say with certainty that the belief is true, we do have enough evidence to say that it is rational to believe, or commit oneself to, or to adopt, or to hold, the belief in question.

Of course, in the case of many of our beliefs we do know that they are true, for instance, that the earth revolves around the sun, that eating high-fat food causes heart attacks in general, that Washington, D.C., is the capital of the United States and so forth. Yet for many of our beliefs, particularly in substantive worldviews, we must settle for rationality because of *the nature of the subject matter*. For the subject matter of worldviews—concerning as it does the nature of reality, the nature of the human person and the nature of moral and political values—is so large and complex that it simply does not lend itself to the kind of proof that we might desire. It is also possible, for any particular belief, to have a disagreement about whether we know the belief to be *true*, or merely rational or probable. For example, two doctors might disagree over whether a particular medicine will bring about a cure, one claiming that it definitely will bring about a cure, the other that it will not. It is also possible, for a particular belief, to have a disagreement about whether the belief is even *rational* or not, for instance, the belief that medical experimentation on animals should always be banned. This happens all the time in the debate between worldviews, and one might argue that it is part of what makes a pluralist democracy vibrant and interesting.

So my claim that many beliefs in substantive worldviews are based on faith is not all that controversial, yet it is one that has played virtually no part in the debate about religion and politics. Nevertheless, the view that some beliefs are based on faith, and therefore not certain, is one of the main motivations behind modern political theories, even if not quite expressed in the way I have expressed it here. But it is a central motivation behind the liberal pluralism of contemporary political thinker John Rawls. Rawls argues that since the debate between different worldviews cannot be settled by appeal to reason and evidence, and since none of us can really be certain of many of our main beliefs, we should therefore try to accommodate as many worldviews as possible in our political structures.[14] We will come back to Rawls's view in chapter six.

---

[14]Of course, this belief that "we should try to accommodate as many worldviews as possible in our political structures" is one about which those who advocate liberal pluralism are fairly convinced, and wish to act on politically in the sense that they wish to give it a central place in the structuring of society and to compel other people to live according to it. It is a value judgment, and it entails that the opposite belief is morally wrong. Many will object to this belief or propose modified versions of it. The discussion about the status of this belief and its justification goes to the heart of the debate about religion and politics and will occupy us in subsequent chapters.

The Rationality of Worldviews

Our analysis so far prompts us to take a moment to consider the question of the rationality of worldviews in general. Some readers might wonder whether, in saying that all worldviews contain some beliefs partly grounded in faith, I am suggesting that all worldviews are reasonable, that we can't really adjudicate rationally between worldviews (and so perhaps I am saying that religious belief is just as legitimate as any other worldview). I want to make it clear that I am *not* saying this. To see this, we can begin by clarifying a little further what we mean by reason.

In the ordinary commonsense use of the term, reason is understood as thinking in a logical way, as trying to be objective, as seeking good arguments, as willing to consider evidence. This is how I am using the term here. I hold that reason is objective, and that all human beings should strive to be reasonable, especially when it comes to discussing questions of great importance, such as those that come up in the debate between worldviews. To be reasonable means that one must offer arguments for one's conclusions in an attempt to persuade others of their truth or reasonability. One should be willing to test one's views in discussion and debate, to consider objections to one's views and to consider all of the available evidence relevant to the subject matter. One must be willing to engage in a rational discussion with one's opponents and critics, and to consider the strongest form of their arguments, not the weakest form or a caricature of their argument. One must strive to be logical and to be willing to follow logical principles and procedures in an argument. This will include seeking positions that are consistent as well as coherent. This is the way a reasonable person should proceed in a debate concerning worldview matters in a pluralist, democratic society.

I have been making the point that one very interesting feature common to all substantive worldviews is that they are ultimately based to some extent on a degree of faith. How rational a worldview is will depend on how much faith is involved in believing especially what we will call its foundational (but even its nonfoundational) beliefs, a subject we will take up later in the chapter. This conclusion will have profound implications for our analysis of the role of one's worldview in public life. Some worldviews are more rational than others. But it might be possible for two or more worldviews to be about equally rational. For example, objectively speaking, some thinkers argue that religious belief and secularism are about equally rational, which is to say that there are arguments and evidence based on certain features of the world which tend to confirm and to disconfirm both positions in equal measure.[15] This presumably is something like the thinking behind a genuine agnostic's position. It is also possible for a person to commit to a religious view on the basis that it is rational, and yet to believe that there is a close to equal measure of evidence to justify another person committing to secularism. Similarly, a secularist might commit to secularism based on the evidence, and yet believe that religious belief is rational for others.[16]

Most importantly, when I say that at least some of the beliefs in a philosophy of life are based partly on faith, *this does not mean that the worldview is irrational*. Worldviews are rational according to how much evidence and argument there is to support their key foundational beliefs, and on how the nonfoundational beliefs are connected to the foundational beliefs. If there is good evidence and argument, then the worldview is rational, if not, not. In addition, there can be disputes over how to weigh the evidence and, even in this age of relativism, disputes over what counts as rational. My thesis about worldviews *does* entail that no substantive worldview can be proven to be true with one hundred percent certainty. This means that in no worldview is it possible to prove all of the key beliefs with total certainty. But I am not implying a relativism about worldviews: we can and do (and must) distinguish between worldviews according to their *degree of rationality* (since we cannot do it according to their truth).

The justification of worldviews is analogous to the justification of scien-

---

[15]The influential contemporary philosopher of religion John Hick holds this view; see his *An Interpretation of Religion* (New Haven, Conn.: Yale University Press, 1989).
[16]The philosopher William Rowe holds this view; see his "The Problem of Evil and Some Varieties of Atheism," in *Contemporary Perspectives on Religious Epistemology*, ed. R. Douglas Geivett and Brendan Sweetman (New York: Oxford University Press, 1992), pp. 33-42. I am interested only in analyzing the position of those who hold a worldview because of argument and evidence, since this is a philosophical analysis. I am not so concerned with other reasons for why people might subscribe to a worldview, such as peer pressure, cultural background, family upbringing, or psychological reasons. Pastors have often noted, for example, that many atheists hold their beliefs for psychological reasons having to do with dislike of their religious upbringing, dissatisfaction with their church's teachings or a need for comfort for their rejection of religious morality. Secularism, at least in our historical context, it should be observed, is almost rebellious by definition, and so there might be more people who subscribe to secularism for psychological reasons than appears at first glance. In short, secularism is not above superstition! There seems to be little research available on the psychology of atheism, but one interesting recent attempt is Paul C. Vitz, *Faith of the Fatherless: The Psychology of Atheism* (Dallas: Spence, 1999). Obviously from the point of view of examining the *rationality* of one's beliefs, all of the reasons for why one holds a view are very important and would have to be taken into account. I *am* interested in the question of justifying a worldview on the basis of authority, and will come back to this possibility in chap. 3.

tific theories in many ways. Scientists today are reluctant to say that a theory is "proved"; although they might say that they are fairly certain of some of the data used to support the theory, the theory itself is a way of organizing the evidence, explaining phenomena, bringing diverse and sometimes disparate data together under one umbrella, etc. The theory can also be said to be either well or poorly supported by the data. Of course, the theory can drive the search for further evidence at some later point, and it can be adopted as a way of looking at the (physical) world. So it is too with worldviews.

I do *not* wish to suggest that, since all worldviews are based partly on a faith commitment, that we cannot evaluate worldviews according to their degree of rationality and must simply recognize them as faith commitments, which are all legitimate and so worthy of playing some role in society. For the fact is that we can judge between worldviews in terms of their rationality. We can assess the foundational beliefs of any worldview and see how much reason and evidence they are based on. Each worldview will have to be judged individually, but in general we can say that we should be suspicious of a worldview that is based on very little reason and evidence and that appears to be based mainly on a faith commitment. Similarly, a worldview founded on a high degree of reason and evidence will probably be a well-justified and rational worldview. Of course, we could (and will) have disputes among worldviews about whether a particular belief is rational or not, or even about whether the whole worldview is rational or not; we may also have disagreements within the same worldview about whether certain beliefs are rational or not.

These disputes will be settled in my analysis *by appealing to reason and evidence.* This is because, on the view being presented in this book, reason and logic are objective; there is objective knowledge; and evidence can be evaluated objectively. I am not saying that the truth is evident to all people all of the time if only they will open their eyes to see. But I am saying that when any worldview makes a claim about the three areas (the nature of reality, of persons, and of moral and political values), this claim is being advanced as being objectively true (and so it would follow that anyone who denies the claim is wrong). But, given this, it is still obvious that people will disagree over many issues. The key question is, *how should this disagreement be handled in the political arena?* I hold that people do not disagree about the nature of reason and logic and about the rules of logical argument;

they disagree about whether the premises of arguments are true or not and about whether conclusions claimed to follow from premises (either with certainty or a with a degree of probability) actually do follow from them. They might also disagree about any relevant data or about what the data shows or how it is to be interpreted. In the discussion over how to handle disagreement in the political arena, we must assume the objectivity of reason and evidence, otherwise we run into problems of relativism and irrationalism.

I am well aware that there is now a major debate raging in the modern university academy which, in varying ways, seeks to challenge the objectivity of reason and logic, to deny that one can have objective knowledge and truth.[17] This movement is evident in philosophy, but it is also present in various other disciplines, especially perhaps multiculturalism, literature, feminism and related areas, even in some areas of theology, though I am not suggesting for a moment that everything in these disciplines is shaped by this approach. There have even been attacks on the objectivity of science, mostly coming from the humanities. Readers unfamiliar with the university academy might be surprised to hear all of this, but those who have even a passing acquaintance with recent scholarship, especially in the humanities, will acknowledge that this is the case. Many scholars in different disciplines have suggested that reason and logic themselves may be relative to one's worldview, or one's perspective on life. Obviously, I reject this view. Unfortunately, it would sidetrack us too much to get into a detailed discussion of this position here; indeed, it would require a book in itself (though, in chapter eight, I will provide a discussion of moral relativism and its problems). For now, I would like to make two points about this position that are relevant to our analysis.

First, there are severe logical and practical problems with denying the objectivity of reason and logic, and of rational argument in general. The main problem is that it opens the door to relativism and irrationalism. If one accepts this general approach, one is committing to the view that one's own worldview is not objectively true, and so its critique of other worldviews (e.g., of traditional religion by feminism) cannot be effective (for the religious believer can simply reply that she does not accept the feminist per-

---

[17]For an overview of various views on this matter, see Lawrence Cahoone, ed., *From Modernism to Postmodernism: An Anthology* (Oxford: Blackwell, 2003); Jean-François Lyotard, *The Postmodern Condition: A Report on Knowledge,* trans. G. Bennington and B. Massumi (Minneapolis: University of Minnesota Press, 1984); Alasdair MacIntyre, *Whose Justice? Which Rationality?* (Notre Dame, Ind.: University of Notre Dame Press, 1988).

spective on such and such an issue, that she comes at the issues from a *different* perspective, etc.). Relativism is hard to avoid here because one would have to explain why one perspective is *better* than another; this will involve an appeal to objective reason and truth, or else one will have to concede that every view is just as good as any other view, a thesis that may eventually end up in complete skepticism, even nihilism.[18]

The second point is that this latter alternative—the view that every perspective is just as good as any other—would, in an odd way, help the cause of the religious believer who wanted to introduce religious beliefs into politics in a democratic society. This is because one could only then critique the religious view from the perspective of *another, different* worldview, and if all worldviews are simply perspectives, then the religious worldview would be just as legitimate as any other perspective and so just as entitled to a place in the public debate. To argue that all worldviews, and their specific appeals to reason and logic, are simply "perspectives" and not objectively true (and so are not applicable to everyone), and then to turn around and deny that the religious view of the world can be a cultural player is a contradiction in terms. Although some of a more postmodernist persuasion seem to welcome this approach[19] and seem to want to get religion a place at the table on this basis, I believe we must reject it. We cannot abandon the objectivity of knowledge without slipping into irrationalism, a cost that is simply too high for most religious worldviews (and indeed most secularist worldviews). It would require religious believers to fatally compromise their integrity because, like most secularists, they are committed to making objective claims about reality and about morality. It would also, again like most secularists, undermine any critique religious believers wanted to make of other worldviews. This would also be an especially difficult problem for secularist-leaning worldviews that reject the objectivity of reason and logic, for undermining traditional worldviews is often one of their main objectives!

Worldviews and Religion

Some readers might be wondering if a worldview and a religion are the

---

[18]For a critique of postmodernism and the view that reason and logic are relative to one's perspective, see my articles, "Lyotard, Postmodernism and Religion," *Philosophia Christi* 7, no. 1 (spring 2005): 141-15; and "Postmodernism, Derrida and *Différence:* A Critique," *International Philosophical Quarterly* 39, no. 1 (March 1999): 5-18.

[19]For an excellent introduction to this debate, see Myron B. Penner, ed., *Christianity and the Postmodern Turn* (Grand Rapids: Brazos, 2005).

same thing. One can see perhaps how a religion could be described as a worldview, but would it be appropriate to describe a worldview as a religion? While it is common to distinguish between a worldview and a religion or, more accurately, to classify religions as subsets of worldviews, I wish to suggest that these terms can profitably be used interchangeably in the debate concerning religion and politics. Before I show why this is appropriate (and will be helpful to us later on), let me first of all consider various definitions of religion. Obviously, one could find hundreds of different definitions depending on which aspects of religious belief one wished to emphasize. But we need only a fairly general definition (a working or operational definition based on how religious people actually live), since we are concerned with worldviews in general and how they relate to each other in a pluralist society. We want a definition that captures the salient points about religion: that it is a complex system of beliefs, is life-regulating (it influences how we live), has an ethical theory, is expressed in certain types of rituals and practices, and is based in significant part on a belief in a sacred, transcendent (unseen) reality. Peter Berger has defined religion as "the human enterprise by which the human cosmos is established." Emile Durkheim saw it as "a unified system of beliefs and practices relative to sacred things." William James draws attention to the ethical component when he says that religion involves "the belief there is an unseen order, and that our supreme good lies in harmoniously adjusting ourselves thereto." Ninian Smart gives a fuller and more useful definition: religion is "a set of institutionalized rituals with a tradition and expressing and/or evoking sacral sentiments directed at a divine or trans-divine focus seen in the context of the human phenomenological environment and at least partially described by myths or by myths and doctrines."[20] There are many other definitions that would probably do as well as these, but I simply want to give a flavor of the types of things included in the definitions. One will notice that there is no standard definition and that many of the definitions overlap, as we would expect.

However, the main point we need to focus on is that there is very little difference between the definition of a worldview we have presented and the definitions of religion surveyed above. They both have the following fea-

---

[20]I am indebted to Irving Hexham's *Concise Dictionary of Religion* (Downers Grove, Ill.: Inter-Varsity Press, 1993), pp. 186-87, for this brief survey of various definitions of religion. See also Roy A. Clouser, *The Myth of Religious Neutrality* (Notre Dame, Ind.: University of Notre Dame Press, 1991), for a very interesting discussion of religious belief as a theory and the nature of theories in general.

tures in common: they are philosophies of life, which are concerned with
the three primary areas (the nature of reality, of persons and of moral and
political values); they contain life-regulating beliefs; not all of the beliefs can
be fully proven; they are exemplified in rituals and practices; they have a
moral code; proponents have various ways of promoting the worldviews;
proponents try to convert people. They differ with respect to only one issue:
a religion of necessity involves a belief in an unseen world, in a sacred
realm, and it usually involves belief in a Supreme Being. Even on this point
though, we have to be careful since there are nontheistic religions that do
not believe that God is a transcendent being over and above the world, such
as nontheistic Hinduism. But, speaking generally, a worldview need not be
committed to this unseen world and sacred realm in order to be a worldview, and so this is the obvious clear difference between the definitions of
worldview and of *religion*. The notion of a worldview is broader than the
notion of a religion; or to put the matter in a different way, religious worldviews make up a subset of the set of all worldviews.

Nevertheless, I am asking that we think about using both terms interchangeably as long as we keep in mind this one key difference—that the
word *religion* is usually restricted to describe a worldview that includes as
part of its structure beliefs in an unseen (sacred) realm. But this is only a
difference in *content*, not a difference in *form*, a difference in what the
worldview teaches, not a difference in its structure when compared to other
worldviews. In fact, all worldviews are similar with regard to their formal
structure on the main issue that really matters for the relationship between
religion and politics: they all include foundational beliefs that require a degree of faith to believe them. So (perhaps occasionally) using both *worldview* and *religion* interchangeably is reasonable and will help clarify the debate about religion in politics because it will help us to appreciate that
secularism, too, is a religion in its own way.

Foundational and Nonfoundational Beliefs

Foundational beliefs in a worldview are, as the name suggests, those beliefs
that provide the foundations for the worldview. They are those beliefs without which the worldview would not be the worldview that it is, beliefs that
give the worldview its distinctive identity and subject matter. They are,
therefore, the most important beliefs in a worldview. These are the beliefs
about which the proponents of a worldview need to be most concerned, es-

pecially in terms of their rationality, consistency, the evidence supporting them and so on. Since these beliefs give a worldview its particular character and determine the philosophical foundation of the worldview, as well as (usually) the particular lifestyle the worldview promotes, they require special attention in the debate between worldviews. Some examples of foundational beliefs include the beliefs listed at the beginning of the chapter in the description of the two major worldviews.

There is an interesting relationship between foundational beliefs and reason. We need to ask if a foundational belief is foundational because it is more rational than a nonfoundational belief, or if it is foundational simply because it gives the worldview its identity and subject matter. The answer is obviously the latter since the foundational beliefs are ones that give a worldview its identity and character. And so while we should all strive for our foundational beliefs to be as rational as possible, it is possible for a foundational belief of a worldview to actually have very little evidence to back it up (e.g., the key belief of the worldview of astrology that the movement of the various planets has a profound effect on human behavior).

Foundational beliefs stand in contrast to the nonfoundational beliefs of a worldview. These beliefs are important, but they are secondary to the foundational beliefs. This is because they do not give the worldview its particular character and identity. It is important to note that the nonfoundational beliefs depend for their support and justification on the foundational beliefs to some extent. But the nonfoundational beliefs are not necessarily derived in a logically strict sense from the foundational beliefs. They are in many cases simply seen as rational given the foundational beliefs. Yet nonfoundational beliefs, in a roundabout kind of way, might give certain worldviews their particular character and identity in the sense that they might *distinguish* one worldview from another very similar worldview. One could argue that this is the case with the various forms of Marxism that exist. However, a full account and description of these worldviews will still show that it is really the foundational beliefs that give them their real character and identity—that make them the worldviews they are—and it is mainly because of cultural considerations that one can distinguish them on the basis of their nonfoundational beliefs.

Let us illustrate these points with a few examples. In the worldview of Christianity, some of the foundational beliefs would be that God exists, that he created all life, that he has a plan for humanity and that Jesus Christ was resurrected from the dead. In the secularist worldview, foundational beliefs would include the beliefs that all that exists is physical, that science can explain everything, that human beings are the sole source of meaning and value, and that human beings are autonomous centers of rationality. A nonfoundational secularist belief might be that morality involves the promotion of the greatest happiness for the greatest number of people, the main principle of the moral theory known as utilitarianism. One might, of course, have a dispute about what the foundational (and indeed the nonfoundational) beliefs actually are in particular worldviews, as well as disputes about the evidence and rationality for these beliefs.

It is important to note also that in order for a worldview to get its distinctive character—at least for some of the well-established, influential and well-known worldviews I am talking about—it is usually necessary to hold a set of foundational beliefs *together*. For instance, if one believes in God, while this is a foundational belief of Christianity, believing this alone is not sufficient to make one a Christian, since many non-Christians also believe in God. We might put this by saying that in the more established worldviews, it is necessary to state several *necessary* conditions (of membership in a worldview) in order to arrive at the *sufficient* condition for being a member of that worldview, that is, the listing of those beliefs that, if one held them, would be sufficient to make one a subscriber to that particular view of the world.

It is not necessarily the foundational beliefs in a worldview that primarily *guide* one's behavior, although it is the foundational beliefs that primarily *explain and justify* one's behavior. It is possible for one's behavior in a worldview to be primarily guided by the nonfoundational beliefs. All of this depends partly on the content of the worldview and partly on the actual beliefs the adherent of the worldview emphasizes in his or her daily life. The nonfoundational beliefs are based on the foundational beliefs, though not in any strictly logically deductive sense. And both types of belief can guide behavior. For example, a nonfoundational belief that guides behavior in the worldview of Christianity may be the belief that premarital sex is immoral. A nonfoundational belief that guides behavior in the worldview of secularism might be that smoking is immoral. Is a worldview better justified if foundational beliefs guide behavior? No, not necessarily. Worldview A would be more rational than worldview B if the nonfoundational beliefs of worldview A primarily guide behavior and are rational and are closely tied to the foundational beliefs, which are also rational, and it is also the case that in worldview B the foundational beliefs guide behavior but these beliefs are not rational. But in some worldviews the foundational beliefs could be more concerned with theoretical matters of justification and the nonfoundational beliefs with practical matters of behavior. But again this would depend on the structure of the worldview in question, and each worldview would have to be analyzed individually to determine where it stands with regard to the questions we have raised here.

Lower-Order and Higher-Order Beliefs

In the analysis of the theoretical structure of worldviews, we also must distinguish between what I call *lower-order* beliefs and *higher-order* beliefs. Although this language is a bit technical, it turns out to be quite helpful when it comes to adjudicating the debate between worldviews in the public square. This distinction should not be confused with the distinction between foundational and nonfoundational beliefs. Lower-order beliefs and higher-order beliefs are distinguished by the *amount of faith* required to subscribe to the belief, with more faith being required for the latter than for the former. A lower-order belief of a worldview is one of those beliefs that, although it usually requires faith (recall that at least some beliefs in all substantive worldviews require a degree of faith), it is still based mostly on reason and evidence, *and so it is more likely to be regarded as reasonable by others.* A higher-order belief is one that requires a great deal of faith (or at least more faith than a lower-order belief) in order for a person to subscribe to it. In a worldview, it is always better from the point of view of the rationality of the worldview for the foundational beliefs to be lower-order beliefs. This is because we obviously want our foundational beliefs to be based on as much reason and evidence as possible and on as little faith as possible (while recognizing that some foundational beliefs in all substantive worldviews will require some degree of faith *because of the subject matter involved*). Lower-order beliefs are more likely to be persuasive to others, and this will have important implications for the debate among various worldviews in the public square. In short, lower-order beliefs are rational beliefs from the point of view of pluralism and of introducing them into political discussion. All worldviews have lower-order and higher-order beliefs.

One might wonder what kind of beliefs could be higher-order beliefs and why anyone would believe them. In short, can higher-order beliefs ever be rational beliefs? The answer to this question is yes, and a few examples will help to illustrate the point. In Christianity, a lower-order belief is that God exists, as I indicated earlier, but a higher-order belief might be a specific belief about the nature of God—that he is three persons in one God, for instance. The Christian philosopher might argue that one can provide a very good argument for belief in the existence of God, which is therefore a lower-order (more rational) belief, but acknowledge that belief in the Trinity takes more faith, is based in part on revelation, and so is therefore more accurately described as a higher-order belief. Indeed, there could be disputes within a worldview about some of these matters. In secularism, the secularist may argue that a lower-order belief of the view, for which there is strong argument and evidence, is that "all of reality is physical," but the secularist might acknowledge that the belief that the human mind is completely physical (a position I call "extreme materialism" about the mind) is a higher-order belief, since it is based more on faith than on evidence. Higher-order beliefs are rational if they are well tied to lower-order beliefs. Thus the Christian might claim that since the belief that God exists is reasonable and the belief that Jesus existed is reasonable, then the belief in the reliability of the Bible is reasonable, and so the belief in the incarnation is reasonable. Similarly, the secularist might argue that since the belief that all that exists is physical is reasonable and the belief in scientific progress is reasonable, then the belief that the human mind is physical is reasonable.[21]

It is, however, obviously possible to have foundational beliefs that are based on a great degree of faith and very little reason or evidence, for example, the foundational beliefs of astrology already mentioned. This means that a foundational belief could be a higher-order belief. In the best worldviews—the most rational ones—most of the main foundational beliefs should be lower-order beliefs (i.e., they are well supported by reason and evidence). The question arises of how one judges or decides if a particular belief in a philosophy of life is a higher-order or a lower-order belief. One can't decide by simply examining the nonfoundational beliefs, especially

---

[21]In suggesting that higher-order beliefs can be rational, I am not denying that religious beliefs can sometimes be irrational. I discuss this matter further in chap. 3. For a few examples of religious beliefs that many people would regard as irrational, see Martha Nussbaum's examples in "Religion and Women's Human Rights," in *Religion and Contemporary Liberalism*, ed. Paul J. Weithman (Notre Dame, Ind.: University of Notre Dame Press, 1997), pp. 93-137. Nussbaum does not give any corresponding examples of irrational secular beliefs, though these would be easy enough to supply.

since the foundational beliefs can be primarily based on faith too. The answer is that we judge this matter on the basis of appeal to objective reason and on an objective analysis of the evidence. However, even if an appeal to objective reason and evidence is made, the proponents of different worldviews could still dispute whether a belief was foundational or nonfoundational and, more importantly, whether it was lower-order or higher-order. For most of the major worldviews we are dealing with here, we can say that at the very least we do know which beliefs are conventionally regarded as foundational and which as nonfoundational. The question of which beliefs are lower-order or higher-order will turn out to be a very important matter for the general discussion of which beliefs it is legitimate to introduce into the political arena, and I will come back to it often in what follows.

Promoting Our Worldview: Belief, Action and Ritual

We have not yet looked at the relationship between belief and action in a worldview. This relationship is momentous in human experience because we all know that it is one thing to accept a belief, to commit to a belief, but quite another thing to live out the belief, to act according to the belief, to regulate one's life and behavior under the influence of the belief (or beliefs). It seems to be a feature of the human condition that, no matter how strongly held, we often find it difficult to live out our beliefs. There are several reasons for this failure, which I would like to briefly mention here; not all of them imply moral culpability, though some do. (One apparent characteristic of much of modern society is a fierce commitment to certain beliefs, but a failure either to live according to those beliefs or to apply them consistently.)

An important point to consider is that there is a relationship between the degree of faith required for a belief and one's willingness to act on this belief, that is, to live according to the belief. It is necessary to distinguish three ways this relationship might be expressed. First, it might require a great deal of faith to subscribe to a particular belief, but, nevertheless, one might be utterly committed to the belief and be convinced of its truth. In this case, one might be willing to act on the belief even though a high degree of faith is required to believe it. For example, a devout religious believer might believe that nothing happens except what God wills, and so be very accepting of personal setbacks. Second, it might take a great deal of faith to subscribe to a particular belief, and because the degree of faith required is very high, this may weaken one's commitment to the belief. That is to say, there may be some element of doubt involved in one's assent to the belief. This doubt may not always be consciously experienced or expressed, but it may be enough, not to make one give up the belief, but to make one reluctant to act on the belief. For example, secularists might believe on faith that there is no afterlife, but continue to have a strong hope that they will see their loved ones again. This hope may be motivated by their doubt of the belief that there is no afterlife. Third, there is often a correlation between thinking that there is very good evidence for a belief and one's willingness to act on the belief; if one considers the evidence for one's belief to be strong, one is generally more likely to live out the belief. For example, the belief that all people are children of God could motivate one to support a variety of social policies in a particular society. These three kinds of cases are obviously crucial, and we need to keep them in mind as we study the formal structure of worldviews.

One might not act on a belief because of human weakness. One might believe very strongly that adultery is morally wrong and yet commit adultery. Or that one must study for one's exam tonight, but come evening one is found relaxing at the movie theater. Or that gluttony is wrong, but reach for that extra piece of pie! This is a very common feature of human experience. Human weakness could be motivated by a need to fulfill one's desires (one's desires rule one's head, as Plato would have put it). It could be the result of laziness; sometimes it is more difficult to be strong than weak, especially when faced with temptation. One's failure to act on a belief might also be due to social pressure, a time-honored cause of people not living up to their beliefs. Another cause of people not acting on their beliefs is legislation, for example, one might be prevented by law from acting on one's belief that taking drugs is moral. And once we introduce legislation into the matter, we can see that this is a widely accepted and perfectly respectable way of getting people to act according to beliefs that they have not acted according to up to now.[22] Of course, in our analysis of worldviews, the matter of legislation would have to be factored into the consideration of the ra-

---

[22]Getting people to act according to beliefs which they have not acted according to is one thing, but getting them to believe the beliefs, to commit to them, to accept them as their own beliefs, is quite another. However, there is some historical evidence for the fact that if one bases a law of the land on a particular belief, over time many people who did not subscribe to the belief will eventually come to accept the belief as true. A good example of this in American history is the abolition of slavery or the principles enshrined in the Civil Rights Act (1964) or perhaps even in our own time the legalization of abortion.

tionality of worldviews.

The beliefs and actions of a worldview are often expressed in various types of rituals. Rituals, as we know, are a very important part of almost all worldviews and therefore of life. And while we are familiar with the rituals of the more established, well-known worldviews, we need to start learning to recognize and appreciate the various rituals and practices of less established worldviews, like secularism. Worldviews are usually exemplified by certain rituals, practices and behaviors, though the extent to which this is essential to the nature of a worldview is a matter for debate. But one can often identify a member of a worldview by noting certain practices and behaviors he or she engages in. Some worldviews may have more rituals than others, and some may be more established than others. Some examples of rituals and practices in the Christian worldview would include going to church every week, or saying a prayer before meals, or reading from the Bible on a regular basis. On the secularist side, rituals and practices might include going to a meeting of the Secular Humanist Society every month, or contemplating the majesty of the universe, or reading often from the works of astronomer Carl Sagan. This is not as much a stretch as it might sound. The secularist Michael Shermer said in a radio interview that he gets a kind of "spiritual" fulfillment from attending and participating in the weekly meetings of his scientific organization "The Skeptics Society." Indeed, as secularism spreads, its need for and development of various types of rituals and practices will surely increase (more on this point in chapter two). It seems to be the case that we all need rituals of a certain kind in order to live, and these are very often tied to our worldviews in some way. Among other things, rituals seem to provide regular reassurance that one's worldview is rational.

There may also be some overlap between the rituals of various worldviews, especially in those worldviews that are quite close in their beliefs about the three primary areas. Rituals express the beliefs of the proponents of the worldview, as well as affirming the worldview and strengthening one's commitment to one's beliefs. So there is a reciprocal relationship between the beliefs of the worldview and the practices these beliefs give rise to in that each can strengthen the other. We should not be surprised at this for it is part of the complicated relationship that obtains between belief and action in human experience.

Worldviews may be promoted in many different ways and in many different venues. In free societies, worldviews have ways of promoting themselves through spokespersons, publications, institutions, interest groups and so on. Some worldviews do this more than others. It would make an interesting study in itself to examine the various ways in which worldviews can and do promote themselves. It is also important to keep distinct the *beliefs* of a worldview from the way in which members of a worldview try to *promote* these beliefs. We also need to keep these two notions distinct from the *attitude* the proponent of one worldview might have toward the beliefs (and the adherents) of another worldview. These three important issues are often confused by people from all sides of the spectrum. A worldview may try to promote itself by holding rallies, distributing literature, taking out TV adverts or trying to get its views adopted in legislation and made the law of the land.

I am often tempted to describe the major proponents of a worldview as its "priests," even if the worldview is secularist, just as I have described (in the definition of the formal structure of a worldview) the institutions founded by and employed by the proponents of a worldview as a "church." But I don't insist on the term *priests* in case it misleads. These terms are meant to convey only that all worldviews have recognized proponents of the worldview, that there are institutions and groups associated with every worldview. Thus, Paul Kurtz and Richard Dawkins could be described as priests of the church of secularism; they are special authorities on this worldview to which others might appeal in order to understand the view better or find arguments to support the view or rally people to the view, etc. This is all I mean to capture by suggesting the term *priests* here; I am not suggesting that they are acting as intermediaries between God and people, or that they have special powers by virtue of their membership in the priesthood. As with the other terms I have used above, my main point always is to illustrate the similarities *in structure* between the religious worldview and the secularist worldview. Although this terminology is obviously more typical of some worldviews than others, nevertheless it can sometimes be appropriate in our discussion. We will see that it can help us avoid making a serious error in our analysis of the structure of different worldviews.

In the last characteristic identified in the definition of worldview, missionary work, I again elect to adopt a traditional religious term to describe this aspect of all worldviews. Again the advantages of this kind of language will become apparent in the succeeding chapters. But the main point is not the issue of terminology, it is the fact that proponents of worldviews do generally try to promote their view to gain new members. This is not necessarily done in a systematic and sustained way. It could be done in a disparate, piecemeal and unorganized way. This depends in part on how coherently expressed a worldview is and how unified its members are both in terms of their beliefs and in terms of the institutional structures of the worldview.

So with our definition and analysis of the concept of a worldview in place, let us now turn to consider an influential worldview in modern culture: the worldview of secularism.

2

The Worldview of Secularism

It is not as controversial as it used to be to argue that secularism is actually a worldview unto itself. Where once this was a disputed claim, more and more people are now beginning to talk this way about secularism, and secularists themselves are beginning to define their beliefs and values more clearly. I think it is fair to say that in the twentieth century, especially the latter half of the century, secularism became a quite significant worldview. It became significant in a number of ways: many more people today subscribe to some version of secularism than did in the past; it is advocated in whole or in part by the members of various interest groups; it influences the attitudes of many people, including opinion-makers, in matters involving moral and political questions and the meaning of life; it is now offered by many as a serious alternative worldview to that of religious belief. It has gained so much recognition and influence that some have even suggested that it is really a type of religion. As Canadian philosopher and secularist Kai Nielsen has recently put it: "What I want most to achieve . . . is to give a perspicuous articulation and soundly reasoned account of a thoroughly secular and as well a thoroughly humanist way of looking at things and of living in the world—our modern, or, if you will, postmodern world."[1] Nielsen goes on to pay particular attention to the social and political implications of secularism.

In this chapter I will try to illustrate these themes. I will appeal to our analysis of the concept of a worldview from the previous chapter to show that secularism is a worldview that competes with religious belief, and that it is quite accurate and useful to describe it as a "religion" because it will

---

[1]Kai Nielsen, *Naturalism and Religion* (New York: Prometheus, 2001), p. 11.

help us to further appreciate that secularism and religious belief have quite similar structures. We will take a detailed look at the worldview of secularism—its main beliefs and values, its main spokespersons in various disciplines and areas of life, both today and in the past, how it differs from secular humanism and from political liberalism. We will also examine secularist trends among religious believers. This detailed account of the secularist worldview will enable us to appreciate the significance of secularism in modern pluralist societies. It will also help us to understand (in the next chapter) what is meant by the attempt to describe or single out a belief as a "religious belief." It will also help show that the attempt to single out religious beliefs as a separate category of beliefs is not justified, and ends up arbitrarily discriminating against the religious worldview.

Secularism Today

The word *secular* (from the Latin *saecularis*) literally means "of or relating to the world," and although this sounds a generally positive, neutral note, it is a word with mostly a negative, even tendentious, connotation. The word *secular* was used traditionally to convey the point that if something is of or relates to the world, then it does *not* relate to the supernatural, religion, the church, the clergy and so forth. Even today secularists are struggling hard to get out from under this connotation. They are now attempting to refine their view in positive terms so that it can command recognition and acceptance in a pluralist society, so that it can have a legitimate place at the table of political discussion in such a society.

Secularists have done quite well in the task of stating their beliefs and values in positive terms, but they have been generally less successful in adopting a positive temperament toward alternative views. Their attitude still remains quite negative and I don't think it is unfair to say that some are too often apt to describe their opponents and their opponents' views in derisory, smug and sometimes sneering ways. They sometimes seem to regard themselves as "enlightened," and members of other worldviews as backward; indeed, they see secularism as a significant intellectual achievement of modern times. This belief mandates a political agenda, and unfortunately sometimes makes the secularist prone to over-the-top rants against religious belief. Recently, Daniel Dennett has condescendingly suggested that secularists start calling themselves "Brights"; further, the mission of the Brights movement involves working "to craft a social awareness that the constituency of persons who have naturalistic worldviews is large enough to have social and political clout, and it wants such persons to be accepted as citizens on a level playing field with those who hold other worldviews."[2]

So while their beliefs may be stated positively, secularist attitudes are still usually negative and antisomething, such as antireligion, anticlerical, antitraditional morality. As a result, secularists often find it difficult to avoid a militant streak; they can be just as full of righteous indignation as religious believers, and can sound like missionaries on a crusade. Unfortunately, the practical effect of this attitude is often seen in an attempt to press the cultural debate with quite poor secularist arguments, arguments that are unfair, do not often engage the substantive issues of disagreement or that are not very well informed. This is particularly true of the work of scientists who write from a secularist perspective such as Richard Dawkins, Francis Crick and Steven Weinberg, but it is also true of Dennett, a philosopher.[3] This is also, I think, a fair description of much of the public-square debates in popular media.

In chapter one, I gave an overview of the main beliefs of the secularist worldview in general on a number of matters. My thesis about secularism is that it is a growing and increasingly influential worldview throughout Western culture, and it is now a major player in moral and cultural debates and in the debate concerning pluralism. And although it is nowhere near as advanced or as influential as traditional religious worldviews, it is gaining members and becoming more significant. Indeed its power and influence in modern culture is truly astonishing when one considers how few people hold this view when compared with the number of people who belong to one or other of the traditional religions.

The secularist outlook does not lack for spokespersons. Contemporary spokespersons for secularism in one way or another would include Steven Pinker, Thomas Nagel, Peter Singer, Ayn Rand, Edward O. Wilson, John Rawls, John Searle, Daniel Dennett, Frederick Crews, Carl Sagan, Ann Druyan, Steven Weinberg, Richard Dawkins, Maxine Greene, Richard

---

[2]Dennett does not seem to be the originator of the term "Brights." See the website of the Brights movement at <http://www.the-brights.net>.

[3]See, for example (in the works referenced in note 4), Crick's evasiveness on the issue of free will, Weinberg's superficial chapter on philosophy, Dennett's exaggerated claims that he has explained consciousness and Dawkins's enthusiastic, but clearly logically fallacious, attempt to explain how order came out of chaos in the universe. At the more popular media level, religious arguments against abortion are often dismissed as being misogynist; against embryonic stem cell research as being antiscience; or against the coarsening of the culture through mass media as being "puritanical," etc.

Lewontin, Michael Ruse, Quentin Smith, Kai Nielsen, Simon Blackburn, Gore Vidal, Peter Atkins, Harold Pinter, Ludovic Kennedy (British author and journalist), Iain Banks (British novelist), Stephen J. Gould, Francis Crick, Michael Shermer, Paul Kurtz and many others.[4] These thinkers are all reasonably well-known contemporary intellectuals; they come from a variety of nationalities, backgrounds and disciplines; all are trying to advance the secularist cause in various ways. Yet this is just a smattering of names who support the secularist worldview; there are many more from all walks of life, many in positions of influence. And because many of these secularists are widely recognized public intellectuals (with many best selling books to their credit) they have significant cultural influence, obviously more than the average secularist, perhaps in some circles even more influence than some well-known religious figures.

Perhaps the best-known public intellectuals associated with an explicitly secularist worldview are the husband and wife team of Carl Sagan and Ann Druyan. Before his death in 1996, Sagan and Druyan worked together on many projects aimed at advancing, through legislation if possible, a naturalistic view of the cosmos and of the human person, and their secularist moral and educational views.[5] Sagan and Druyan are best known for their 1980 PBS TV series *Cosmos,* which was watched by millions of people; it continues to be shown on various channels and is part of educational curricula at many institutions across the country. This is an excellent TV series, well

---

[4]Some representative works include Steven Pinker, *How the Mind Works* (New York: Norton, 1997); Thomas Nagel, *The Last Word* (New York: Oxford University Press, 1997); Paul Kurtz, *Living Without Religion* (New York: Prometheus, 1994); John Searle, *Minds, Brains and Science* (Cambridge, Mass.: Harvard University Press, 1984); Daniel Dennett, *Consciousness Explained* (Boston: Little, Brown, 1991); Richard Dawkins, *The Blind Watchmaker* (New York: Norton, 1987); Francis Crick, *The Astonishing Hypothesis* (New York: Touchstone, 1995); Steven Weinberg, *Dreams of a Final Theory* (New York: Pantheon, 1992); Kai Nielsen, *Naturalism and Religion* (New York: Prometheus, 2001); Carl Sagan, *Cosmos* (New York: Random House, 2002); Edward Wilson, *Consilience: The Unity of Knowledge* (Cambridge, Mass.: Harvard University Press, 1988); Michael Ruse, *Darwin and Design: Does Evolution Have a Purpose?* (Cambridge, Mass.: Harvard University Press, 2003); John Rawls, *Political Liberalism,* paperback ed., with a new preface (New York: Columbia University Press, 1996); Michael Shermer, *How We Believe* (New York: Henry Holt, 2000); Quentin Smith, "The Metaphilosophy of Naturalism," *Philo* 4, no. 2 (2001): 195-215.

[5]Sagan and Druyan were cowriters of the *Cosmos* TV series. They also cowrote *Shadows of Forgotten Ancestors* (New York: Random House, 1992). Druyan was a producer of the film *Contact,* about the search for extraterrestrial intelligence, which was based on the novel by Carl Sagan. See also the book by Carl Sagan based on the TV series, *Cosmos;* and his *Billions and Billions* (New York: Ballantine, 1997) for his views on a variety of topics, including religion and science, the environment, abortion and his battle against illness.

worth watching, but there is no doubt that it is promoting the secularist worldview. The series opens with the famous line "the cosmos is all that is or was or ever will be," and it later claims that "we are made of star-stuff" and are born "ultimately of the stars." Sagan believes that deep down we know that we came from the universe and that this "may trouble whatever gods may be."[6] The series is also full of moral pronouncements, especially concerning Sagan's pet topics: the state of the environment, global warming and the production of nuclear weapons. Sagan, for instance, asks regarding the environment "Are we willing to tolerate ignorance and complacency in matters that affect the entire human family?" and an episode in the series (a chapter in the book) is devoted to the perils and foolishness of nuclear arms build up. I mention these moral issues not necessarily to disagree with Sagan, but simply to note that he is advancing a secularist worldview, part of which includes a moral agenda, much of which would require legislation to be implemented. The whole series also has a religious aura to it, and Sagan wonderfully conveys the spiritual enthusiasm of the secularist scientist contemplating the mystery and beauty of the universe. He clearly holds that one can still have some kind of spiritual life even if one is a secularist (of which more later)—indeed, Sagan's life and work are a kind of "religious" witness to his worldview. He also rarely has a good word to say about traditional religion, never misses an opportunity to portray it in an unfavorable light and treats it with a barely concealed contempt.[7]

Sagan's wife, Ann Druyan, has been more forthcoming about her aims as a secularist in recent years. In a revealing interview in the *Skeptical Inquirer* magazine, she gives an honest and frank overview of her secularist worldview.[8] Her worldview has three main themes: that science can explain everything, the critique of religion, and the attempt to promote her worldview, including her moral beliefs, politically. She is very disparaging of the creation story in the Bible and believes that the image of God that is portrayed there is of a "terrifying" figure. She notes that human beings often find the universe a disquieting place, so "as a society we lie to our children. We tell

---

[6]See Sagan, *Cosmos,* pp. 4, 12, 5.

[7]Though in his *The Demon-Haunted World* (New York: Ballantine, 1997), Sagan is a little more "ecumenical" toward religion, suggesting that perhaps religion and naturalism (secularism) might at least be in dialogue.

[8]See Ann Druyan, "Ann Druyan Talks About Science, Religion, Wonder, Awe . . . and Carl Sagan," *The Skeptical Inquirer,* November/December 2003, pp. 25-30; see also her epilogue to Sagan's *Billions and Billions,* pp. 268-75.

them a palliative story, almost to ensure that they will be infantile for all of their lives."[9] In the struggle between religion and science over the centuries, we eventually reached a kind of truce, she holds, where "the churches agreed to stop torturing and murdering scientists and the scientists pretended that knowledge of the universe has no spiritual implications," meaning that scientists pretended that science was no threat to religion.[10]

Yet like Sagan, Druyan believes that secularism has a spiritual side, which involves that "soaring feeling that we experience when we contemplate 13 billion years of cosmic evolution and four and a half billion years of the story of life on this planet."[11] She wonders why it is that the message of science does not grab more people and give them the kind of emotional gratification that religion has given to so many. She suggests turning planetaria all over the country into places of worship, where people could find "inspiration in the revelations of science." Druyan says she got this idea from her experience cowriting the script for two planetarium shows (one on the history of the universe; the other on the search for extraterrestrial life) for the Hayden Planetarium in New York. These shows are "the greatest virtual reality theatre on Earth; completely immersive in the experience of travelling through the universe."[12] They got her thinking, she says, about how

> we might offer something that would be at least as compelling as whatever anyone else in the religion business is offering. We get to take you through the universe, and through the history of not only the Milky Way Galaxy but also the larger universe, and to tell something . . . about the nature of life. It's a very uncompromising message about evolution and I think very directly promotes the kind of values and ideas that I think we share. Every kid who goes to a city public school gets taken to these shows.[13]

Ann Druyan is here articulating her secularist vision, which is founded on a naturalistic worldview, and which, in her version at least, has as part of its agenda the debunking of the religious worldview. She also wants many of her moral views established in law, not just about the environment, science education or nuclear weapons but also about drug taking. Druyan is a board member of NORML, the National Organization for the

---

[9]Ibid., p. 28.
[10]Ibid.
[11]Ibid.
[12]Ibid., p. 29.
[13]Ibid.

Reform of Marijuana Laws in the United States.

Turning to some other secularists, Pinker, Searle, Dennett and Crick are thinkers from different disciplines all working hard to advance the thesis that the human mind is a physical entity. They do so in order to remove the possibility that the mind is nonphysical "stuff" and so not just a property of the brain; if they succeed in this objective, they will have helped to further cement the secularist claim that all of reality is physical. Pinker is a psychologist, Searle and Dennett are philosophers, and Crick is a scientist. Dawkins, an evolutionary biologist and one of naturalism's most ardent polemicists, is trying to show that evolutionary theory can explain much in the universe, and so we do not need God. He argues that life itself has a biochemical, naturalistic origin. British philosopher Simon Blackburn in his work on language is attempting, among other things, to show that language and abstraction (and so the workings of the human mind) can be explained in naturalistic, scientific ways. Indeed, the obsession with philosophy of language and the philosophy of mind in contemporary Anglo-American philosophy can be seen as attempts to explain problematic areas of the human person—language and mind—in naturalistic terms, in order to preclude nonnaturalistic explanations (thereby lessening the probability that God exists). It is not a coincidence that in the age of secularism, the philosophy of mind, for example, is a huge area of research within the discipline of philosophy.[14]

Secularism, Politics and Seculocracy

There is no question that many secularists today want to establish what I call a *seculocracy*. This term refers to a state where many of the laws are based on a secularist ideology or worldview (just as we often describe a state

---

[14]There are no limits to how far secularists will go to avoid traditional religious conclusions. One only has to think of the philosopher W. V. O. Quine's attempt to get rid of universals (general, abstract terms) from language because of the difficulties he faced in trying to explain universals in naturalistic terms, or of philosopher David Lewis's bizarre theory of possible worlds. Lewis believed that in addition to our world there are untold numbers of possible worlds in which we all exist and are actualizing all of the possibilities we do not actualize in our current world. Why propose such a strange theory? Because, Lewis says, "talk of [possible worlds] has clarified questions in many parts of the philosophy of logic, of mind, of language, and of science—not to mention metaphysics itself." Or to put it another way, his hypothesis allows us to handle better many difficult philosophical problems while still retaining our secularist worldview, that is *while avoiding appeal to the existence of God.* See Quine, *Ontological Relativity and Other Essays* (New York: Columbia University Press, 1977); Lewis, *On the Plurality of Worlds* (New York: Blackwell, 1986).

based on a religious ideology a theocracy).[15] To use the language of the U.S. Constitution, what secularists want is a state where their views on significant political, social and moral questions are *established* in law. Our overview of the secularist worldview in chapter one illustrates this point clearly, as does our survey of the work of various secularist thinkers above, especially the work of Sagan and Druyan. It is clear that secularism is not a negative doctrine; it is now a positive doctrine with significant political implications, and it therefore needs and relies upon organized groups, spokespersons and fund-raising initiatives in order to promote its beliefs and values in the political arena. It is because secularism is not a negative or a neutral thesis about reality and human persons that throughout this book I will usually prefer to use the terms *secularism* and *secularist* to describe this view and its proponents, rather than using the term *secular*. It is very important to underscore the *positive* nature of secularism in the discussion about religion and politics, and the word *secular* generally fails to do this.

Secularism is not, of course, a new doctrine, though it has become a significant player as a worldview in itself only in recent times. Yet its indirect influence over the past one hundred years has been truly enormous. Thinkers of the past who have championed some form of secularism include Voltaire, Denis Diderot, Friedrich Nietzsche, John Stuart Mill, Charles Darwin, Sigmund Freud, B. F. Skinner, Karl Marx, Oliver Wendell Holmes, H. L. Menken, John Dewey, Corliss Lamont, Sidney Hook, Walter Lippmann, Bertrand Russell, Jean Paul Sartre and Simone de Beauvoir. Each of these thinkers actively promoted secularism as a way to transform society, and their ideas became increasingly influential over time. Russell famously said, for instance, that "religion prevents our children from having a rational education . . . it is possible that mankind is on the threshold of a golden age; but if so, it will be necessary first to slay the dragon that guards the door, and this dragon is religion."[16] Marx held that religion was the opium of the people, and that we needed to debunk it in order to motivate political revolution. These and other similar ideas influenced many people in many areas of life who then went about in their own quiet way affecting the secular transformation of society. Yet it is not the origins of secularism that interest us so much in this

---

[15]The concept of theocracy is often misunderstood and is much abused in contemporary arguments concerning religion and politics. The concept is regularly thrown around as a substitute for reasoned debate. For a good discussion of the concept, see Paul Marshall, *God and the Constitution* (Lanham, Md.: Rowman & Littlefield, 2002), pp. 65-70.

[16]Bertrand Russell, *Why I Am Not a Christian* (Penguin: London, 1927), p. 37.

book as its content and influence in contemporary culture. Various reasons can be given for its origins—from being understood primarily as a way of dealing with religious strife, to the view that a main motivation behind it was the wish to legitimize extramarital sex, to the view that it is really a neutral position among all other ideologies, to the view (which is becoming dominant today) that it is a substantive, positive and superior worldview to that of religious belief.

Christian Smith has edited a fascinating book on the history of what he calls "the secular revolution" in America. Smith, a sociologist, and his fellow contributors have challenged us to look again at why secularism became so politically dominant in U.S. culture over the last hundred years. Smith argues that there was a fairly well articulated, coherent attempt to overthrow the nineteenth century's mainline Protestant establishment. This "rebel insurgency consisted of waves of networks of activists who were largely skeptical, freethinking, agnostic, atheist, or theologically liberal; who were well-educated and socially located mainly in knowledge-production occupations; and who generally espoused materialism, naturalism, positivism and the privatization or extinction of religion."[17] The essays in Smith's book discuss and explain in detail how various areas of life were affected by the secular revolution.

The revolution occurred in seven main areas: (1) religion and science: science was promoted by secularists as the way of enlightenment, knowledge and progress, and religion was seen as backward, oppressive and superstitious; (2) higher education: many institutions of higher education, as the historian George Marsden has shown,[18] were transformed from religious institutions into secular ones; (3) mass primary and secondary education: schools were transformed from offering their mainline Protestant program into offering a "neutral," nonsectarian, secular educational curriculum, from which religion is excluded; (4) public culture and philosophy: mainline Protestant custodianship of public culture, with its emphasis on Christian America and moral integration, was supplanted with liberal political theory, with its emphasis on pluralism, relativism and procedural justice, while again

---

[17]Christian Smith, ed., *The Secular Revolution: Power, Interests, and Conflict in the Secularization of American Public Life* (Berkeley: University of California Press, 2003), p. 1. For an interesting and influential overview of the struggle between the secularist and religious mindsets in the modern world, see Peter Berger, *The Sacred Canopy* (New York: Anchor, 1967).
[18]See George Marsden, *The Soul of the American University* (New York: Oxford University Press, 1994).

excluding religion; (5) law: the view that religion had no place in public and social policy decisions, often made by the courts, was vigorously promoted, and a "wall of separation" between religion and politics was gradually established by the judiciary; (6) the religious view of the self: the understanding of the self as a spiritual and moral being concerned with caring for the soul in which the churches would play a major role was replaced by a naturalistic, psychologized model of human personhood, over which therapists and psychologists are the authorities; and (7) print and broadcast media: the media marginalized religion and adopted a (supposedly) religiously neutral approach to news and opinion.

Smith suggests that all of these transformations, which, taken individually, are well documented and uncontroversial in themselves, can nevertheless collectively be described as a "revolution." And not simply as a revolution that happened by accident or that was the inevitable result of modernization, but one that was intentionally promoted by many working in these individual areas of life, who knew what they were doing, and devoted themselves to bringing about their moral and political objectives. Smith argues, for example, that the "warfare" (or "conflict") model of the relationship between religion and science is not an accurate portrayal of the history of this relationship, but was deliberately exaggerated as a way of undermining religious belief and promoting secularism. It was, in short, largely motivated by secular ideology.[19]

Coming back to the present, Kai Nielsen, as noted earlier, is one of the few contemporary thinkers grappling seriously with the political and moral questions one must face if one adopts a secularist position on reality. Arguments against abortion and euthanasia and in favor of the death penalty mostly come from religion, Nielsen suggests, and he wants to move us toward what I have called a seculocracy where his own views on these matters are established in law, motivated by his secularist worldview. He recognizes that secularists will have to address these issues seriously in the future.[20] I predict that we will increasingly see works that involve an attempt to combine naturalism (the view that all that exists is physical) with the old secular humanism (the view that human beings themselves are the source of all meaning and value); this is, I think, the inevitable next step for modern atheism.

Indeed, the various Humanist Manifestos are just such an attempt.

---

[19]See Smith, *Secular Revolution*, pp. 1-12.
[20]See Nielsen, *Naturalism and Religion*, p. 15.

Humanist Manifesto I (1933) and *Humanist Manifesto II* (1973) were documents produced in the United States by groups of like-minded individuals eager to promote humanism as a worldview and as a religion. This worldview, particularly in the second manifesto, did expressly link humanism with a naturalistic, reductionist account of human life, and also with a liberal, democratic political theory. Supporters claimed that human life was the result of "unguided evolutionary change," and that they would "work to uphold the equal enjoyment of human rights and civil liberties in an open, secular society and maintain it is a civic duty to participate in the democratic process and a planetary duty to protect nature's integrity, diversity, and beauty in a secure, sustainable manner." The second manifesto was originally signed by 114 leading intellectuals, and many others added their names later. Among the original signers were Isaac Asimov, Paul Blanshard, Francis Crick, Arthur Danto, H. J. Eysenck, Maxine Greene, Sidney Hook, Paul Kurtz, Corliss Lamont and B. F. Skinner. John Dewey was the best-known signatory of the first manifesto. A third manifesto appeared in 2000, *Humanist Manifesto 2000*. The supporters of this one include Richard Dawkins, Daniel Dennett, Edward O. Wilson and Eugenie Scott (director of the National Center for Science Education, Oakland, California).[21]

Yet in describing secularism as a worldview, I am not especially thinking of the formally organized secularist groups or societies that exist (especially in U.S. society). Such groups include those mentioned who published the various Humanist Manifestos, along with the Council for Secular Humanism, Ethical Culture, American Atheists, various Eupraxophy groups and so on. In Britain, there is the National Secular Society, which campaigns for religion to be taken out of public life. Moreover, a think tank with close ties to the Blair Labour government has recently proposed that children should learn more about atheism and secular humanism in high school religion education classes (in part because the vast majority of people in Britain do not attend a weekly religious service).[22] Indeed, many countries now have formal secularist societies. It is interesting to note that many of these groups are mod-

---

[21] See *Humanist Manifestos I and II* (New York: Prometheus, 1973), pp. 7-10; 13-24; see also *Humanist Manifesto 2000*, ed. Paul Kurtz (New York: Prometheus, 2000).

[22] See *The Independent*, February 15, 2004. For a very brief but informative overview of the history of humanism, see Edwin H. Wilson, "Humanism's Moral Dimensions," in *The Humanist Alternative*, ed. Paul Kurtz (New York: Prometheus, 1973), pp. 15-19. Wilson believes that scientific humanism (what we have been calling naturalism) can be traced back to Francis Bacon's *Novum Organum* (1620).

eled after religions, some even espousing forms of spirituality. Nevertheless, it is still the case that the vast majority of secularists, or people inclined toward secularism, do not belong to any organized group representing secularism. (Let us not forget, also, that atheistic communism was once a worldwide movement.)

I am not saying that all of the above thinkers have thoroughly embraced the secularist agenda, though I think many of them have. There is as yet no unified voice of secularism, and may never be (perhaps the mainstream media and Hollywood come closest—at least on moral matters—since they are consciously and vigorously promoting many secularist causes in a systematic and pervasive way on a daily basis).[23] But all of these thinkers are working within a broadly secularist worldview and outlook, and are advancing their own distinctive part of it in their research and writing. While some secularists today emphasize the scientific side of things, and some emphasize the moral and political side of things, eventually these two areas will have to come together to form a full theory of secularism, a theory which will then have to be defended against religious belief. Secularists and religious believers are just beginning to enjoin this debate in a sustained way, and it is obviously a crucial debate for the issue of religion in politics. Indeed, this book is an attempt to contribute to this debate and to propose one way it might go.

Perhaps some of the thinkers mentioned would deny that they are secularists. That is fine; it is only necessary to show that their work aids and easily fits into a secularist worldview. Indeed, just as many religious believers may not think of secularism as a worldview, this may also be true of secularists themselves! As H. J. Blackham has noted, talking about what he calls humanism (what I have been calling secularism), many people are humanists "without knowing it"; he then goes on to argue that humanism requires

---

[23]When Mr. Mel Martinez was nominated as Secretary of Housing and Urban Development by President George W. Bush, he said the following: "Today for me is the fulfillment of the promise of America, the promise that regardless of where you come from, what language you speak, the color of your skin, or your economic circumstances, if you share the dream of a brighter tomorrow, and you're willing to pursue it with respect for others and an abiding faith in God, all things are possible." Several major newspapers, including the *St. Louis Post Dispatch, St. Petersburg Times, Bergen County Record* and the *Dallas Morning News,* ran this statement but without the reference to an abiding faith in God. Somebody decided to omit this. For what reason? Interestingly, Hugh Brogan notes how the Founding Fathers came to realize, in the various debates surrounding the beginning of the republic, that the press could be almost as influential as the pulpit! See his *Penguin History of the United States* (New York: Penguin, 1985), p. 98.

a political agenda.[24] Even today, there may still be a certain coyness about identifying oneself as a secularist. This is not just because one may not realize what one believes, or, more accurately, what view of the world is entailed by one's more specific moral and political beliefs, but because it can help one move more toward a seculocracy if one acts as if one's view is neutral (and therefore privileged), rather than just another worldview seeking to influence the public debate.

Some secularists today may be tempted, for public relations reasons, to play up the cultural perception and indeed confusion that their view is a neutral worldview. In this way, one can more easily avoid the debate on substantive issues, especially with religious believers. One can avoid the debate if one refuses to identify one's position, refuses to identify one's metaphysical commitments and foundational beliefs, than if one comes out in the open and admits that one is working for the cause of secularism. For instance, on the subject of abortion it might be more politically expedient for a secularist to argue that he does not hold a view on abortion himself, that he simply wants to legalize the practice and let people have a choice, in contrast to the religious believer who does hold a position on it and wants to make the practice illegal for everyone. This may be more expedient for the secularist than to acknowledge that he *does* hold a position on abortion and wants to shape the culture according to his own values. That is why one has to have a certain admiration for thinkers like Dawkins, Crick, Sagan, Druyan and Nagel who lay their cards honestly on the table (although Dawkins has an unfortunate tendency to engage in rants rather than reasoned debate). This way everyone knows where everyone stands. Many have charged that organizations like the National Academy of Sciences and the American Civil Liberties Union are largely covert secularist organizations that, at least sometimes, use science and a legal attack on religion in U.S. public life, respectively, to advance secularist causes.

In short, some secularists like Nielsen and Dawkins actively promote it, others like Rawls and Stephen J. Gould are more subtle; some emphasize science, like Crick and Pinker, others emphasize politics and the human

---

[24]See H. J. Blackham, *Humanism* (Harmondsworth, U.K.: Penguin, 1968). Blackham provides a very clear and readable overview and defense of a type of humanism that is clearly heading in a strongly naturalistic, scientific direction, and he addresses a series of interesting objections to the doctrine, many of which would be raised by religious believers. For the debate between humanism and other worldviews, see Lewis Vaughn and Austin Dacey, *The Case for Humanism: An Introduction* (Lanham, Md.: Rowman & Littlefield, 2003).

person, like Ruse and Nielsen. Some see themselves clearly as secularists with a fairly developed agenda, like Sagan and Druyan; others are less sure. Some are involved in formal societies, like Paul Kurtz's Eupraxophy Society or Daniel Dennett's "Brights"; others do not belong to any society or group. Some mainstream prominent publications and groups also follow the secularist line such as the *New York Times,* the *New York Review of Books,* much of national broadcasting and Hollywood. And there is at least one center of higher education, the Center for Inquiry, founded by Paul Kurtz, housed at the State University of New York at Buffalo, which offers research fellowships aimed at the promotion of philosophical naturalism (though there are many research grants in different disciplines that are primarily used for the promotion of naturalism and secularism, even if not explicitly so identified).

The secularist worldview is not confined to academia or media, however. As Rowler, Hertzke and Olson point out, if secularism is defined fairly broadly, say to include those who no longer attend church services or participate in their official religion, the number of secularists in the United States might range anywhere from fifteen to thirty percent of the electorate (many of these are highly concentrated on the east and west coast).[25] They combine "with infrequent attendees [to church] to create a sizable secular and near-secular portion of the voting population."[26] In short, secularists in the United States at least, as well as trying to establish control of much of the establishment (the universities, the courts, the media, the law schools, TV and Hollywood) are also gaining political clout as a voting block in their

---

[25]To give one interesting example in terms of places, among the largest worldviews in New York city are Catholicism and secularism, and so one might expect much of the public debate on various issues in this city to be influenced by these perspectives.

[26]R. Fowler, A. Hertzke and L. Olson, *Religion and Politics in America* (Boulder, Colo.: Westview, 1999), p. 107. In their overview of the various religions in America, although they nowhere consider the view that secularism is a worldview in itself, these authors at least consider what they call the "secularization thesis"—the thesis that American society is becoming more secular, especially among the elite classes, and that this fact has considerable political significance (pp. 255-56). Compare this to a book like Diana L. Eck's *A New Religious America: How a "Christian Country" Has Become the World's Most Religiously Diverse Nation* (San Francisco: HarperSanFrancisco, 2001). Eck gives detailed accounts of the movements of Hinduism, Buddhism and Islam in contemporary American society and how these movements are radically changing the religious landscape. She occasionally comments—usually in terms of the constitutional issue (not the moral question) of the separation of church and state—on the effect of these new religious movements on American pluralism, but never once considers the question of whether secularism is a worldview and how the *presence* of secularism in the debate will also change the pluralist landscape in a very significant way.

own right. It is also true that there are increasing numbers of secularists in many European countries.

Needless to say, all of these thinkers, groups and ordinary citizens do not necessarily hold the same beliefs; they surely have many disagreements among themselves. Nor is it always easy to identify when the secularist worldview is being asserted or appealed to (though this is changing). However, I think there would be fairly broad agreement among secularists on the foundational beliefs that all of reality is physical, that the human person is to be understood in a reductive, naturalistic way, that we need secularist accounts of morality and politics, and that, at the very least, traditional religion must be relegated to the private sphere. In short, they would probably all subscribe to the view that the secularist agenda must define and dominate the public square. As the well-known American intellectual and secularist Sidney Hook put it, "Religion as a system of over-beliefs about the existence of God and related views, I regard as a *private* matter."[27] Secularists of all stripes usually agree that their worldview not only should dominate public and social policy matters, but that religious beliefs should have little or no role in these matters (and, as we will see later, they hold that wherever secularist and religious views disagree, secularist views should be presumptive).

The secularist outlook may also apply to those who are antireligious is some lesser way, to the attitudes of those who would not go so far as to advocate an alternative secularist worldview (though they may be committed to this, in part, and simply not realize it). As I indicated, sometimes the word *secular* is used to convey the point that a view is simply not religious; it is also sometimes used to refer to the fact that when we engage in a public discussion today we don't all share the same foundational assumptions. But the word *pluralism* is a better word to convey this latter point. I am arguing that when we recognize that our pluralist society also includes as a key player in cultural and moral debates the worldview of secularism, then our understanding of religion and politics will have to be significantly revised.[28]

It is important to note that secularism is not the same view as political

---

[27]Sidney Hook, "The Snare of Definitions," in *The Humanist Alternative,* ed. Paul Kurtz (New York: Prometheus, 1973), p. 33.
[28]In chap. 4, I will consider the objection that what is sometimes called "secular reason" is really neutral between worldviews and is not the same thing as *secularism*.

liberalism, although perhaps political liberalism dovetails more easily with secularism than it does with religious belief. (Some in the United States might describe secularism as *liberalism without religion,* or perhaps accompanied by a version of religion that is devoid of religious doctrine or that does not take its creed very seriously, that is mainly cultural and "spiritual.") I am using the term *liberalism* in this book in the sense derived from the thought of John Locke and John Stuart Mill. Liberalism is a political theory that advocates a significant realm of personal freedom for human beings and that in general elevates the freedom of the individual over the common good of society. Mill also advocates the relativistic view that every human being has his or her own philosophy of life; so one of the practical challenges for modern democracies is how to arrive at a workable political system given the diversity of worldviews (John Rawls's political theory is one response to this problem, as we will see in chapter six).[29] As a matter of fact, in the United States secularism is liberal in outlook, though it need not necessarily be so in theory. And we should not forget that secularism is also regularly allied with various forms of Marxism.

The Influence of Secularism on Religion

It is interesting to note that many religious believers today are themselves quite secularist in outlook. This means that they either accept or are very influenced by some of the key beliefs of secularism (perhaps on moral questions), and these beliefs edge out and trump their religious beliefs whenever the two clash (e.g., they might hold that abortion is immoral but agree to legalize it). Members and supporters of Americans United for the Separation of Church and State, an organization presently led by Mr. Barry Lynn, fall into this category. Like many religious people, they are under the sway of the secularist mindset. A recent Gallup poll showed that religious believers today experience an intense religious hunger, but they seem in general not to be sure about what they believe and why. Many believe in God, but admit that this belief is not the first thing they appeal to in many aspects of their lives. They also say that their religious beliefs have little impact on their own lives or in society. One reason for these attitudes is the increasing secular-

---

[29]For an excellent, clear overview of the various forms of liberalism and for a critique of liberalism as a whole, see John Kekes, *Against Liberalism* (New York: Cornell University Press, 1997); see also David T. Koyzis, *Political Visions and Illusions* (Downers Grove, Ill.: InterVarsity Press, 2003), chap. 2.

ization of society.[30] The practical effect of the influence of secularism on traditional religion and the influence of groups like Barry Lynn's is to produce an influential group of (liberal) religious believers who further advance the secularist cause by watering down their religious beliefs[31] and by calling for the elimination of religion from politics. Americans United is perhaps an extreme instance of this view in action.

Why do some religious believers think that religion should be curtailed in public life? After all, there is no corresponding attitude among secularists—there are no secularists calling for the restriction of secularism in public life. One reason could simply be that many religious believers are confused about issues surrounding religion and politics, and about the political implications, in particular, of some of their own beliefs, and so they are unwittingly aiding the cause of secularism. Another reason is that many religious believers in the United States in particular have been very influenced by the *legal* history of the relationship between religion and politics. The First Amendment to the U.S. Constitution calls for freedom of religion; over the last few decades the courts—ably abetted by many interest groups and the mainstream establishment—have usually interpreted this to mean "freedom from religion." This interpretation has gradually intimidated many religious believers into compromising their beliefs in various ways, into becoming very deferential to secularism, into thinking there is something not quite right about their own beliefs.

Yet a third reason is the one already alluded to in our brief mention of Americans United. Many religious believers are suspicious of, even hostile to, *other religions,* particularly those with which they do not agree on some important moral questions, and so there is a tendency, especially in liberal religious groups, to use the rhetoric of church and state separation as a way of *restricting* the influence of the groups with which they disagree in the political arena. Usually, a consequence is that their *own* religious views

---

[30]See the overview of recent surveys of people's religious beliefs in George Gallup Jr. and D. Michael Lindsay, *The Gallup Guide: Reality Check for 21st Century Churches* (Loveland, Colo.: Group Publishing, 2002).

[31]Sometimes this watering down can take radical forms, such as in the various fideistic views found in the work of the English theologian Don Cupitt or the Welsh philosopher D. Z. Phillips. These thinkers deny that God exists as a transcendent being, that the soul exists and that there is life after death. I believe that one reason they adopt such radical views is due to the influence of modern science and the secularization of modern society. For more on Phillips's fideism, see my "Commitment, Justification, and the Rejection of Natural Theology," *American Catholic Philosophical Quarterly* 77, no. 3 (summer 2003): 417-36.

(those of the liberal groups) will prevail in public policy. Thus, for example, supporters of Americans United believe that abortion should be legal, but often rather than arguing for this view directly, they use the rhetoric of church-state separation in an attempt to *exclude* the view of those who hold that abortion should be illegal, and so in this way they believe that the Americans United view is more likely to win the day.[32]

To take another example, a Kansas City-based group called the Mainstream Coalition threatened to visit churches in the Kansas City area during the election season of 2004 to make sure local ministers were not telling their congregations how to vote on certain issues, thereby violating tax-exemption rules for churches. Were the motives of the (tax-exempt) Mainstream Coalition pure? Were they really worried about violations of tax laws relating to the separation of church and state, or was this an indirect (but not so subtle?) way of attempting to promote *their own political views* by attempting to silence their opponents? (And these views may well be *religiously* inspired.) In U.S. society, church-state separation is almost always invoked by liberal groups against conservative groups. As Stephen Carter has noted, "It is a matter of simple fact that the rules are almost always invoked against churches and other groups that fall toward the right end of our rather narrow political spectrum; the left is all but immune."[33] These examples show that it would be a mistake to conclude from the fact that some religious believers favor a strict separation of church and state, that it follows from this that these groups do not want to promote their religious views in politics, or that the public square really is neutral, or that the secular state is not antireligious.

In the arguments and discussion that follow in this book, for the sake of simplicity I will refer to arguments that seek to exclude (or restrict) religious belief from public life as secularist arguments, while recognizing that some of these arguments might also be proposed by liberal religious believers.

---

[32]A fourth reason sometimes offered by religious believers is that restricting religious beliefs in politics is *good* for religious belief; among other advantages, it protects the religious worldview from political corruption. Although this is an important point, it is not a sufficient reason for restricting the role of religion in politics, as I argue in the last section of chap. 5.

[33]Stephen L. Carter, *God's Name in Vain* (New York: Basic Books, 2000), p. 70. The strategy of groups like the Mainstream Coalition and Americans United reminds us of an earlier use of the same strategy in U.S. history. Carter illustrates that nineteenth-century pro-slavery politicians argued in various ways for the separation of church and state because most of the arguments against slavery were coming from religious groups and leaders, and "the separation of church and slavery" was a way of putting a brake on abolitionism (see p. 21 and pp. 83-89).

(Similarly, when I said above that the secularist outlook controls much of the U.S. establishment, I also include the outlook of liberal religious believers in this judgment.)

Secularism as a Worldview

Let us bring some of these points together to further illustrate my claim that secularism is now a worldview in its own right. Secularism satisfies well the definition of a worldview that I laid out in chapter one. Secularism is obviously a philosophy of life, which contains beliefs about the three primary areas (the nature of reality, the nature of the human person, the nature of moral and political values). The secularist holds that all of reality is physical, that human beings are purely physical beings and that some political structures are more morally preferable to others. Secularism contains life-regulating beliefs, such as "human beings are the source of all meaning and value," or "everyone should have the freedom to live as they see fit, as long as they do not harm others," and so on. Carl Sagan, as we have seen, wanted tougher laws protecting the environment, and Kai Nielsen wants to make euthanasia legal.

It is also fair to say that secularism has certain rituals, as pointed out in chapter one. And although it does not have nearly as many established rituals and practices as traditional religion, which has been around so much longer, this will change when it becomes more widespread, and is changing even as we read these words. We have seen that the naturalist Michael Shermer has acknowledged that he gets a kind of spiritual uplift from attendance at the weekly meetings of his scientific group.[34] But my main point is that secularism has rituals and practices that express, confirm and reinforce the secularist's "spiritual enthusiasm," if you will, for his or her beliefs and lifestyle. Carl Sagan is a witness to this type of spirituality in his narration of

---

[34]For some very perceptive social commentary on secular rituals, rites and beliefs, see David Brooks, *Bobos in Paradise* (New York: Simon & Schuster, 2001), where he argues that secularism is infused with spiritualism and rituals aimed at firming up one's metaphysical self! One is also reminded of John Dewey's distinction in *A Common Faith* (New Haven, Conn.: Yale University Press, 1962) between "religion" and "the religious," where *the religious* "denotes attitudes that may be taken toward every object and every proposed end or ideals" (p. 10), even though one rejects the supernatural and organized religion. I do not wish to insist upon the point that the secularist worldview includes such attitudes, but there is surely something true in Dewey's observation that "militant atheism is . . . affected by lack of natural piety" (p. 53). Most atheism is not militant, and so the average atheist would not have shut himself off from the experience of this natural piety.

Cosmos. Secularists could even be said to take comfort from their beliefs in the way that all members of worldviews do (although this comfort is a consequence of one's beliefs and not an initial reason for holding them). Indeed, the philosopher Robert Solomon has recently proposed a spirituality for the skeptic, "a model of vibrant, fulfilling spirituality that embraces the complexities of human existence and acknowledges the joys and tragedies of life."[35] Rejecting organized religion and the realm of the supernatural, Solomon's proposal is yet another contribution to the growing body of work aimed at filling out all of the facets of the secularist worldview, metaphysical, moral, political and now what Solomon calls "naturalized spirituality." As in other worldviews, rituals both express and reinforce the worldview.

It is also obvious that secularism promotes a theory of morality. Although many secularists favor utilitarianism, the specific content of this theory can vary with the particular form of secularism, just as it can with the particular form of religion, though like religion, the various secularist views will have much in common with each other, especially concerning the foundational beliefs. Perhaps one of the more obvious, defining features of modern secularism is its proponents' attempt to morally shape society and culture according to their version of the good life, as seen for instance in Ann Druyan's work aimed at legalizing marijuana use.

Finally, secularism is promoted by various organs and outlets; it has its "priests," and they are engaged in missionary work, in trying to recruit people to that worldview. Many of them are trying to show that their worldview is the most rational option and that other worldviews, especially religious views, are mistaken. Richard Dawkins is trying to show in his book *The Blind Watchmaker* that evolutionary theory can explain all of reality, and those who deny this or who believe that there is some overall purpose to the universe are wrong. As Dawkins has famously put it, "Darwin made it possible to be an intellectually fulfilled atheist."[36] Francis Crick, who did pioneering work on the structure of DNA and is author of *The Astonishing Hypothesis,* argues in that book that there is no soul, that the human mind is a totally physical entity, and those who believe otherwise are misguided: "The Astonishing Hypothesis is that 'You,' your joys and your sorrows, your memories and your ambitions, your sense of personal identity and free will, are

---

[35]Robert C. Solomon, *Spirituality for the Skeptic* (New York: Oxford University Press, 2002), quote taken from the dust jacket.
[36]Dawkins, *Blind Watchmaker,* p. 6.

in fact no more than the behavior of a vast assembly of nerve cells and their associated molecules."[37] Crick has clarified matters for us even more in his recent statement that "I went into science because of [a distaste for religion], there's no doubt about that. I asked myself what were the two things that appear inexplicable and are used to support religious beliefs: the difference between living and nonliving things, and the phenomenon of consciousness."[38] This may well be a little bit of personal historical revisionism by Crick, but it indicates that he sees himself as being on a bit of a crusade! These are just obvious examples; many other cases of secularist "missionary work" could be cited.[39] All of these thinkers are doing missionary work for secularism through their various publications, public lectures, TV and newspaper interviews and so on. They are trying to spread the word that secularism is true, to convince people of its truth, and to get people to adopt this view over other alternatives, such as traditional religious worldviews.

Secularism as a Religion

I want to propose that not only does secularism satisfy the definition of a worldview, but that, with appropriate clarifications, it also satisfies the definition of religion. The first reason for describing secularism as a religion is that it satisfies the definition on all of the main points. It is therefore appropriate to describe secularism as a religion, as long as we recognize *one* difference. The one key difference between traditional religion and secularism is that the latter does not accept belief in God (in any sense of the term) or in an unseen sacred realm, but on all of the other *formal* features of a worldview, it mirrors exactly the traditional religious view of the world, as we saw in chapter one.

The second reason for describing secularism as a religion is that in the twentieth century it has become a positive worldview in a way that it had not

---

[37]Crick, *Astonishing Hypothesis*, p. 3.

[38]As quoted in an article in the *Washington Times*, "DNA Pioneers Lash Out at Religion," March 24, 2003 <www.washingtontimes.com>.

[39]As a further example, see Simon Blackburn's derogatory remarks about religion in his review of philosopher Hillary Putnam's *The Threefold Cord: Mind, Body and World* in the *New Republic*, April 17, 2000, where, among other things, he says that "I have heard it said, unkindly or not, that Putnam's project in recent years has been to make the world safe for religion," and he reminds us of the "attitudes that cling to the religious spirit, such as exclusiveness, sanctimoniousness, sectarianism, hostility to science, admiration for wishful thinking" <www.tnr.com>. He adds that religious beliefs are found wanting or even risible upon critical examination. This kind of caricature is not likely to lead to a meeting of minds between the worldviews!

been in the rest of history. By a positive worldview, I mean that secularists have become more sophisticated in the last few decades and have begun to try to state and defend their beliefs in positive terms. They want to do this to give secularism a more prominent place in the debate between worldviews, to distinguish it and themselves from traditional religion more sharply, and because they believe it will help in bringing more converts to their view and in the overall critique of religion. In this sense, secularism must be distinguished from atheism, although it does have much in common with atheism. But in the past, the atheist defined himself, if you will, in opposition to religion, rather than as a positive adherent of a different worldview.

Atheism was negative in at least three ways. First, the atheist, who was very much in the minority, defined himself in terms of what he was not, rather than in terms of what he was. So in the past an atheist might say, when asked what he believed, that he did *not* think that God existed or that he *rejected* religious morality, and he might go on to distinguish himself from all of those religious believers who believed the opposite. Second, he often defined himself negatively, in the sense that his identity was often bound up more with who he was not (i.e., a religious believer), than with who he actually was (i.e., an atheist)! Third, the atheist also defended his view negatively, by attacking religion and arguments for religious belief, a kind of negative strategy. He did this rather than presenting positive arguments in favor of atheism.[40] In this way, atheism was usually perceived, correctly it seems, as being primarily antireligious. This might also explain why many religious believers have a quite negative view of atheism, more so than they have of, say, secular humanism.

However, in the twentieth century all of this changed, and this marks in general the transition from atheism to secular naturalistic humanism. The negative approach was no longer appropriate, and a new image was needed. Now a secularist is much more likely to present secularism as a positive thesis, one that identifies what he believes rather than what he does not believe. For example, secularists will say they believe that human life is the outcome of a purely random, naturalistic process (evolution), and that all of

---

[40]Of course, in the history of thought there were pockets of positive atheism and of naturalistic attempts to explain reality, such as those of Lucretius (first century B.C.) and the early atomistic philosophers (fifth century B.C.). However, such views were very much in the minority and had little or no influence on religion or society; it was not until the modern era (especially during the Enlightenment) that such views began to have a creeping and eventually dominant influence on political and civil matters.

reality is physical. And, very importantly, their defense of these beliefs now will not consist simply of attacking the arguments for religious belief. They will offer positive arguments for the view that all of reality is physical, arguments perhaps based on an appeal to cosmology, evolution, genetics (as in the work of Carl Sagan).

The fact that secularism is now presented as a positive thesis, which its proponents are prepared to defend by appeal to positive evidence, makes it even more legitimate not only to describe it as a worldview but also, as I have been arguing in this section, as a "religion." The fact that it is a positive thesis identifies its adherents as people who have a different worldview from that of traditional religion and who wish to highlight this fact. The move to secularism is in part a way of making atheism more respectable and of presenting it as a serious alternative to traditional religion—as, in fact, an alternative "religion." Indeed, atheism can't remain negative always; there will come a time when atheists will be forced by circumstances to develop their views in positive ways and to broaden their beliefs out into a coherent worldview. That time is upon us. Kai Nielsen, as we have seen above, is an example of one atheist who is in the vanguard of the attempt to respond to the challenge of making atheism more positive, comprehensive and defensible.[41]

The third reason we can describe secularism as a "religion" is that, like all substantive worldviews, some of its key beliefs are based on *faith,* in the first sense of that term described in detail in chapter one. Members of every religion accept beliefs they cannot *prove* but to which they pledge their commitment, and these beliefs help regulate their behavior. Because of this (as we will see in the next chapter) it can be appropriate to describe secularist beliefs as "religious beliefs." This is an important point because the phenomenon of beliefs being based partly on faith is often used to put religious views in a different category from secularist views; however, it cannot be used to do this because both views have this feature in common. So my main point here is that there is nothing really inaccurate about describing secularism as a religion because it captures the salient points that it is a worldview, that some of its beliefs are based on faith, and that it is competing in the marketplace of ideas with other worldviews. To put this point another way, the main differences between traditional religious worldviews

---

[41]See also recent attempts to explain altruism from an evolutionary perspective, such as Elliot Sober and David Sloan Wilson, *Unto Others: The Evolution and Psychology of Unselfish Behavior* (Cambridge, Mass.: Harvard University Press, 1998).

and secularism are differences of *content* and not differences of *form;* differences in what the worldviews teach or hold and not differences in their respective structures. Both worldviews have the same formal structure, as we have seen, but certainly differ with regard to their content. Their similarity of structure will nevertheless have profound significance for our understanding of the role of religion in politics.

Finally, the fourth reason we can appropriately describe secularism as a religion is that, like all substantive worldviews, it does lead to a significant change in one's life. This change has always been an integral part of the religious worldview. Traditional religious belief has usually led, upon its adoption in a person's life, to a radical change in that life.[42] This change comes about not just in terms of the theoretical beliefs one holds, but also in terms of one's moral and spiritual life. That is to say, upon becoming a religious believer one does not just begin to believe different things that one did not believe before, such as that God exists, for example, whereas one previously believed that God did not exist, or that Jesus rose from the dead, whereas one previously believed that the resurrection never occurred. These theoretical beliefs are also accompanied by and intimately tied to (in terms of justification) a transformation in how one lives one's life. Adopting a new religion usually leads to a quite noticeable change in one's moral and spiritual behavior. This is clearly an important feature of adopting the traditional religious view of the world. Of course, such a change will not necessarily come about, but it is usual in the religious worldview.

Yet it should not be overlooked that this transforming aspect of adopting a new worldview is also an important feature of any substantive worldview, including the worldview of secularism. Suppose one converted from, say, Orthodox Judaism to secularism, how would this affect one's life? It would lead to one adopting a set of new beliefs such as the belief that all that exists is physical, that we must choose our own moral values (since there is no God), that there is no soul, that extramarital sex is not necessarily immoral and so on. All of these beliefs will affect how one lives. A person who made this kind of conversion (say after lengthy reflection on Richard Dawkins's missionary works) will begin to look at the world in a secular way and be-

---

[42]See the interesting account of the lives of C. S. Lewis (the religious worldview) and Sigmund Freud (the secularist worldview) contrasted side by side in their search for happiness and fulfillment based around their respective worldviews in Armand M. Nicholi Jr., *The Question of God: C. S. Lewis and Sigmund Freud Debate God, Love, Sex, and the Meaning of Life* (New York: Free Press, 2002).

have accordingly, rather than continuing to look at the world in a religious way. This will affect many aspects of one's personal behavior and attitudes, from the area of human relationships to moral values to political issues. I am here reminded of a young woman I once heard about who converted from Catholicism to secularism and shortly afterward moved in with her boyfriend, causing her mother much grief, both personally and in the small community in which they all lived. She also supported a campaign to legalize euthanasia and took up other secularist causes. And so, since secularism does lead to such a transformation in one's life, this is all the more reason to regard it as a religion. Let us not forget that the word *religion* is often interpreted to mean "a way of life." And secularism is a way of life just as much as traditional religion is, although it is not as widespread or as well established as traditional religious belief (though this will no doubt change in the future).

I would like to conclude this section with a point about terminology. I have been describing secularism as a religion to illustrate the point that it has much in common with traditional religious belief, especially the very features that it has often used to deny traditional religion a place in the public square. However, if the arguments of this book are correct, it would be better *in the long-distant future* for the purposes of clarity to generally describe each position as a worldview instead of as a religion because the term *worldview* helps us avoid confusions concerning the status of the worldview, and especially concerning why religion is supposed to be (formally) different from secularism.

In the general debate between worldviews, it is often more helpful to refer to the views in question by their generic name of *worldviews* instead of putting them into subsets of worldviews, such as the subset of traditional religions or the subset of secularisms. That might be the best way to proceed in the future. Yet old habits die hard, and it will be initially strange for us to think about religion and politics in the new categories and terminology I am proposing here. In what follows, I will often refer to religious worldviews as "traditional religion" to distinguish them from secularist worldviews. I will sometimes use the general term *religion* to refer to any worldview, even if the worldview has exclusively secularist content, in order to emphasize the structural similarity of worldviews and to further illustrate the usefulness of looking at things this way for the debate concerning worldviews and politics.

Having therefore analyzed fully the notion of a worldview in general and discussed the worldview of secularism in particular, it is now time to turn to the religious worldview. We must consider the questions of what makes a belief "religious" and what is supposed to be wrong with "religious beliefs" from the point of view of introducing them into politics before turning to the question of whether the worldview of religious belief is a *reasonable* worldview.

3

Religious Beliefs and Reason

An old college friend of mine is a strong opponent of euthanasia. He used to argue against it all the time during our seminars in ethics and political philosophy. Although he could marshal several arguments against the practice, his favorite one was that life is a gift from God and that it would be wrong for us to reject that gift, no matter what the circumstances. Hence all forms of suicide are immoral. Although he was a Christian believer, my friend did not get this argument from the Bible, but from Plato. It was easy to lose count of the number of times he brought this argument up in our seminars, with different professors, only for almost all of them to dismiss it without any discussion. The reason they would invariably give was that it was a "religious" argument. And religious arguments, they held, are simply not appropriate in philosophical or political discussions. Now this response to my friend's argument, and to similar arguments that make an appeal to religious beliefs, is not unusual. In fact, it is probably fairly typical for our society; one might even say that it is the default view right now among various groups in our culture, especially among the intelligentsia.

But what do we mean when we describe a belief as a religious belief? It is a description we use all the time, but are far from clear about its meaning. And what is wrong exactly with beliefs that are religious beliefs, so wrong that one should not bring these beliefs into politics? We are asking what is meant by the term *religious* when it is used in statements like "For religious reasons, the couple are opposed to abortion" (this phrasing is used frequently, for example, in the *New York Times*); or, "one should not impose one's religious views on extramarital sex on everyone"; or, as the pro-euthanasia side argued in the 1997 debate in Oregon, the argument against euthanasia is a religious argument, and the argument in favor of euthanasia is not a religious argument (and so the religious argument should not be introduced into the political debate on euthanasia, just like my friend's argument). In these cases, the word *religious* is not simply referring in a descriptive way to a traditional religious worldview or to religion-related content, but to some *quality* the beliefs have that makes them distinctive from other, secularist beliefs. The word *religious* is not just telling us that the beliefs come from a religious worldview, but that there is something about the belief, some quality or characteristic it has, that makes it problematic in a democratic society. We need to identify what this quality is and bring out its implications for the debate between worldviews. This will be helpful because the secularist usually insists that traditional religious beliefs are not worthy of inclusion in the political debate because they are "religious." Our discussion of what it means for a belief to be a "religious" belief will also lead appropriately later in the chapter into the question of the rationality of religious beliefs. (Keep in mind that we are interested in the moral question of why religion should be excluded from politics, not the legal question of whether it can be, say, according to the U.S. Constitution.)

What Does It Mean to Describe a Belief as "Religious"?

I have argued above that all worldviews are "religious," because at least some of their beliefs are accepted on faith, and so secularism is just as much a religion as any traditional religion. Examining the ways in which a particular belief or view might be described as religious will help us to elaborate these points further. (I should note that I am primarily referring to how secularists and those opposed to any significant role for traditional religion in politics use the term *religious;* most religious believers are unlikely to use the term in any kind of negative or derogatory way.) The meaning of the term *religious* has been subject to no sustained analysis in the literature on religion and politics; this is a serious omission because the meaning of the term has crucial relevance for determining the rules (and therefore the outcome) of the public-square debate concerning moral, political and social matters.

When a particular belief or view is described as religious, what is normally meant is that it is supported by or based upon or derived from some of the following sources[1]: (1) a text, such as the Bible, the Qur'an, John Stuart Mill's *On Liberty*, Karl Marx's *Das Kapital*, John Rawls's *A Theory of Justice*; (2) the institutional church(es), including representatives such as the priests and other authorities of the worldview (e.g., Billy Graham as a spokesman for Protestantism or Richard Dawkins as a spokesman for secularism); (3) a profound personal experience of some kind (e.g., the experience that God is near, the experience that people are fundamentally equal, etc.); (4) the *tradition* of the church in question (e.g., in Judaism by appeal to the Talmud; in secularism by [selective] appeal to the works of philosophers John Locke, Immanuel Kant or John Stuart Mill); (5) appeal to faith alone (e.g., believing that life is a gift from God on faith; believing that there is a scientific answer to the question of the origin of the universe on faith).

The reader will have noticed that I have deliberately included secularist examples of these sources, as well as examples from traditional religion, in order to illustrate that it is quite possible for a secularist to hold and to promote a belief based on these sources; these sources are not confined to religious believers. As long as a secularist belief is based on a similar type of appeal to the kinds of sources that religious believers might also use, then the arguments used to exclude religious beliefs because they come from these sources will also apply to secularist beliefs that come from the same kind of sources. Contemporary political theory, as we will see in chapter six, appeals frequently to the authority of liberal political *tradition* to support some of its important, indeed crucial, claims. These examples also serve to remind us and to emphasize again one of my main claims: that secularism is also a religion, and that it has the same formal structure as traditional religious belief.

The secularist, and those opposed to the introduction of religious beliefs into politics, usually want to claim that beliefs based on these five sources *are not worthy candidates for inclusion in political debate.* This is because these sources are not reliable, or are irrational, or are nonrational, or cannot be proven, or are rejected by many reasonable people and so on. Appeal to a religious text is controversial because we cannot be sure the text represents genuine revelation from a supernatural source; further, many reject the

---

[1]I have been influenced in my description of some of these sources by Robert Audi's discussion in his *Religious Commitment and Secular Reason* (Cambridge: Cambridge University Press, 2000), p. 116. Audi refers to some of these sources as sources of religious obligation; I think it is more accurate to describe them as sources to which one might appeal to justify the rationality of religious belief.

text as a reliable source of religious knowledge. The same goes for religious authority figures or institutions. Appeal to a tradition can also be controversial because the origins of traditions are often morally questionable, there are different traditions in different parts of the world, and sometimes tradition means little more than custom—all good reasons, it is claimed, to be skeptical of tradition as a source for political arguments. Similarly, an appeal to a profound personal experience is not acceptable to those who have not had the privilege of the experience and who will surely doubt its validity. An appeal to faith (in the sense of believing without evidence) is also rationally unacceptable.

To elaborate these reasons a little further, the secularist holds that in a pluralist society one cannot *reasonably* expect others who are not already members of the particular religious worldview in question to be guided by beliefs in the public political arena that are derived from any of these five sources. This is a *moral* argument; it means that morally and rationally one should not introduce religious arguments into public debate if they come from any of these sources. Of course, in most democracies one can, as a matter of free speech, introduce almost any argument one likes into the public square. But the proponents of the (general) moral argument against introducing religious arguments into politics hold that although legally it is permissible to do so, morally one should not do so. (There are good reasons for having a fairly permissive free speech law, as we will see later.)

The attempt to morally exclude religious beliefs from politics has led to what Richard John Neuhaus has called the "naked public square":

> What is relatively new is the naked public square. The naked public square is the result of political doctrine and practice that would exclude religion and religiously grounded values from the conduct of public business. The doctrine is that America is a secular society. It finds dogmatic expression in the ideology of secularism.[2]

Neuhaus goes on to argue that the doctrine is not only false, but dangerous. What is pernicious about this secularist doctrine is that it attempts to sideline the religious only by failing (or refusing) to acknowledge that secularism too is a worldview, and that, logically, there is no such thing as a naked public square, as we will see as our discussion unfolds.

So the use of the term *religious* today to describe a belief (especially by

---

[2]Richard John Neuhaus, *The Naked Public Square* (Grand Rapids: Eerdmans, 1984), p. vii.

the secularist) is meant to convey that the belief is based on *one or a combination of the five sources mentioned above.* When a belief is described as "religious" this means it is based on appeal to a text, tradition, authority, experience or something of that order. In this way, the term *religious* is often used in a pejorative sense in an attempt to distinguish traditional religious beliefs and views from secularist beliefs and views, in order to exclude traditional religious beliefs from politics. (The *New York Times* would not report that "for secular reasons, the couple is opposed to abortion." Or even "for secular reasons, the couple supports abortion.")

For the purposes of my discussion in this book, I am prepared to make a major concession to the secularist on this matter, a concession some religious believers, I acknowledge, would not be willing to make. I am prepared to agree that *one should not introduce into the public square religious beliefs based on the above five sources.* I will add two provisos to this restriction: The first is that one *may* introduce beliefs into the political arena based on these sources if one is prepared to debate the rationality of the source rather than simply appeal to the source as authoritative without a rational argument to support its claim to authority.[3] The second proviso is that the secularist also cannot introduce beliefs into politics if they come from these five sources. Although I know it will be controversial among many religious believers,[4] my reason for granting that we should not introduce beliefs based on the first five sources into politics is that I am persuaded by the argument that one cannot reasonably expect others who come from different tradi-

---

[3]This debate might include an argument that the Bible, say, was an authoritative book. The argument for this might be offered before one comes to the public-square debate, as it were, and not explicitly in the public square, where it might be simply assumed. But the argument itself would have to be, and usually would be, public in the sense that it would appeal to objectively available sources such as logical argument, archeological evidence, historical evidence, eyewitness testimony, etc. This argument cannot be dismissed by members of other worldviews because it is *not* an argument based on privileged claims to knowledge, claims that only the religious believer can know. Nor can it be dismissed by facile rejoinders along the lines that "that was an awful long time ago, and we can never be sure that it all really happened." I mention this here because arguments for the historicity of the Bible are well established in both Catholic and Protestant theology, but they are usually dismissed without a hearing by secularists, who are almost always not themselves biblical scholars.

[4]One philosopher who argues for a much more permissive view of which religious beliefs can be included in politics is Paul Weithman, in his *Religion and the Obligations of Citizenship* (New York: Cambridge University Press, 2002). He would allow into the public square religious reasons based on the five sources listed. Although I find his view overall very refreshing, I support a more restrictive view for religion in politics for the reasons given in this section.

tions, cultures or worldviews to be persuaded by these sources.[5] I am persuaded that one cannot reasonably expect a Muslim, for instance, to be convinced by an argument that relies on an appeal to the Bible, and that one cannot reasonably expect a Christian to be convinced by an appeal to the authority of the Qur'an. Or for a secularist to be persuaded by the Talmud, or for a Hindu to be persuaded by an appeal to recent liberal political tradition (as in Rawls's political theory).

The fact that one cannot expect a Christian, say, to be convinced by an appeal to the authority of the Qur'an does not mean that the claims made in the Qur'an are false. Or that, vice versa, the claims of the Bible are false. Or that the claims of liberal political tradition are false. It means only that, *without further argument,* they are unlikely to be persuasive to members of other worldviews. It is also essential to appreciate that the claim that people introduce their religious beliefs into the public square based solely on what a text says or on what a church authority says is not quite so obviously true as it may at first appear. It is true that people often appear to be doing just that—basing their moral and political arguments on an appeal to a religious authority, or figure, or institution, but one must ask if this is what they are really doing. Remember that we are talking about reasonable people here (not fanatics). These would be people who may appeal to the Bible because they trust it (perhaps because of how its teachings have worked in their own lives), trust their church and its history, know (vaguely) perhaps that biblical morality has a long history of influence and support, know that many great philosophers and theologians, whom they regard (rightly) as authorities, have defended it with strong philosophical arguments, who admire greatly the moral character of their religious leaders, both past and present, and so on.

In short, I am suggesting that many people who appeal to the authority of a text may be doing so as *a shorthand way* of appealing to some combination of these other arguments simply because they don't have the time, training, expertise or confidence to engage the debate on a more pluralistic

[5]Of course, it is difficult to specify what we mean precisely by a rational or a reasonable person. I will come back to this matter later in the chapter, but it would have to include a certain level of (not necessarily formal) education, life experiences, etc. The crucial point, as we will see, is that the majority will ultimately decide what is rational (even though they could be wrong), rather than some special minority (e.g., university professors) because the latter course runs the great risk that "rationality" will (arbitrarily) turn out to equal secularism, or at least the political views of the select group.

level. I think it is possible that the modern debate on these issues has over-played the claim that appeals to questionable sources (from the point of view of pluralism) are the basis of most religious arguments today. It is just as plausible that people are assuming the rationality of their view in the ways I have suggested here without bothering to argue the fact, in just the way that most people do (or so I claim) who believe in God—because they believe (deep down) that it is rational to do so, even though they may never articulate their specific reasons for believing or ever engage the philosoph-ical debate about the existence of God. There is a difference, after all, be-tween *having* a reasonable belief and being able to *show* that your belief is reasonable. Of course, these latent *arguments*—when made explicit—could still be wrong, and might well be rejected by people from other worldviews. But this simply brings us back again to the general debate between world-views in a democratic society.

Kent Greenawalt has distinguished between grounds (or reasons) that are accessible to fellow citizens and grounds that are not accessible in his argu-ment for restricting religious views in politics. He believes some reasons are accessible to most people, but that others are not. In the latter category, he focuses especially on "feelings, attitudes and insights developed mainly in re-sponse to personal experience," and he asks, "If some ethical views seem to come down to idiosyncratic personal expressions of attitudes or emotions, if they have no objective basis that can be established, should they provide any ground for coercing others?"[6] Greenawalt's description of what might count as nonaccessible grounds is here too broad, for it would surely also apply to the idiosyncrasies of secularists, who have generally struggled in trying to jus-tify the ethical views they hold with so much confidence and passion. But the five sources above seem to me to be a defensible way of trying to draw a limit between accessible and nonaccessible grounds.[7] I acknowledge that this is controversial, and I don't want to completely close the door on appeal to these sources in politics, though in this book I will not defend the view

---

[6]Kent Greenawalt, *Private Consciences and Public Reasons* (New York: Oxford University Press, 1995), p. 24.

[7]In *The Naked Public Square*, Richard John Neuhaus appears to agree with the kind of restric-tion I am arguing for here, although he does not give an analysis of the types of beliefs that would be restricted. But in his criticism of what he calls "the new religious right," he says that "it wants to enter the political arena making public claims on the basis of private truths. The integrity of politics itself requires that such a proposal be resisted. Public decisions must be made by arguments that are public in character" (p. 36). I take it that Neuhaus's "private truths" relates to claims made on the basis of the first five sources I have identified.

that one should be able to appeal to them. In addition, as we will see later, despite this restriction it will still be possible to legitimately introduce one's religious beliefs into political discussions on a host of issues, especially those regularly debated in U.S. society (e.g., on abortion, euthanasia, social welfare policy, workers rights, exploitation and the morality of war).

Although I will go on to argue in this chapter that religious believers can offer rational arguments for religious conclusions in the political arena, it would be unrealistic to expect every religious believer to be able to do this. Many will not have the time or the ability or the confidence to engage in a rational defense of their positions, even privately, let alone publicly. But it is sufficient that they know that there is a rational argument available, that there are people whom they trust as authorities on various issues pertaining to their worldview. For example, a religious believer could vote against a law permitting abortion based on a rational argument given by Pope John Paul II (in the encyclical *Evangelium Vitae* perhaps). In this case it would be important that the pope actually provide a rational argument (and not just an appeal to biblical authority or Church tradition, though these sources might be alright as I have indicated as long as they are rationally justified as authorities, which elsewhere the Catholic Church argues they are). It is especially important to have a rational argument if he wants his view to be persuasive to other democratic societies (this is why I think Pope John Paul was careful to include a rational argument against abortion that appeals to scientific evidence, among other things, in *Evangelium Vitae*).

It is quite acceptable for many people to rely on authorities in our culture as their source for rational arguments for various positions; indeed, given that many public arguments often rely on complex data, data that is not immediately available to most people, reliance on authorities will be not just acceptable, but necessary in many cases (e.g., arguments about many economic policies rely on predictions based on different types of data about how the policies will affect jobs, businesses or the economy generally, etc.). It is incumbent on those appealed to as authorities to actually have and to be sincerely convinced by rational arguments and evidence. This applies to all worldviews. Indeed, it will be the duty of those gifted enough to be leaders in the various worldviews to not only provide rational arguments and evidence for their positions but also to make these arguments available to the population as a whole. Also, they must be people of high moral character and trustworthiness because in many instances, especially after their followers come to know and rely on them, people will simply accept the fact that there is a rational argument available on a certain issue just because the authority says so, and not because they are familiar with the arguments (for instance, a secularist might rely for his view that homosexuality is genetic on arguments offered by secularists working in various science disciplines). We must not forget that worldviews are often quite complex, secularist ones no less than religious ones.

Thomas Nagel has argued that one cannot reasonably expect someone who rejects religious revelation to accept a belief based on revelation (especially if the belief is used as the basis of coercive legislation).[8] That is to say, it would not be reasonable for a religious believer to expect a secularist to be *persuaded* that, for example, he should not become a vegetarian because the Bible clearly says we have dominion over animals. A religious believer, according to Nagel, should agree that it is not reasonable for him to ask the secularist to be persuaded by this appeal to the Bible (and so one should not morally introduce this belief into the political arena and should not try to influence legislation with it). I am inclined to agree with Nagel on this point, as long as the two provisos mentioned above are observed. But the crucial mistake that secularists (and indeed many religious believers) make is to think that *all* religious beliefs come from these sources and from no other source. Greenawalt himself moves dangerously close to this view and generally does not consider sufficiently the rationality of the religious worldview (nor of the secularist worldview). It would be awfully convenient for the secularist if, amidst the complicated task of sorting out one's beliefs, supporting them, defending them to others and trying to influence society in various ways by means of them, it turned out that one could never do this with religious beliefs, and so they should not be introduced into politics! But it will not turn out this way, as we will see.

---

[8]See Nagel's very insightful discussion in his "Moral Conflict and Political Legitimacy," *Philosophy and Public Affairs* 16 (summer 1987): 215-40. See also Joseph Raz's challenging reply to both Nagel's and Rawls's arguments in "Facing Diversity: The Case of Epistemic Abstinence," *Philosophy and Public Affairs* 19 (winter 1990): 3-46. See also Nagel's *Equality and Partiality* (New York: Oxford University Press, 1991), chap. 14, where he acknowledges the force of some of Raz's criticisms of his position. Bruce Ackerman makes a similar argument (to Nagel's) in his restriction of religious belief in a liberal democracy; he considers only religious beliefs that are based on an appeal to what God has revealed, and never entertains any other kind of possible support for religious belief. See his *Social Justice in the Liberal State* (New Haven, Conn.: Yale University Press, 1980), p. 281. Ackerman's arguments are one of the most obvious examples of religious caricature that one will find in the literature on this subject and, I suggest, are arguments that are simply nonstarters with religious believers.

Reason as a Source of Religious Beliefs

This secularist claim that all traditional religious beliefs come from the five sources mentioned above is too superficial, and no reasonable religious believer should accept it. In identifying these five sources, the secularist is simply assuming that there can be no other source for traditional religious beliefs, and he is also assuming that secularist beliefs never come from these sources.[9] Both of these assumptions are false. The secularist has failed to distinguish between two quite different senses of the word *faith* (identified in chapter one): the sense that describes believing on faith alone without regard to the evidence and the sense that describes *believing on the basis of reason and evidence as much as possible* (a rational faith, the first sense of faith in chapter one). He narrowly defines the meaning of the term *faith*, with the implication that the term only applies to religious belief and that religious belief is nonrational in some important sense.[10] He does not recognize that faith can be rational and that *his own views are based on faith*. It is not that the secularist or those religious believers who take a secularist position on these matters provide an argument that faith can't be rational or show that their own beliefs do not involve faith, it is more that they have simply *ignored* these crucial matters. As Neuhaus has said, "[Authentic religion] raises the question of faith, and most liberal secularists are in deep denial about their articles of faith and acts of faith."[11] The secularist conveniently ignores the issue of the rationality of religious belief, or superficially

---

[9]In his book *How We Believe,* the skeptic Michael Shermer recounts the story of how he once debated my friend Doug Geivett on the question of the existence of God. Shermer was surprised when Geivett devoted most of his time to presenting arguments for the rationality of religious belief, and also by the fact that the audience demanded that Shermer address these arguments directly. Shermer admits that this surprised him because he had "always understood religious belief to be based on faith, the notion of 'proving' one's faith seemed oxymoronic" (p. 90). In a belated response to the audience's demand, Shermer then goes on in his book (pp. 91-98) to give an embarrassingly weak summary and critique of the various arguments for the rationality of religious belief, the kind of critique I contend that does not challenge religious belief.

[10]It is important also to remind ourselves that the view that religious beliefs are based on "faith" (in the pejorative sense identified in chap. 1) is not confined to secularists, but can be found all too frequently even among sophisticated religious believers. One can made a good case that George Marsden, in his otherwise excellent and timely book, *The Outrageous Idea of Christian Scholarship* (New York: Oxford University Press, 1997), writes from the standpoint of accepting religious beliefs on faith, as does Kenneth Miller, on the different but no less relevant subject of religion and science, in his *Finding Darwin's God* (New York: HarperCollins, 1999).

[11]Richard John Neuhaus, "Why We Can Get Along," *First Things,* February 1996, p. 27.

denies that religious beliefs can be rational, or fails to compare the rationality of religious beliefs with that of secularist beliefs. This leads us to introduce a *sixth source* of religious beliefs—beliefs based on rational argument, evidence and human experience.

To help us understand these points further, we must distinguish between a belief's being religious because it was arrived at by means of a religious *process* and a belief's being religious because the *content* of the belief is of a religious nature. This is a crucial distinction, yet it is almost always overlooked. A belief can be described as religious if it was arrived at by means of a religious process, and by religious process I mean the *six* sources now identified above. The word *process* describes *the way in which or the manner in which a person arrives at the belief.* So, for example, Joe's belief that Jesus was resurrected from the dead because it is reported in the Bible, which he believes is the Word of God, is a belief arrived at by means of a religious *process* (i.e., by appeal to a text). Sarah's belief that God created the world, which she arrived at by means of a rational reflection on experience, is a religious belief because it was arrived at by means of a religious process—rational reflection and then reasonable commitment to the belief (the *sixth* source above). So a belief can be described as religious if it was arrived at by means of a religious process.

On the other hand, a belief can also be described as religious if the *content* of the belief is of a religious nature, irrespective of the process by which the belief was arrived at. Thus Joe's belief above that Jesus rose from the dead is religious because it has religious *content* in the sense that it is one of the beliefs of a traditional religious worldview concerning the activity of God. Sarah's belief is religious because it is about a transcendent God, so it too is religious in content, since it is about the transcendent, unseen world. Secularists and religious believers alike, in all walks of life, fail to distinguish between these two quite different meanings of the term *religious,* leading to much confusion as a result, especially in the debate over the role of religion in politics. My claim here is that not all beliefs that were arrived at by means of a religious process are unworthy of inclusion in political life. More specifically, beliefs that were arrived at from *rational argument*—by appeal to rational argument, evidence and human experience—are worthy candidates for inclusion in politics. I will come back to this point in the next sections; I simply want to lay out the main points of the argument in this section.

A serious confusion with serious implications occurs frequently in the debate concerning traditional religion in politics because we continually fail to distinguish between the two senses of the term *religious*—process and content —in the way that I have clarified them here. When the term *religious* is used it usually refers to the process by which the belief was arrived at, with the implication (especially if the term is used by a secularist), that the process is somehow illegitimate. However, I am claiming that there is a perfectly respectable process for arriving at religious beliefs—this involves appeal to rational argument, evidence and human experience—and then commitment to the beliefs. This process is usually ignored or downplayed by the secularist (and even by some religious believers). Yet it is also the process used by the secularist to arrive at his own beliefs! (As we have seen in chapter one, even this source does not bring certainty for beliefs concerning the three areas, and this is true for all worldviews, not just traditional religions.)

A crucial implication of what I have said so far is that a belief can be described as religious *irrespective* of whether its content comes from the worldview of traditional religion or comes from the worldview of secularism. A secularist belief arrived at by means of any of the six sources above is also religious. For example, say one believes, as John Rawls does, that certain moral and political values are implicit in our political tradition, and that these values should be used to regulate public political discourse. This is a religious belief in my sense because it is based on an appeal to tradition. Or if one believes, as Richard Dawkins does, that human beings do not differ in kind but only in degree from other animals, this also can be described as a religious belief because, although it might be based on reason and evidence, it requires a degree of faith to believe it (just like belief in God).

So if beliefs from any of these sources turn out not to be worthy candidates for inclusion in the public square then secularist beliefs arrived at from the same sources will also not be worthy candidates for inclusion in the public square. Similarly, any argument that is used to allow a place for secularist beliefs based on the process by which they were arrived at will also apply to traditional religious beliefs *that were arrived at by means of the same process.* In short, secularist beliefs are also religious beliefs because they must come from one or more of the sources mentioned. And it is appropriate to call beliefs that come from the sixth source *religious* because they still require a degree of faith to believe them.

Michael Perry is one thinker who does not appreciate the distinction between a belief's being religious in terms of the process by which it was arrived at and being religious in terms of its content. Perry defines a religious belief in terms of content: "a religious belief . . . is either the belief that God exists . . . or a belief about the nature, the activity, or the will of God."[12] Although Perry provides an insightful and provocative discussion of the relationship between traditional religion and politics, his analysis suffers from failing to make this distinction. He refreshingly presents a more balanced, fair reading of the First Amendment establishment clause than most, and he agrees that this clause means that religious arguments can be presented in public debates by public officials, yet he still believes that ideally public policy should be made only on the basis of secular arguments. But by failing to distinguish between the process by which one arrives at a belief and the content of the belief, Perry implies, even if he does not quite say so explicitly (though he often comes close), that traditional religious beliefs and arguments are inferior to secular beliefs and arguments. Perry does not discuss the vitally important matter of the rationality of religious beliefs. He simply assumes that religious beliefs are not as rational as secular beliefs, and he does not appreciate the further point that secular beliefs, too, are often based on faith.[13] (I will discuss Perry's position further in later chapters.)

Another thinker who holds a superficial view of religious belief is Stanley Fish, whose position on truth claims in general is very close to relativism. Commenting on the evidence for the various miracles reported in the Bible, Fish says, "If you tell a believer that no one can walk on water or rise from the dead or feed five thousand with two fishes and five loaves, he will tell you (in the mode of Tertullian) that the impossibility of those actions for mere men is what makes their performance so powerful a sign of divinity. For one party the reasoning is, 'No man can do it and therefore he didn't do it'; for the other the reasoning is, 'Since no man could do it, he who did it is more than man.'"[14] But this account of the debate concerning miracles is quite superficial and mainly relies on the (contradictory) claim that reason and logic and evidence are relative to each worldview. Fish believes that every worldview is a presupposition, a matter of faith, and he talks as if the religious worldview and the secularist worldview can never have a serious debate because they have no common ground. Although for most of his ca-

---

[12]Michael J. Perry, *Religion in Politics* (New York: Oxford University Press, 1997), p. 31.
[13]Ibid., chap. 1 and pp. 66-82.
[14]See Stanley Fish's debate with Richard John Neuhaus, "Why We Can't All Just Get Along," *First Things*, February 1996, p. 37.

reer Fish has been clearly in the relativist camp, I think the best way to read his view here is as a subtle attack on religious belief, an attack based on the implication that one cannot *reason* with a religious believer.

We have seen that when we use the word *religious* to describe a belief we equivocate between referring to the process by which the belief was arrived at and the content of the belief, what the belief is about. In the future, when we refer to a belief as "religious" we should keep in mind the process by which the belief was arrived at, not just the content of the belief. For the belief in question could have either traditional religious content or it might have *secularist* content. This new terminology underscores again the structural similarity of both worldviews, since both of them can be described as religions and since both have "religious" beliefs. *The main difference between a secularist view and a traditional religious view is not the process by which the beliefs were arrived at, but the content of the beliefs.* As indicated in chapter two, I don't wish to insist upon the point that secularist beliefs should be called religious beliefs, or even that secularism should be called a religion, but want only to emphasize that it would be quite appropriate to use both terms since they highlight one of our main points: the structural similarity between religion and secularism.

Let us now turn directly to the question of the rationality of religious belief.

The Rationality of Religious Belief

As discussed in chapter one, major claims in my overall argument are that all worldviews are faiths to some degree, that religious belief is a rational faith and that it is more rational than secularism. I also showed in chapter two that secularism is a worldview/religion that relies in part on faith, and in the earlier sections of this chapter I suggested that religious beliefs based on reason have a legitimate role to play in politics. I will devote the next two chapters to a full discussion and critique of the various arguments offered by some influential thinkers against introducing religious beliefs into politics. But for the remainder of this chapter, I would like to elaborate further on what I mean by the rationality of religious belief and explain why reasonable religious beliefs can be part of politics. Obviously, I cannot take time here to establish the rationality of religious belief. That would be much too large a project and would require a study in itself. It would also take us too far away from our present task. But I would like to indicate more specifically what I have in mind when I say that religious belief is rational, and how this conclusion will affect public debate in a democratic, pluralist society such as ours.

I am claiming only that *the general religious view of the world* is reasonable, that many of the more basic, foundational beliefs associated with religious belief are reasonable and can legitimately play a role in public political and social debates. Religion in general, as we saw earlier, usually involves a belief in a transcendent, unseen, sacred realm. It also typically involves all or some of the following beliefs: God (or the Supreme Reality or Realities) exists; God created the universe; God created all life; human beings consist of body and soul; the soul can survive after death; human beings differ in kind from other animals; human beings have free will; the human mind is nonphysical; there is an objective moral order; the objective moral order requires the existence of God for its justification; there is a human nature; human beings are social beings by nature and not by choice; and so forth. It also includes various moral beliefs, many of which flow from these more basic beliefs, such as the belief that human life is extremely valuable and so abortion and euthanasia are immoral. Most of these beliefs—or similar beliefs—are shared by the major world religions, and indeed by most smaller mainstream religions as well.

The general religious view of reality recognizes that the world is not our own, that life is a gift and has a fundamental value, that our eternal destiny is beyond the world and is bound up with how we live our lives now. This means that a religious believer will emphasize matters of the soul, the spiritual and moral life, over the life of pleasure and of consumerist materialism. It means also that we are our brother's keeper and not selfish egoists. In a pluralist society, there will be disagreement among religions themselves about how to promote and achieve religious goals and, when secularism enters the picture, even about whether they are worthy goals, but the main point is that religious believers must be part of this debate.

To use the language of democracy, we might say that human rights and responsibilities flow out of the traditional religious view of the human person. This is why some have argued recently that the Judeo-Christian view of the human person may support a democratic political structure. Robert Kraynak has pointed out that Christianity stresses human dignity, from which rights and responsibilities can be derived;[15] it also stresses freedom,

---

[15]See Robert Kraynak, *Christian Faith and Modern Democracy* (Notre Dame, Ind.: University of Notre Dame Press, 2001), p. 153.

equality, conscience and the idea that civil law is based on natural law, which is in turn based on God's eternal law (to use the language of the natural law tradition). Secularism usually denies most of the above-mentioned beliefs and the moral values associated with them. For example, secularists deny that there is a human nature and so support changing definitions of the family, as in allowing gay marriage.

I have identified only the most basic religious beliefs here, and while I am approaching these beliefs from the worldview of Christianity, it is true that most of these beliefs are common to most religions. I am claiming only that these beliefs are very reasonable, and more reasonable than their opposites. This is not to deny that there are interesting, sometimes divisive, debates within and between religions on some of these matters. But again it would take us too far afield to get into these, and, more importantly, they are not particularly relevant to my overall argument. I simply wish to emphasize my assessment that the religious view of the world in general is more rational than the secularist view of the world. I find very problematic various secularist beliefs such as that everything in the universe may ultimately have a scientific explanation, including the nature of the human person and the phenomenon of free will. I find this view of the universe and of human life very difficult to accept from a rational point of view. And so when I come to the political arena, my thinking on moral, social and political issues will be informed by my worldview. It would not be reasonable for me to allow a worldview that I myself do not hold to trump my own worldview or to be the basis of the political structure.

I do not think that religion is any threat to democracy; on the contrary, it has much to add to the public-square discussion. This is why (democratic) politics needs religion, not just because to be truly democratic it must be concerned with promoting fairness and equality among worldviews, but also because the religious view of the world can make valuable contributions to modern debates concerning a host of issues. For example, I hold that the religious view overall provides a greater grounding for objective morality and for supporting political values, such as human rights, which are an extension of the moral order into the political order. Secularism has struggled with the whole question of objective morality and has had difficulty in avoiding moral relativism. If one believes that there is no overall purpose to the universe and that human life is a random accident, it seems evident that it will be difficult to avoid relativism and even skepticism, especially in the practical area of ethics and politics, where one is often concerned with the question of how society should be organized, with how people should live. This is why liberal political theory today has moved in a relativistic direction. I am not suggesting that secularism is based on relativism and skepticism, as I indicated above in my description of this worldview, but I do think it struggles with these matters (quite overtly) in a way that religious belief does not. As Ann Druyan has put it: "I'm sure most of what we all hold dearest and cherish most, believing at this very moment, will be revealed at some future time to be merely a product of our age and our history and our understanding of reality."[16] This relativistic tendency is here revealingly well expressed by a scientist even as she presents her own clear moral agenda by which she wishes to shape society and culture, as she attempts to move modern politics toward a seculocracy!

In the political arena, in particular, I think that religious belief can do a better job than secularism of defending the notion of human rights, a dominant theme in contemporary moral discussions. The religious worldview better explains and justifies why all human beings should have basic human rights—because we are all created in the image of God.[17] One example of secularist difficulties with this matter was the 1947 decision by the American Anthropological Association to object to the United Nations Declaration on Human Rights because it was an attempt to impose "western morality" on other cultures (a position they later reversed with a new 1999 statement). The religious worldview supports an objective moral order and a moral account of the human person, and so can provide a clear answer to the question of where human rights come from in the first place and why we should be concerned with them. They are based on natural rights that all human beings share by virtue of being a human being. The religious worldview also has a moral schema that helps us with the content of these rights (and so the view that all people are made in the image of God has political implications for how people should be treated). This is why it is no accident that some of the foremost thinkers on natural rights, such as Locke, held a religious worldview, something that modern discussions of Locke's views often conveniently overlook.

---

[16]See Ann Druyan, "Ann Druyan Talks About Science, Religion, Wonder, Awe . . . and Carl Sagan," *The Skeptical Inquirer,* November/December 2003, p. 26.
[17]Paul Marshall eloquently defends the view that the basic message of Christianity has a political dimension; see his *God and the Constitution* (Lanham, Md.: Rowman & Littlefield, 2002), pp. 33-63, where he surveys Old and New Testament views of the role of religion in politics.

One of the greatest challenges facing secularists today is in the area of human rights, ironically an area in which they are often most vocal. The challenge they face is to provide an objective foundation for their ethical and political views concerning human rights. They will surely have to work more at this in the future. Of course religions have not always lived up to their beliefs, and there is often disagreement among various religious views of the world on moral and political matters; religions have also developed and refined their views from time to time (for the better). This is true of every worldview, religious or secularist, and indeed is part of the debate between worldviews. But my point for the purposes of our discussion is simply that what we have here is a debate between the religious worldview and the secularist worldview on various matters (human rights and objective morality, purpose, free will, human nature, etc.), and my position is that overall the religious worldview is more rational than the secularist worldview, and that is a significant part of the reason why I am a religious believer.

The history of philosophy is full of arguments about each of the beliefs I have mentioned, and I refer any reader who wants to pursue these beliefs further to these discussions. I am thinking, in particular, of the various arguments known in philosophy of religion as "natural theology," the attempt to use rational arguments and evidence to show that it is reasonable to believe that God exists.[18] Much of the history of philosophy has been concerned in one way or another with the rationality of religious belief versus the rationality of secularism. I acknowledge that one can raise interesting and sometimes good objections against some of the steps in the various arguments on the religious side (just as one can for the arguments on the secularist side); that some reasonable people are not convinced by them; that they do not tell us everything about God or cover all of the myriad issues separating the world's religions. All of this I cheerfully grant.

All I am claiming is that it is reasonable to hold the beliefs I identified. These foundational beliefs are based on reasonable arguments and on evidence. They are, therefore, in the terminology introduced in chapter one, *lower-order beliefs* (i.e., rational beliefs). I hold that these religious beliefs

---

[18]For contemporary discussions of these arguments, there is no better proponent than British philosopher Richard Swinburne, who has written a series of books laying out the rational case for religious belief (all published by Oxford University Press). See, among his books, the following: *Is There a God?* (1996), *The Existence of God* (1991), *The Coherence of Theism* (1990), *The Resurrection of God Incarnate* (2003), *Revelation: Metaphor and Analogy* (1992), *Providence and the Problem of Evil* (1998) and *The Evolution of the Soul* (1997).

are more rational than the foundational beliefs of secularism. I suggest that the history of the discussion on this matter bears this out since there are countless millions throughout history who have been and are convinced of the rationality of religious belief. This does not guarantee that religious belief is rational, of course, but the idea that religious belief is rational is not an unreasonable conclusion. And this is my main point. It would be different if religious belief were a marginal view, but this is not the case. Some version of the above beliefs have been held by most of the smartest thinkers in history and by millions of ordinary, reflective, decent people, full of common sense. And it is simply not true that ordinary people accept religious belief mainly on authority. They accept religious beliefs also because the evidence supports a religious view of reality, even if their arguments are often inchoate or superficial, and even if they could not do them justice in the public square or the voting booth. The religious view of reality is deeply ingrained in the human heart. This does not guarantee that our religious beliefs are true, since the majority is often wrong. But it is a good place to start. As the philosopher Thomas Nagel candidly puts it in a recent book reflecting on his career in philosophy: "I want atheism to be true and am made uneasy by the fact that some of the most intelligent and well-informed people I know are religious believers."[19] This uneasiness—honestly admitted to by Nagel—is all we need to give religion a legitimate place at the political table on the basis of its plausibility and reasonability.

It is important to point out, to take a slight tangent at this point, that I am assuming the truth of the basic principles of democracy, and that the public-square discussion will be governed by these principles. Obviously, when we debate a theory, view, moral position or political issue in the public square, we need a set of rules to regulate this debate. These rules will not be value-free; rather, in our modern state they involve appeal to the principles of democracy. In short, a commitment to democracy includes a commitment to a set of moral values and principles. Everyone concerned with fully develop-

---

[19]Thomas Nagel, *The Last Word* (New York: Oxford University Press, 1997), p. 130. Quentin Smith is another naturalist who is up front about the fact that he is advocating naturalism for moral, political and cultural reasons. He believes that contemporary naturalists have been too quick to assume the rationality of naturalism without actually debating theism and theists, and have consequently adopted a position that is not as well argued or as easy to defend as they think. He says, "the great majority of naturalist philosophers have an unjustified belief that naturalism is true and an unjustified belief that theism (or supernaturalism) is false." See "The Metaphilosophy of Naturalism," *Philo* 4, no. 2 (2001): 195.

ing their worldview will eventually have to ask themselves how they justify
or rationally support *these* moral values and principles and what role and
status they have overall in their worldview. My answer to this question,
which I will discuss in chapter six, is that if one accepts the principles of
democracy, one must justify them from *within one's worldview.*

It goes almost without saying that I am not claiming that *all* religious beliefs are rational. Certainly there is no shortage of irrational religious beliefs,
just as there is no shortage of irrational secularist beliefs. I also recognize
that many religious beliefs are higher-order beliefs, as I indicated in chapter
one. I have already mentioned that there is a fascinating and ongoing discussion and debate between various world religions on doctrinal and textual
matters (perhaps less so on moral matters). This is an important part of the
panorama of ideas that one finds in a pluralist democracy. But it is not a
debate we need to get into here.

Introducing Reasonable Religious Beliefs into Politics

I indicated in the first section of this chapter that I would insist only on including in the public square religious beliefs for which rational arguments
can be given, and this includes the list of basic religious beliefs constituting
the general religious view of reality stated above. So my proposal is quite
modest for which religious beliefs can be introduced into politics. I would
exclude two sets of religious beliefs from public arguments: beliefs based
on the first five sources mentioned above and higher-order beliefs (many of
which will get their justification from these sources). This is significant for
the debate in U.S. society in particular, because in U.S. society higher-order
beliefs are not usually introduced into politics by the various religions (large
and small).

Most of the debate is about moral issues (not doctrinal issues), and these
usually involve *only very basic religious beliefs.* So a religious believer could
offer an argument in the public square against the legalization of abortion,
on my view, and could argue for this conclusion by appealing to religious
content: specifically that God exists and is the Creator of life, that life is extremely valuable, and that the fetus is an innocent human life and should be
protected in law. This is a reasonable argument, I contend, whether or not
everyone is persuaded by it in the public-square debate. One could offer a
religious argument in the public square in favor of government assistance
for the homeless, along the lines suggested in the introduction: that each

person has a basic dignity and integrity by virtue of being created by God, and that the homeless state, with its poverty and hopelessness, compromises this dignity. One could argue against a nuclear arms build-up on the grounds that such action is more likely to lead to war and that this is against God's plan for humanity. These are all religious arguments because they appeal to religious content. I hold that these and similar type arguments are rational arguments—and that is all that is necessary for them to have a legitimate place in the political arena. So we need not be particularly concerned with public debates about higher-order beliefs for the most part; these can be engaged privately and at a later time. In fact, we do not need to get bogged down at all in debate about the rationality of doctrinal beliefs of any kind; we are usually only concerned with the debate over *moral issues,* especially those involving coercive legislation. Of course, higher-order secularist beliefs and secularist beliefs based on the first five sources must also be excluded from public arguments.

Higher-order beliefs of traditional religion might include most doctrinal beliefs, while the basic beliefs mentioned above would be lower-order beliefs. Kraynak has suggested that Christianity in particular has three themes relevant for political discussion: creation, the Fall of humankind from an initial ideal state, and redemption. He argues that these three themes are reasonable to hold, and more reasonable than secularist alternatives. For example, the doctrine of the Fall better explains evil, suffering and death than any liberal account of evil, which holds, with Rousseau, "that man is good by nature, but that society makes him bad through its unjust and oppressive institutions."[20] While it would take us too far afield to get into a debate with Kraynak on the themes he suggests, I agree with him that the more basic religious beliefs are rational, and more rational than secularist beliefs. But I am stressing the *rationality* of religious belief far more than Kraynak does in his overall argument.

Reasonable people can disagree about which beliefs are rational. It is simply a fact of life that reasonable people often see things in different ways. We must strive to justify our views to others, especially if we wish them to become the basis for coercive legislation, while recognizing that our justification may not always persuade others. But we must also recognize that, as Nagel has put it, "arguments that justify may fail to persuade, if addressed

---

[20]Kraynak, *Christian Faith and Modern Democracy,* p. 40.

to an unreasonable audience; and arguments that persuade may fail to justify."[21] Paul Weithman has correctly noted that "my appeal to reasons others
would recognize as good is not supposed to persuade them that I am right.
It is supposed to show them that I am *reasonable*."[22] Everyone's overall aim
though should be to be reasonable, and to try to persuade the reasonable.[23]

This involves offering arguments and evidence for one's conclusions in
an attempt to persuade others of their truth. These must be "public arguments" insofar as this is possible—meaning, among other things, that they
should not be based primarily on the five sources identified above because
these sources do not seem to provide an appropriate basis for *public* arguments. One must strive to give reasons and to be logical whenever one
wishes to coerce others into following one's views or whenever one wishes
others to live in a society that will be shaped in part by one's views. One
should try one's best to give reasons that others will find convincing, while
recognizing that this is not always going to be possible. (Otherwise we
would already have total harmony!)[24] I am not naively insisting that human

---

[21]Thomas Nagel, "Moral Conflict and Political Legitimacy," *Philosophy and Public Affairs* 16
(summer 1987): 218.

[22]Weithman, *Religion and the Obligations of Citizenship,* p. 196 (emphasis added).

[23]Persuading the reasonable can get quite tricky in an increasingly polarized society such as
ours, where there are serious conflicts on major issues rooted in different ways of looking at
the world. This is why the question of whether a person is being reasonable or not can be
hard to answer. Whether we regard somebody as reasonable might be a reflection on us as
much as it is on them. But the more we regard our fellow citizens as being unreasonable, the
more likely it is that the public debate will not be fruitful. This may tempt people to resort to
raw political power to achieve their moral aims in society, rather than persuasive rational argument. In U.S. society in particular, this may further fuel the appeal to constitutional and
legal methods of solving contentious questions, thus further obscuring the moral question. I
am suggesting that we try our best to have a reasonable debate with those who disagree with
us, in the way I have suggested in this chapter.

[24]There is some literature in philosophy on the question of what would count as a "public justification" for a political or moral argument. This debate is too abstruse for us to get into here.
But one thing evident from this literature is that it has proved extremely difficult for liberal
political philosophers to state adequate criteria for public justification, criteria which do not
discriminate arbitrarily against religious beliefs, the kind of beliefs "justificatory liberals" usually take as the paradigm case of beliefs that fail the test of public justification. One of the
most problematic ways to define public justification is to say that it must be based on principles *all* rational citizens would agree to (this is basically the Rawlsian view). But this is obviously too idealistic, because it would disqualify most arguments from counting, secularist as
well as religious. By far the best discussion of the question of public justification is to be
found in Christopher Eberle, *Religious Conviction in Liberal Politics* (New York: Cambridge
University Press, 2002), chap. 7. Eberle's is one of the few books in philosophy that also argues for a significant role for religious beliefs in politics, but he does so in quite a different
way from the way I propose in this book.

beings can be simply reasoning machines; we do need to be always aware of both the fallibility of human reason and the fact that human emotion and commitment will sometimes play a part in one's motivation in politics. I am reminded of a Baptist minister I once heard give an impassioned argument at a public meeting against spending money on nuclear arms. His emotional approach was moving, even powerful, but it was accompanied by rational arguments as to why spending money on nuclear arms was a mistake, arguments that gave many pause and that undoubtedly led most present to recognize he was a reasonable man, even if he did not convince everybody. Like this minister, I think we should try our best to be reasonable in our public arguments, especially those that are aimed at convincing others of the truth of our views. Treating human beings with dignity and respect involves giving them the best reasons we can for our views.

How Should We Handle Reasonable Disagreements?

Given that it is a fact of life that reasonable people disagree on important matters, we sometimes have a gray area within which the rationality of a belief can be disputed. This gray area gives rise to the following question: what do we do if there is a dispute about whether a belief is higher order or lower order? Suppose, for example, that you are not convinced that religious belief is rational, that you tend to think all religious beliefs are higher-order beliefs, or worse? Some might have begun reading the previous sections expecting a robust defense of the rationality of religious belief, and perhaps some were readying their objections so that they could boldly assert that they were not convinced by my arguments. *However, it is crucial to recognize that it is not necessary for me to convince the secularist that religious belief is rational in order for religious beliefs to have a role in politics; all that is necessary is that I hold that they are rational.* And, we might add, that I can convince a significant number of people of this fact or, more accurately, that a significant number of people are *already convinced* of this fact, especially if the beliefs are to have any impact on public-square debates. As indicated earlier, it is an important point that most people in history have genuinely regarded religious belief as broadly rational, even though they often disagree about the details, just as secularists do. This is one of the facts of life about the debate between worldviews. The secularist cannot reject the source—reason—of the religious beliefs I am proposing, he can only reject the conclusion. But what's new? I reject his conclusion too.

Let us not forget that we are not debating the rationality of religious belief versus the rationality of secularism here, we are debating *only* whether religious beliefs can be introduced into the political arena (not, legally, of course, as I have already mentioned since in democratic societies freedom of speech laws would normally allow this to some extent, but morally—is it morally appropriate to introduce religious beliefs into politics?). In addition, the debate about whether a particular belief is rational or not, and so about whether or not it could play a role in public and social policy issues, is *itself* a public-square debate. If there is a dispute about whether a belief (be it secularist or religious) is rational or not (i.e., whether it is lower order or higher order), then *this dispute* also must be part of the debate in the public square. At least four reasons can be offered for this conclusion.

First, from a practical point of view, there is no way to deal with this matter other than to discuss it in the public square because one can hardly expect a person in worldview A, who holds that belief X is rational, not to introduce that belief into public discussions because a member of worldview B believes it to be irrational or is otherwise not convinced by it. It would be irrational for A to defer to B on this matter, and for B to defer to A if the situation were reversed. Therefore, discussion of whether the belief is rational or not would have to be part of the *public* discussion.

Second, it is also reasonable to air this kind of dispute publicly because one can benefit from the variety of perspectives that might be part of a vigorous public discussion. One can learn of new reasons and arguments either for or against one's position and can believe and act accordingly. Many people would also agree that there can be some good in a worldview even if we don't accept the worldview as a whole. In this way worldviews can benefit from healthy debate with each other.

Third, there is also a reason of self-interest for adopting the conclusion that this kind of dispute should be a matter for the public square. One is sure of a hearing for one's *own* views if one adopts this principle, rather than if one agrees to submit to some authority, such as the courts, to settle the matter. This way one is assured that one's view gets heard in the public debate, even if it carries little influence in the end or is not finally adopted. One will generally not want to accept any principle that would lead to the initial suppression of any idea or view from the political arena in case this principle is eventually applied to one's own views! So we need to be cautious —for reasons of self-interest—in agreeing to principles for the regulation of public discussion that would involve the initial suppression of any view. The actual debate in the public square will consist of all parties explaining and defending their views and of trying to convince enough people that their view is reasonable. In this way, their beliefs, claims, views, values may gain enough public acceptance to have political influence and to guide public policy.

But, fourth, the most important reason of all for settling this issue publicly is that any type of suppression of a view *before* a public debate is held violates the basic principles of democracy, especially of freedom and equality. It is a violation of democratic principles if A decides in advance that B's view is irrational, and so B's view should not be part of any public discussion. However, if B's view is discussed in the public square, and A can convince a majority that B's view is irrational or dangerous or undesirable for some other reason, then B's view might be restricted. This is proper democratic procedure. Of course, this does not mean that the majority have necessarily made the right decision, since the majority can be wrong. I have also indicated that the principles of democracy themselves will have to be justified in the end, and that this must be done from within one's worldview.

This is why it is wise for any worldview to allow a significant realm of free speech in a democratic society, a realm where minority, controversial, even objectionable views can be introduced publicly, even though many might think it immoral to bring up such views (as many do of religious views). A recent example that springs to mind is the emergence of the idea that nature, especially biological nature, shows evidence of intelligent design, a view promoted by what has become known as the Intelligent Design (ID) movement. Despite the fact that many in the establishment in science, religion and philosophy are strongly opposed to the ideas of the ID movement and frequently argue that it is really a religious view in disguise and so, morally, its proponents should not introduce it into public arguments, it has still managed to gain a foothold in American intellectual culture. This is because of our free speech laws, which permit the expression and public debate of ID. Of course, it has a long way to go, and it might fail in its bid to be accepted as a rational view by a majority—at least as regards having any influence on public policy (say in education)—but this is all part of the messy (but perhaps beautiful?!) process of democracy.

It is for this reason also—support of free speech laws—that many who present moral arguments against religion in public life are often at pains to point out that they are not denying religious believers their right to free speech. They all pay lip service to this point. Perhaps they are a little embarrassed by, certainly feel uneasy about, their proposals to exclude or restrict religion, and are often acutely aware that it looks like they are advocating arbitrary discrimination (from the point of view of their liberal political theory) against a particular worldview, simply because they disagree with its moral and political views.

All of this applies to secularism too. I have indicated that I believe the secularist view is irrational, that the secularist arguments do not convince me. But I cannot use this fact to exclude secularist arguments from the public square, for the same reasons offered above. I hold, for example, that the secularist view that there is no human nature is irrational, but the secularist disagrees. So this dispute must be aired in the public square whenever an issue comes up that might involve the notion of human nature (such as gay marriage, for example).[25]

Some American readers might be surprised that I am drawing attention to and emphasizing the rationality of religious belief in this chapter. This would be regrettable, but it is a symptom of the attitude of many toward religious belief in the United States. This nation has a long history of treating religious belief as a matter of faith, in the third and even fourth senses identified in chapter one, a matter in which one simply identifies what one believes and suggests that these beliefs are outside of reason. Forms of American evangelicalism in particular helped to promote this view following the publication of the "five fundamentals" in the 1920s, which led to the movement that came to be known as fundamentalism. This movement sometimes promoted a separation of religion from what they regarded as an increasingly corrupt culture.[26] Yet strands of this emphasis can be found in all religions in the United States. This way of talking pleases secularists

---

[25]One could identify many secularist beliefs as irrational, or at least as very controversial. Stanley Hauerwas has pointed out, for example, that secular liberalism cannot offer any convincing explanation of why bearing and raising children is a positive good. See "The Radical Hope in the Annunciation: Why Both Single and Married Christians Welcome Children," in *The Hauerwas Reader,* ed. John Berkman and Michael Cartwright (Durham, N.C.: Duke University Press, 2001), pp. 505-18.

[26]See James C. Livingston and Francis Schüssler Fiorenza, *Modern Christian Thought: The Twentieth Century,* 2 vols., 2nd ed. (Upper Saddle River, N.J.: Prentice Hall, 1997-2000), 2:390-408, for an overview of this movement. Supporters of this movement were sometimes inconsistent because they often did take political positions on issues such as gambling and alcohol consumption. The evangelical leader Carl Henry later argued against the separationist approach and for more involvement of Christian evangelicals in politics.

to no end today, and they are very happy to perpetuate it.

This way of talking about one's religion, which is not nearly as common in Europe and Latin America, has backfired badly. Many people now do not take religion seriously when it comes to dealing with substantive matters of public policy, including many religious believers. Many religious believers themselves have been thoroughly seduced by the view that religion is a matter of faith and should not interfere in politics. Indeed, the mark of a "progressive" religion today is often seen in how much it has marginalized itself from political life, in how little its beliefs affect or influence the way people actually live their lives in society. Specific religions can sometimes be so compromised by adopting this attitude that they often come across as irrational, as not worth taking seriously in politics, as sounding like they should have no public expression or influence. This understanding of religious belief has done much to advance the cause of secularism, since removing religious arguments from public life is essential to the success of the secularist agenda. My point is that this is a mistaken approach and that we need to emphasize again the rationality of religious belief and the significance of this point for politics.

In the United States in particular, it would be helpful if we moved away from the culture of thinking of religious belief purely as a nonrational, even irrational, "faith." It is even very misleading, I think, in the present political climate, to describe one's religion as a faith, because it cements in people's minds the notion that religious beliefs are not as worthy as secularist beliefs. I am arguing that the religious view of the world in general has nothing to fear from rational scrutiny (although some specific religious beliefs in various religions might not survive rational scrutiny, just as many secularist beliefs surely would not). In fact, *we should positively welcome rational scrutiny as reasonable people trying to build a better world*. Further, we will find that secularism too is a faith, and that it does not fare too well in the overall debate with religious belief! In short, the religious believer has a responsibility to engage in reasonable political debate; otherwise we cede the political arena to the secularist.

I have been arguing that religious belief has a legitimate role to play in politics because it is rational. Let me conclude by emphasizing several other points that underscore the reasonability of religious belief and its value for democratic societies. First, it can be argued that religious belief contributes to a person's moral maturity, in the sense that it teaches values and attitudes

broadly based around the golden rule, and that it is good for public policy
to be influenced in this way (e.g., in formulating policies for regulating Wall
Street or for allocating health care). Second, as a matter of fact religious belief has important, substantive, reasonable things to say about many of the
political and social topics of the day. Fr. Brian Hehir has pointed out that
there are six major problems currently confronting U.S. society and that Catholicism and other mainstream religions have important things to say
about each of them.[27] Religion has made a profound contribution to the
abortion debate, for example, and has kept alive the view that abortion is
a grave moral evil. Martin Luther King Jr. (and long before him Sojourner
Truth) were strongly motivated by religious belief in their work for civil
rights.[28] Charles Colson, inspired by his religious worldview, founded the
group Prison Fellowship, which partners with local churches across the
United States to work with a group that society often scorns and neglects:
prisoners, ex-prisoners and their families. They also work toward reforming
the criminal justice system. And let us not forget Pope John Paul II's three
influential social encyclicals in the last twenty-five years.[29] Who can doubt
that these views and the work they inspire are worthy of being present in
the public square?

    Third, religion is a safeguard against what many rightly see as the ex-
cesses of secularism, secularism run amok in our society, such as genetic en-
gineering programs not mindful of ethical concerns (cloning, embryonic
stem cell research); gay marriage; sexual promiscuity (activism against sexual abstinence programs); educational fads and so on. Fourth, in the contemporary world, especially in U.S. society, religions are increasingly trying
to promote consensus on as many topics as possible, whereas secularism is
almost necessarily confrontational, since it opposes religions on so many
questions. Examples of religious dialogue and cooperation on doctrinal and

---

[27]I have been unable to find the original source of Fr. Hehir's remark. A recent Gallup poll of
1,004 adults found that 61 percent of Americans believe "religion can answer all or most of
today's problems," although 64 percent felt that religion is losing its influence on the nation.
As reported in *The Washington Times*, November 17, 2004.

[28]See David Chappell, *A Stone of Hope: Prophetic Religion and the Death of Jim Crow* (Chapel
Hill: University of North Carolina Press, 2004). For an interesting discussion of historical religious arguments against slavery, especially the antislavery arguments of John Wesley versus
the racism of David Hume, see Vincent Carroll and David Shiflett, *Christianity on Trial* (San
Francisco: Encounter, 2002), pp. 26-31.

[29]See *Centesimus Annus* ("The Hundred Year," meaning one hundred years after Pope Leo
XIII's *Rerum Novarum*, "On the Condition of the Working Classes"), 1991; *Sollicitudo Rei So-
cialis* ("On Social Concern"), 1987; and *Laborum Exercens* ("On Human Work"), 1981.

moral issues include the recent "Catholics and Evangelicals Together," an initiative of the Institute on Religion and Public Life (which publishes *First Things* magazine) and the "Joint Statement on Jews and Christianity."[30]

I will elaborate further many of the points made above in the next two chapters, where I turn to a full discussion and critique of the various moral arguments offered by liberal political theorists and others for why traditional religion should have little or no place in politics in a liberal, democratic society.

---

[30]See Charles Colson and Richard John Neuhaus, eds., *Your Word Is Truth: A Project of Evangelicals and Catholics Together* (Grand Rapids: Eerdmans, 2002). See also James S. Cutsinger, ed. *Reclaiming the Great Tradition: Evangelicals, Catholics and Orthodox in Dialogue* (Downers Grove, Ill.: InterVarsity Press, 1997). See also the papers in *Dialogue and Universalism* 10, no. 11 (2000), on the topic of "Christians, 'Non-Believers,' Jews: Towards Complementarity," especially the Jewish statement "*Dabru Emet* 'Speak the Truth': A Jewish Statement on Christians and Christianity." This statement was signed by two hundred eminent Jewish scholars and rabbis. (The statement was reprinted in *First Things*, November 2000.)

4

Keeping Religion Out of Politics I

One reason for occasionally using traditional religious terminology to describe certain features of all worldviews is that it enables us to see how much secularism formally has in common with religion and enables us to look in a new light at the arguments for keeping religious beliefs out of politics. The worldviews do differ with respect to their content, but they are similar with regard to their form, and that is the point we have been emphasizing. The differences in their content are obviously important, though, and I will come back to them from time to time. But the arguments offered to exclude traditional religion from public life are almost always arguments about how worldviews differ with regard to their structure, with the implication that there is something wrong with the religious worldview. Yet since these worldviews do not differ with regard to their structure, we will see that these arguments do not work.

There are at least eight main arguments offered to exclude religion from politics. These include the arguments that religious beliefs should be excluded because they are irrational or are not quite rational enough to take seriously, because they are dangerous, are sectarian, are against the U.S. Constitution, or because the public-square debate should be a "neutral" debate. These arguments are offered by a variety of thinkers, including philosophers John Rawls, Robert Audi and Richard Rorty, and legal thinkers Michael Perry and Kent Greenawalt, all of whose views I will refer to along the way. Less sophisticated versions of these arguments are also extremely popular among the intelligentsia and the media, and consequently various forms of them have found their way into popular culture.

Not everyone who offers the arguments considered in this and the next chapter are secularists. Audi and Perry, for instance, are religious believers, yet they give priority to secularist arguments in an important sense and seem to regard arguments that make appeal to religious beliefs as somehow inferior, as we will see. Religious individuals and groups sympathetic to this view are sometimes referred to as the "religious left," and this might include groups such as the National Council of Churches and the Southern Christian Leadership. For the sake of simplicity, I will refer to all those arguments that seek to exclude (or restrict) religious belief from public life as secularist arguments (while recognizing that not all who propose these arguments are secularists). I wish to emphasize also that I am not implying that in modern democracies the state is necessarily a secularist state, but only that those worldviews that get to compete in the public square and to influence policy will shape what kind of public culture we live in. The state is never neutral with regard to the promotion of the values that shape our lives. In particular, I want to avoid the mistake of confusing the notion of "secular reason" with the notion that the state is neutral between worldviews.

Let us elaborate these interesting points in the rest of the chapter by turning to consider four major arguments for excluding religious beliefs from politics.

Religious Beliefs Should Be Excluded Because They Are "Religious"

The secularist often argues that we should exclude religious beliefs from politics because they are "religious," and this quality makes it illegitimate for these beliefs to influence public policy. In describing a belief as "religious," the secularist means that it originates from one or more of the *five* problematic sources identified in chapter three, namely, that it is grounded by appeal to a text, an institution, an experience, a tradition or on faith alone. Now as I indicated in the previous chapter, I am prepared to grant this argument in general to the secularist (with several qualifications). I do not wish to insist that traditional religious beliefs based on these five sources have a role to play in politics. I am arguing only that religious beliefs that come from the sixth source, reason and evidence, have a role to play in politics. So even if we grant the argument that religious beliefs based on the five sources mentioned ought to be excluded, it will not succeed in excluding *all* religious beliefs from politics.

As we noted in chapter three, there are several reasons why beliefs that are arrived at by means of the first five sources might be problematic candidates for inclusion in the public square. The first reason is that one cannot reasonably expect others who do not already follow the traditional religion in question to be guided in the public square by beliefs originating from the first five sources. The essence of this case is that beliefs arrived at from the first five sources are questionable. They are grounded, for example, on an appeal to an authority such as the Bible, an institutional church or church tradition, all problematic sources to those not of that religion. It is not so much, the secularist might argue, that the authority should be rejected, but as Plato's "Euthyphro question" illustrates (in the dialogue *Euthyphro*), superficial appeal to an authority is inappropriate because it seems to bypass the legitimate question of why we should accept the authority in the first place.

Second, there is also the serious problem of dealing with conflicting authorities coming from different religious traditions, and even conflicting interpretations of the authorities within the same religion. Which text do we follow, the secularist might ask, the Bible or the Qur'an? And what do we do with conflicting interpretations of the same text? Or with disputes about which Bible to use, Protestant or Catholic? In general, a simple appeal to an authority as a source of a belief seems to leave out the legitimate question of the justification of the belief. This is a major problem, the secularist will argue, in a pluralist society, especially concerning those beliefs that may influence public policies, debates and arguments, more so if the debates are about coercive legislation. The secularist might also add that beliefs based on religious experiences or on faith alone are too private, controversial, unsupported by evidence, nebulous, to reasonably expect a person who questions their source to follow them or to acquiesce to public and social policies based on them.[1]

Yet we must point out that if traditional religious beliefs based on these problematic sources are not worthy candidates for inclusion in political debates, then secularist beliefs from similar sources must also be excluded from these debates. And secularists do often appeal to these five sources to justify their beliefs, something that is often overlooked. It is usually presumed that it is only the religious believer who appeals to questionable sources. But this is not true. For example, a secularist might appeal to the authority of a text, such as John Stuart Mill's *On Liberty,* rather than the arguments in the text, to support some of his beliefs about freedom. Secularists do frequently appeal to authority to justify their views, especially ordi-

---

[1]But recall the argument in the first section of chap. 3, where I suggest that arguments from authority are often much more than that.

nary secularist believers, who might appeal to Sigmund Freud or Richard Dawkins or Charles Darwin in the same way that an ordinary religious believer might appeal to St. Thomas Aquinas or Billy Graham or Martin Buber. Or they might appeal to the tradition of liberal political philosophy from Locke onwards to support some of their arguments about democracy (as political philosopher John Rawls does). Secularists might even hold a belief on "faith alone," for example, that freedom is an absolute value.

It might be thought that the fourth source, religious experience, does not apply to secularism. But I am not so sure about this. For secularists do sometimes appeal to experiences to justify their beliefs, at least in part. For example, the secularist might argue that it is just obvious that individual freedom is more important than the common good. While these are not religious experiences in the sense that they involve an appeal to an unseen, transcendent world, there are similarities to religious experience in the sense that they are nonperceptual, privileged experiences (not everyone has the experience) and privatized experiences (other people do not undergo the experience at the same time as the secularist is undergoing it!). I do not wish to insist upon this point, but simply to raise it as worth considering and to emphasize that secularists cannot use privileged experiences of one sort or another as a source of justification for those beliefs they wish to include in the public square (or to exclude).

Of course, the secularist might not argue in these ways. But should secularists appeal to any of the first five sources to support a belief, which they sometimes do, then these beliefs would be subject to the same criticisms to which secularists claim religious beliefs are subject. But, most important of all, this reason for excluding religious belief fails because not *all* traditional religious beliefs originate from these five problematic sources. It is to this point that we now turn.

Traditional Religious Beliefs Cannot Be Based on Reason and Evidence

Often what the secularist has in mind when he disparages religious beliefs, even if he does not say so explicitly, is that religious beliefs are really not rational enough to be taken seriously, at least at the political level. Crucially, this conclusion is seldom debated by the secularist; it is rather an assumption he makes, and it has to be said that it is an idea that has some footing in our culture as a whole (even among religious believers themselves). This new argument recognizes the inadequacy of the first argument above for excluding religious belief from the political arena. And so this second objection tries to reject the *sixth* source mentioned in chapter three—reason, evidence and human experience—as a possible source for religious beliefs (but not as a possible source for secularist beliefs, of course). There are two emphases in this new argument: first, the suggestion that traditional religious beliefs are based on faith; second, the suggestion that religious beliefs are not rational beliefs—secularist beliefs are, in fact, more rational than religious beliefs. Let us take each emphasis in the argument in turn.

The first emphasis is often one of the main reasons given by secularists today for distinguishing between traditional religions and secularist religions. Their claim is that since many traditional religious beliefs are based on faith they are not worthy candidates for inclusion in political debates. Recalling our discussion of the meaning of the term *faith* in chapter one, this objection suggests that traditional religious beliefs are not based on argument or evidence but are accepted on trust (second and fourth meanings of *faith*). This comes close to saying that only those beliefs of which we can be certain are worthy candidates for contributing to political debates. It is suggesting that religious beliefs in general, including the belief that God exists, cannot be proven, and so should not influence public policy. Yet this argument is not very convincing because at least some secularist beliefs are also based on faith in the sense that they cannot be shown to be true (in the way described in chapter one). So if the secularist were to insist that only beliefs that were known to be true with certainty (and so did not require faith) could influence the law of the land, then it would be impossible to establish any laws; by this reasoning his own view would have to be excluded too. In this objection, the secularist is simply being naive in implying that traditional religious belief is based on "faith" and in thinking that his own view is superior to any view based on "faith."

We can illustrate this abstract point with a concrete example. For the secularist, the belief that everything that exists is physical is based on faith in part; it cannot be fully proven by rational argument or by appeal to the evidence. In particular, the secularist has not proved that the human mind (consciousness, thoughts, ideas, etc.) is physical. Of course, he might believe that it is physical or hope to prove it one day (a misguided hope, I hold), but right now he believes this on faith. He might claim that it is a rational faith; whatever about this point, it is still a belief based partly on faith.

Similarly, many of the beliefs the secularist advances about human behavior or about moral and political values are based partly on faith because of the nature of the subject matter. For instance, if the secularist believes that extramarital sex is morally acceptable, this again is a belief he cannot *prove*. Of course, reasons can be offered for it (just as reasons can be offered against it). Nobody disputes that. But the issue is not whether reasons can be offered for it, but whether it can be *proved*. If not, then it is based on a degree of faith, like traditional religious beliefs, and according to the secularist argument in this section, it should therefore be a purely private affair.

The second line of reasoning the secularist offers for rejecting the sixth source as applying to religious belief is to argue that religious beliefs are not rational beliefs, that secularist beliefs are more reasonable than religious beliefs. Because the secularist often recognizes the untenableness of the argument that religious beliefs cannot be proven, he adjusts his rather superficial claim that religion is based on faith to a more modest one. He might acknowledge that while both religious and secularist claims are based partly on faith, religious claims are based on an irrational faith, but secularist claims on a rational faith, and so only claims based on a rational faith can enter into politics. This claim can sound harsh when expressed like this (especially if it comes from a secularist who elsewhere questions the objectivity of reason and knowledge, as many do, such as literature professor Stanley Fish and philosopher Richard Rorty).[2] So for public relations reasons a secularist might put this point by saying not that religion is irrational but that it is nonrational or that faith is outside of reason, or some argument along these lines.

It is worth noting that traditional religious believers themselves are often seduced by this kind of talk. Michael Perry, for instance, agrees with the secularist that public officials should not rely on religious arguments in the public square unless they believe that a persuasive secular argument reaches the same conclusion. Further, they must *themselves* find the secular arguments persuasive. However, in his defense of this view, Perry seems to think that

---

[2]Rorty has written that we should make it seem like bad taste to bring our religious views into public life. It has to be said that this is a bit rich coming from a philosopher who has spent most of his career denying the objectivity of knowledge! See Rorty's "Religion as Conversation Stopper," in his *Philosophy and Social Hope* (New York: Penguin, 1999), p. 168. Like Ackerman's argument mentioned in chap. 3, this is an example of an argument that I believe is simply a nonstarter with religious believers. In general, liberal political thinkers must make a better attempt to engage the arguments of religious thinkers.

all religious arguments are based on an appeal to faith or religious experience or to what God has revealed, and he believes such arguments won't be convincing to those who are not already inclined to accept them. But Perry's analysis and discussion of religious arguments is quite superficial; he does not consider that one can make a very good case for the rationality of religious beliefs. He certainly implies that religious arguments are inferior to secularist arguments.[3]

Robert Audi is another influential thinker on religion and politics who does not give sufficient attention to the question of the rationality of religious beliefs. A large part of Audi's argument for restricting religion in politics is based on his view that religious beliefs are not rational enough to introduce them into the public square. As he puts it, "If fully rational citizens in possession of all the relevant facts cannot be persuaded of the necessity of coercion—as is common where that coercion is based on an injunction grounded in someone else's religious scripture or revelation—then from the point of view of liberal democracy, the coercion lacks an adequate basis."[4] As we saw from our discussion in chapter three, this claim is very implausible in the absence of a discussion of the rationality of religious belief, and also of the rationality of secularism.

Audi does provide a detailed analysis of what should count as adequate secular arguments and motivations, one of the most comprehensive treatments of this issue in the literature. He argues that whenever a traditional religious believer introduces an argument into the public square that would restrict the human conduct of others (e.g., if he argued that abortion should be illegal), he must follow two principles.[5] The first, the principle of secular

---

[3]To be fair to Perry, he has since modified his view on this matter and now believes that the secularist's reasons for excluding religion from politics are not very persuasive and that it is sometimes legitimate to introduce religious arguments into public debate. However, he still seems to have a quite negative view of the status of religious arguments, to give secularist arguments the presumption of being in general more rational than religious ones. He also conspicuously fails, it seems to me, to acknowledge the rationality of religious belief, and settles for offering arguments explaining why religious believers should show restraint in being guided by the Bible in political matters and why Catholics should not necessarily be guided by their official Church teaching. See Perry's discussion in *Religion in Politics* (New York: Oxford University Press, 1997), especially pp. 9-42; and his later discussion in Michael J. Perry, *Under God: Religious Faith and Liberal Democracy* (New York: Cambridge University Press, 2003).

[4]Robert Audi, *Religious Commitment and Secular Reason* (Cambridge: Cambridge University Press, 2000), p. 123. (Hereafter *RC.*)

[5]Ibid., pp. 86-100.

rationale, says that one should not restrict human conduct for religious reasons unless one is willing to offer "adequate secular reason for this advocacy or support (say for one's vote)."[6] But this principle is not enough, according to Audi. One must also follow what he calls "the principle of secular motivation." This principle calls for one not just to offer secular reasons to support one's position, but says that one must be mainly *motivated* oneself by these reasons in one's commitment to the position advocated.[7] In other words, when a religious believer presents an argument in the public square for X, the religious believer must not only offer secular reasons for X, but must himself be *motivated* by these reasons. He must find these reasons convincing himself and be mainly convinced by them. He can't simply be offering them to appease the secularist (to cloak his religion in secularist guise), but deep down be motivated by religious reasons (e.g., by what the Bible says) all the time. A secularist reason is a reason that makes no appeal to religious content (such as the existence of God).

Audi qualifies the restriction somewhat to say that religious believers can introduce religious arguments into politics as long as adequate secular reason can be given as well. These reasons could even be motivationally *stronger* for the religious believer, as long as the secular reasons provide *adequate* secular motivation. One could also introduce one's religious beliefs if they were not being used to support coercive legislation. However, despite these qualifications, the end result is the same: one cannot introduce religious beliefs in order to influence the shape of society through coercive policy or legislation unless one presents them in secular terms and finds these terms motivational oneself. This amounts to saying that the religious content is not necessary to justify the beliefs (but if a believer thinks it is that's fine, as long as he does not try to convince others of this in the public square).[8]

Audi's failure to give sufficient attention in his overall argument to the rationality of religious belief and to the difficulties with the overall justification

---

[6]Ibid., p. 86.

[7]Ibid., p. 97.

[8]Audi defines a secular reason as one whose status "does not evidentially depend upon the existence of God (or on denying it), or on theological considerations, or on the pronouncements of a person or institution qua religious authority" (*RC,* p. 89). His oblique parenthetical reference to "or denying the existence of God" indicates that he thinks his position is neutral with regard to religion and secularism, but as I have been arguing, it is not because his arguments rely on the fact that religious beliefs are inferior in some way and that "secular reason" *cannot reach* religious conclusions that would be sufficiently rational to allow one to introduce them into politics.

of secularism leads to problems with both of these principles. The principle of secular rationale should be unacceptable to religious believers because, as I have tried to show, religious arguments are just as reasonable as secular arguments on many topics, but especially on the topic of abortion, one of the main examples to which Audi appeals to illustrate his two principles. Audi's main reason for the principle of secular rationale seems to be that traditional religious believers would not like it if they were coerced into certain types of behavior, such as dietary laws and dress practices and so on. But this is not a very strong reason to support the principle. Surely a principle with such far-reaching implications as this needs an illustration of why secular reasons are *better* than religious reasons in a way that is not simply arbitrary (i.e., Audi needs a discussion of the rationality of religious belief). I have argued that no such argument can succeed. We must also note that all positions that are made the basis of law—whether secularist or religious—restrict human conduct. This is true even if an activity is made legal (and not just illegal). If abortion is legalized it also restricts the conduct of religious believers in the sense that although they want to live in a world where abortion is illegal, they are forced to live in a society where it is legal. Almost everyone who contributes to public debates wants some aspect of their views imposed (usually by law) on those who disagree with them.

Audi's principle of secular motivation (which Perry also accepts) might be read as an almost sinister way of removing the last vestiges of religious belief from public life since, despite Audi's qualifications, it still calls for religious believers to have secular motives, not just secular arguments. Not only should religious believers use secular arguments stripped of all religious content to justify their views publicly, but they must also find these arguments convincing themselves. So even if one has religious reasons, there is little point in bringing them up in political discussion. Despite Audi's qualifications, it would simply be a nuisance (especially in our society) to introduce publicly religious beliefs if one does need them to motivate or justify one's position and if one thinks they will not motivate or convince others. It would only exacerbate the problems Audi's principles are designed to solve.

The only thing that could justify Audi's two principles would be an argument that religious beliefs are irrational or dangerous or worse.[9] And al-

---

[9]See *RC,* pp. 100-103, for Audi's negative views of religion, religious institutions and religious leaders.

though I think it is fair to say that both Audi and Perry have a fairly low view of religious belief in general, even though they are religious believers, neither offers any such argument.[10] Further, both fail to appreciate the crucial point that many religious beliefs have political implications, as we will see later, and that it would be irrational for a religious believer to ignore or suspend these implications in the public square. There are many religious beliefs that simply cannot be practiced privately without the belief being seriously compromised or tacitly accepted as nugatory or irrational by those who hold it (a religion so private, as someone once said, that the guy would not impose it on himself!). Indeed, one interesting way that some bemused religious believers try to deal with the political discrimination against their beliefs in U.S. society is, as one religious couple from Kansas put it: "even if we can't directly proselytize—because of the separation of church and state—we can let our lives become our witness." Religious believers have always been aware throughout history of the immense power of witness in promoting religious beliefs politically.

Audi's overall discussion implies that religious beliefs are basically irrational, but he does not defend this view. The defense of Audi's two principles would require a detailed discussion of the rationality of both religion and secularism, as well as an analysis of what a "religious" argument is.[11] But Audi does not give sufficient attention to these vital matters. It is also worth reminding ourselves that it is a cultural fact that secularism is often motivated by dislike of religion, especially of religious morality. (This is why to-

---

[10]See Paul Weithman, *Religion and the Obligations of Citizenship* (New York: Cambridge University Press, 2002), chap. 6, for a very insightful critique of Audi's two principles. While I find myself in strong agreement with Weithman's arguments here, I think his analysis would benefit significantly from a consideration of what it is about religious arguments that Audi finds objectionable (the answer, as I have suggested, is that he does not think they are reasonable).

[11]Audi does ask the question of what a religious argument is, and he gives the following answer: "an argument is religious not because of what it says but (roughly speaking) because of how it must be justified" (*RC*, p. 71). He elaborates, saying an argument would be religious "provided that (a) its premises, or (b) its conclusions, or (c) both, or indeed (d) its premises warranting its conclusion cannot be known, or at least cannot be justifiably accepted, apart from reliance on religious considerations, for instance scripture or revelation or clerical authority" (*RC*, p. 71). There are two problems with this definition: it ignores the issue of whether religious arguments can be based on reason only, and, second, it ignores the issue of what to do with secular arguments whose premises and conclusions are based mainly on an authority (e.g., John Rawls's, and indeed Audi's—who is a disciple of Rawls—appeal to recent liberal political *tradition*). This definition of a religious argument clearly suggests that religious arguments are inferior to secular arguments.

day it is often in attack mode, and why traditional religion is often in defense mode.) So we could say that a secularist who gives a "neutral" argument against a particular religious belief must also be free of an *antireligious motive*. For example, a secularist who argued that the religious teaching on extramarital sex should be rejected, might not be convinced by the actual secularist argument he is offering for this, but might be motivated by a desire to rationalize his own behavior. He could also be motivated by a general animus toward religion. In this case, he would have a *secular(ist) motive*, even if he presents his argument in as neutral a way as possible.

An example of "neutral" (and legal) arguments being used to mask antireligious motives is the objection by the antireligious group Freedom From Religion to a Missouri statute in 2001 that permitted various Missouri county governments to add the phrase "so help me God" to tax forms. The group objected on two grounds: (1) that the statute was discriminatory because it did not appear on all Missouri tax forms and (2) that, of course, it violated the First Amendment. Yet, if one examines the "About Us" mission statement of Freedom From Religion (which includes the following: "The history of Western civilization shows us that most social and moral progress has been brought about by persons free from religion"), one can clearly see that the group's real motive for opposing the Missouri court judgment is antireligious, and their goals include the promotion of secularism.[12] So although I reject Audi's two principles, I think he fails to appreciate that the secularist too can have questionable motives.[13]

This is why the secularist argument that religious beliefs are not reasonable is often couched in language intended to obfuscate the insult that religion is irrational, but the end result is the same: traditional religious beliefs are excluded from the public square. This softens the critique of traditional religious belief for public relations reasons, which are crucial here because

---

[12]See op-ed article, "Tax Form No Place for Religion," by Annie Laurie Gaylor of the Freedom From Religion Foundation, in the *Kansas City Star,* March 17, 2001. For the group's "about us" statement, see their website at <http://www.ffrf.org>. My view on this matter is that tax forms are generally not an appropriate place for statements reflecting one's worldview (religious or secularist). This Foundation has also more recently brought a lawsuit against the University of Minnesota to try to prevent them from offering a tax-supported university program that combines health and spiritual wellness (see *Science and Theology News,* June 2005, p. 15).

[13]Audi does acknowledge that he means also to rule out antireligious motivations (see *RC,* p. 98). But one cannot do this, I contend, until one provides a full analysis of secularism as a worldview and one considers the issue of religion in public life from the point of view of the debate between religious worldviews and secularist worldviews.

if the secularist were to come right out and say overtly that traditional religion is irrational, this would expose the fact that his argument is based on content and not formal structure, and so his case for excluding religion collapses. (He would be trying to exclude religious arguments simply because he disagreed with their political implications.) However, despite the secularist's attempt to soften the blow, we need not worry too much because his argument that religious beliefs are irrational fails.

So we have seen in this section that religious beliefs and secularist beliefs are both based on faith, that religious beliefs can be supported by reason just as much (if not more so) than secularist beliefs. We also rejected Perry's and Audi's arguments. These arguments imply that religious beliefs are not really as reasonable as secularist beliefs, without actually discussing the rationality of religious belief or of secularism. Indeed, both thinkers fail to appreciate or consider the fact that secularism itself is a significant worldview in contemporary culture.

"Secular Reason" Does Not Imply Secularism

Audi and others might object that an appeal to "secular reason" does not necessarily mean that one is advocating secularism. The use of the term *secular reason,* it might be argued, simply means that one appeals to reason and evidence in one's arguments on various issues. The word *secular* means only that one is making no appeal to traditional religion; the word is used purely in its negative sense, as it were, to describe what one's argument is not, not to describe what it is. "Secular" does not mean secularism; so a thinker who argues that one should appeal only to secular reasons in politics, or who, like Audi, argues that one should employ only secular reasons and motivations in one's public arguments, is not covertly suggesting that *secularism* should be the default worldview, and so arbitrarily prejudicing the debate against traditional religion.

For example, on the issue of euthanasia, thinkers like Perry and Audi are inclined to argue that the public argument about this matter should be conducted exclusively in terms of secular reason, yet they suggest that this means only that when one gives an argument in favor of or against euthanasia one may only appeal to reasons and evidence *that do not make any reference to traditional religious content.* So one could argue publicly, for instance, that euthanasia should be illegal because it could not be adequately regulated in legislation, as long as one's argument appealed only to evidence concerning whether and in what ways euthanasia might be abused (and so did not appeal to religious content). But one could not argue publicly that euthanasia should be illegal because life is a precious gift from God. This latter argument has religious content, namely, appeal to the existence of God.

Although neither Perry nor Audi are clear on this issue, their respective positions suggest that they believe the former argument is secular only in the (negative) sense that it does not appeal to religious content; it is not secular in the (positive) sense that it appeals to or assumes a contentious secularist worldview. Audi implies, for example, but never discusses clearly, that he does not mean to say that religious belief should take a back seat but secularism should not; he is saying only that we should appeal to "secular reason," which cannot include any appeal to religious premises or conclusions. Perry's analysis suffers because he does not consider in detail whether secularism itself, as a worldview, might be established in law (thereby promoting a seculocracy) instead of traditional religious belief, or more generally the status of those values he promotes (to the exclusion of their opposites). He does raise this matter obliquely in a footnote, but it merits a more extensive discussion in his overall argument.[14] Perry holds that "no religious argument about the requirements of human well-being is a persuasive basis of political choice for religious nonbelievers."[15] By arguing this way, Perry, however unwittingly, is installing the secularist worldview as primary, as the default view. In order for the secularist worldview not to be regarded as primary here, the secularist would have to be subject to the same requirement—no secular argument about the requirements of human well-being would be a persuasive basis of political choice for religious believers. The only way to make Perry's view consistent is to argue that religious belief is irrational, or at least not as rational as secularism.[16] Audi falls into a similar problem.[17]

---

[14]See Perry, *Religion in Politics,* p. 120 n. 80.

[15]Ibid., p. 75.

[16]As pointed out above in n. 3 of this chapter, Perry has since modified his views on some of these matters.

[17]In an extraordinary admission, Audi says that he does not think that religion is irrational, nor even that there cannot be cogent arguments for God's existence from nonreligious sources (i.e., from secular reasons), but he adds that religious believers should commit to the principles of secular motivation and rationale. He does not seem to realize that this admission basically destroys his case for excluding religious arguments from politics. He fails to realize this partly because he does not consider sufficiently the status of "secular reason," or that secularism is a worldview in itself.

The crucial point, though, is that the argument that one should only appeal to secular reason in politics is not sufficient to rule religious arguments out of public life. The phrase "secular reason" has two possible meanings here. If the phrase "secular reason" just means "reason," which is how Audi and Perry intend to use it, then reason can be used to establish the rationality of basic religious beliefs, in the manner explained in chapter three. That is to say, reason can be used to establish the rationality of basic religious premises and conclusions. The only way secular reason could be used to exclude religious belief from public life is if one could show by secular reason to most people's satisfaction that religious beliefs *are not as rational* as secular beliefs. But I have argued that no argument along these lines can succeed. *To say that an argument that appeals to reason only can't have (in principle) a conclusion with traditional religious content is really just to say that religious beliefs are irrational, or at least not as rational (and so not as worthy) as secular beliefs.* One might, of course, be convinced of this oneself, but this is not enough; one has to convince the religious believer too if one wants to restrict religious belief in politics, and that is why no such argument can succeed.

On the other hand, if secular reason does imply secularism (and the view that secularism is more rational than religious belief), this too is unacceptable to the religious believer, who will argue just the opposite. In any case, even if there is a lively and ongoing debate about which beliefs are more rational, it must still be a *public-square* debate, as I have already argued.

It is essential to point out, however, that secular reason *must* inevitably mean secularism, on some issues at least. If one insists that arguments that have religious content cannot be appealed to, this is often tantamount to saying that the secular*ist* position on the issue in question must prevail or be regarded as the default view. This would be the case, for instance, in arguments concerned with whether human beings differ in kind or only in degree from other animals, a debate relevant for a host of topics, including body/soul questions, the nature of mind, the purpose of human beings in the universe, animal rights, sexuality and so forth. If the arguments that God created the world and all life, including human life, for a particular purpose, and that human beings are the highest form of life—if these arguments are ruled out from the beginning because they have religious content, and it is insisted that the religious believer present only secular arguments, which means arguments with only secular*ist* content—then the existence of God,

God's creating the world and the status of human beings are all *ruled out* of the discussion. If such arguments are prohibited and the religious believer can only draw on secular arguments on these matters, this will prejudice the debate toward the secularist position, which is that human beings differ only in degree from other animals (the view of Dawkins and Sagan, for instance).

Such a mandate to use only "secular reason" would mean in short that we should debate these issues as if God does *not* exist, or as if, say, there is *no* soul, and not just from a position of neutrality on these issues. This is true even if the argument only implies that there is no soul but does not say so explicitly (e.g., if it said something like: animals have rights because superior rational capacities in human beings are not sufficient to justify discrimination among life forms on the basis of their worth, an argument that *assumes* that the soul is not the basis of these superior rational capacities, that these capacities are not evidence of nonphysical properties in human beings). In short, when you debate an issue *as if* God does not exist you are essentially debating as if secularism is presumptive, as if religion is inferior, as if secularism is true. Religious believers are sometimes accused of smuggling God into various issues, but I hope I have shown that it is just as possible to smuggle God *out* of an issue (i.e., to smuggle secularism in!). Indeed, as Nicholas Wolterstorff has noted, it is much easier in general to spot the presence of religious arguments in a debate than it is to spot the presence of secularist arguments.[18]

A secularist once pointed out to me that our local newspaper, the *Kansas City Star,* is biased toward the traditional religious worldview, a claim that surprised me! When I asked him in what way it was biased, his answer was instructive. He replied "because they have a religion section ["Faith and Values"] each Saturday, and no corresponding secularist section." While this no doubt appeared to him to show a bias toward traditional religion, in fact it shows just the opposite, a bias toward secularism. This is because the *Star* is (unwittingly perhaps) marginalizing religion in life generally by relegating it to a small section once a week. They are feeding the stereotype that religious belief is simply a matter of faith, and while significant in the sense that many people subscribe to it (the religion not the paper), it is not sufficiently important to influence what goes on in the rest of the paper, including analysis of the news stories of the day, contribu-

---

[18]See Robert Audi and Nicholas Wolterstorff, *Religion in the Public Square* (Lanham, Md.: Rowman & Littlefield, 1997), p. 105.

tions to the various political and moral debates and so forth.

This last point is vital, and is another clear way in which "secular reason" really means secularism, in some contexts. For newspaper editorial writers, including those at the *Star,* do not usually bring religiously based arguments into their editorials, say into their arguments that embryonic stem cell research should be legal, or that partial birth abortion should be legal, or that the death penalty should be abolished in Missouri and Kansas. They present arguments for these views based on reason and exclude, arbitrarily I am claiming, religious content on these matters. For instance, in their argument in favor of research that involves the destruction of human embryos, they exclude automatically the view that life is a gift from God. And one cannot argue that the death penalty, say, is immoral in principle and that it should be illegal without bringing in one's worldview somewhere along the line. *And newspaper editorials routinely exclude the religious worldview from this debate.* Moreover, as I have emphasized, if editorial writers claim that they are simply appealing to reason, this won't be enough to exclude religious arguments, since they too are reasonable. The reason the *Star* is not biased toward religion even though it has a special religion section is that everything else in the paper concerning ideas, beliefs and arguments relating to worldviews is written from largely a secularist perspective. For all practical purposes, secular reason in this context means secularism.

Advice columns in the mainstream press are often good places to find secularist values masquerading as something else. These columns often promote a definite, usually secularist, view of morality, human relationships and so on. Anyone who writes in expressing a traditional view is usually criticized and subtly encouraged to change to adopt a more liberal view. For example, a newspaper advice columnist once ran a letter from a young woman who asked for advice about premarital sex, saying that she was worried about engaging in it for several reasons, the main one being that it is immoral according to her Catholic religion. The advice columnist replied by saying that the column was obviously not the place to give advice about the young woman's religious beliefs, and advised her to be cautious, responsible, and to go ahead when she was very sure it was what she wanted! What is significant about this exchange is that the columnist rejects the woman's religious beliefs without mentioning them by name, and also advised her to do the same. She advises the young woman to follow *her* beliefs (the advice columnist's) on premarital sex. The fact that most people would be slow to notice this when reading the column at first glance is testimony to the way we have compartmentalized religion in modern democracies.

Might there be cases where a traditional religious believer would not appeal to arguments with religious content in the political arena, but appeal only to arguments based on secular reason? This is possible. A religious believer might think that in a debate with secularists, and even members of other religions, it would be more pragmatic or irenic from the point of view of passing legislation favorable to his beliefs, or simply for his beliefs to have some influence, to couch his argument purely in secular terms (i.e., in terms that do not appeal to any religious content). This means only that he might attempt to present his views in more neutral language (i.e., he decides not to appeal to religious content), not that he should compromise his beliefs (i.e., not believe the religious content). However, he would not be acquiescing in Audi's principle of secular motivation here; this would simply be a pragmatic judgment.[19] Yet in the long term, this approach might be dangerous for the religious believer because it might be taken to imply that religious belief is somehow irrational and not worthy of being a player in the political arena. The long-term aim of the religious believer, in U.S. society especially, should be to restore the legitimacy of arguments with religious content to the public square; so religious believers should be careful not to be too much influenced by the contemporary climate that stigmatizes these arguments.

This is the reason that I am cautious about the approach of John Finnis and other modern-day natural law theorists, such as Joseph Boyle, Germain Grisez and Robert George,[20] who have nevertheless done excellent work in developing a natural law approach in the context of the contributions it can make to the political discussion in a liberal, democratic society. Their emphasis has been on developing purely secular style arguments based on reason and natural philosophy (with no appeal to religious content) on the moral and social debates of the day (though their conclusions are consistent

---

[19]Pope John Paul II has adopted something like this strategy in his various encyclicals, although he has been careful to offer both religious arguments (arguments that appeal to religious content) and secular arguments (arguments that do not appeal to religious content). See, for example, the arguments against abortion in *Evangelium Vitae* ("The Gospel of Life"), 1995.

[20]See John Finnis, *Natural Law and Natural Rights* (Oxford: Oxford University Press, 1980); Germain Grisez and Russell Shaw, *Fulfillment in Christ: A Summary of Christian Moral Principles* (Notre Dame, Ind.: University of Notre Dame Press, 1991); Robert George, *The Clash of Orthodoxies: Law, Religion and Morality in Crisis* (Wilmington, Del.: ISI Books, 2001); also his *In Defense of Natural Law* (New York: Oxford University Press, 1999).

with religious morality). I have no problem with this approach per se, and I think they have succeeded well in developing persuasive secular arguments for moral conclusions that are consonant with religious morality. George, in particular, expertly develops a theme I have been emphasizing in this book: that secularist views often fail the test of reason and that religious views are more rational than secularist views. Yet my reservation is that the traditional natural law approach is, in the context of modern liberal societies, essentially *defensive* in character. It often concedes an essential point to liberal political theory—that one should not bring one's religious beliefs into the political arena. It tries to make up for this by saying that this restriction is not so much of a problem because one can still give philosophical (i.e., secular) arguments for (religious) morality. The secularist has usually replied to this approach by simply dismissing natural law conclusions (and the default approach among moral philosophers today is generally to ignore the natural law tradition). My reservation with this natural law approach, as I have argued, is that one should be very careful about conceding to the secularist the conclusion that religious beliefs are not appropriate in politics. One should introduce one's religious beliefs and defend them by appeal to reason.

The natural law theorists are right, though, to insist on a key philosophical point in the discussion about the basis for morality—that moral values, even if supported by secular reasons, still need appeal to the existence of God in the end for their ultimate justification. Finnis puts this point well:

> the fact that natural law can be understood, assented to, applied, and reflectively analyzed without adverting to the question of the existence of God does not of itself entail either (i) that no further explanation is required for the fact that there are objective standards of good and bad and principles of reasonableness (right and wrong), or (ii) that no such explanation is available, or (iii) that the existence of God is not that explanation.[21]

It is an important part of the argument for the superior rationality of the religious worldview over the secularist worldview that the objective moral order requires appeal to the existence of God for its ultimate justification. This is a point also made forcefully by J. Budziszewski, who has emphasized the "general revelation" of the natural law to human beings in his work on natural law, that is, the view that human beings, through reason and expe-

---

[21]Finnis, *Natural Law and Natural Rights,* p. 49.

rience, can rationally arrive at moral conclusions and also at the conclusion that God exists.[22] Rejection of this whole way of thinking is one of the reasons secularism sails so close to moral relativism on so many issues and why modern political theory is essentially relativistic in character (as we will see in our later discussion of the work of John Rawls).

I think a secularist could also adopt a pragmatic approach in the sense that he might propose an argument in the public square expressed in as neutral a way as possible, which means that it would suppress key premises and conclusions that come from his secularist worldview, although he is in fact motivated by these premises and conclusions. So, for instance, a secularist might believe that because human beings do not differ in kind from other animals, that killing animals is wrong. But when he presents these arguments in public he might argue for the conclusion that killing animals is wrong because it is cruel, or causes pain, or because *our* moral values require us not to kill or harm animals, but never mention his underlying belief that there is no substantial moral difference between human beings and animals. In this way, he is trying to influence public policy on the basis of a secularist belief disguised as something else. Or a secularist might hold that the theory of evolution is strong evidence against the existence of God and that once people fully appreciate the theory, they will see this (as Darwin's friend Thomas Huxley held). This might be his main motivation for supporting strong teaching of evolution in public schools, hoping that it will lead to a rejection by many, or at least to a watering down, of their religious beliefs over time. Yet in public debates on these matters, for pragmatic reasons, he might defend the teaching of evolution in science curricula purely on the grounds that we should teach the latest scientific theories.

In addition, religious believers and secularists might try to reach consensus on an issue in the public square if it was possible or if they thought it might be politically expedient to do so. In short, they might not always bring their worldviews into the debate in a direct way. All participants in the public political discussion must be political realists, especially in a pluralist culture (and all must engage in *realpolitik*). As noted in the previous chapter, we should not only try to give people reasons if we are trying to coerce

---

[22]See J. Budziszewski, *Written on the Heart: The Case for Natural Law* (Downers Grove, Ill.: InterVarsity Press, 1997). This book is an excellent and very readable introduction to the natural law tradition and its thinkers and arguments.

them, but to give them reasons they are likely to find persuasive insofar as we can do this. So, for example, on the question of animal rights, religious believers and secularists might try to come to some consensus without having to get into the full debate about whether human beings differ in kind from other animals, though the full justification of the position of each side may well come back in the end to their views on this question. Although this kind of consensus is possible on some issues, it is not possible on all issues, nor is it desirable on all issues. For on some issues, consensus will involve too much of a compromise of one's foundational, basic beliefs. Richard John Neuhaus has argued that some issues in a democracy are best fudged for the sake of political order, and perhaps this is true and we must all do our best to live with it. But, Neuhaus goes on eloquently, the fudging should not be a form of deception, but rather,

> a readiness to patch things together that may not quite exactly fit, to live with a few loose ends not tucked in. Forgiving is not forgetting, to be sure, but in everyday life forgiving includes an element of fudging. People who compromise in accordance with the discipline of the democratic process know that they are compromising. That is, they do not tell themselves or others that it does not matter, that there was no principle at stake, that there was not a reasoning that had been stopped short of its logical end. . . . Democracy is the product not of a vision of perfection but of the knowledge of imperfection. . . . The person who makes a compromise is making a moral judgment about what is to be done when moral judgments are in conflict.[23]

What compromises one is willing to make will depend on the topic; some will not come easily; and some may be impossible. But whatever the outcome, it is a discussion that must include religious arguments as well as secularist ones.

Kent Greenawalt has asked if people would actually debate the existence of God and other related matters in the political arena.[24] He thinks that this would not be the best forum for such a debate. In general, some might argue that I have a too lofty view of the kind of debate that could take place in our public square, which twenty-four-hour news TV channels, in particular, have reduced to the lowest common denominator when it comes to political discussion. There is some truth to Greenawalt's point, but some disagree-

---

[23]Richard John Neuhaus, *The Naked Public Square* (Grand Rapids: Eerdmans, 1984), p. 114.
[24]Kent Greenawalt, *Private Consciences and Public Reasons* (New York: Oxford University Press, 1995), p. 87.

ments will come down to a public-square debate in the sense that one would have to bring in the key foundational beliefs of one's worldview, religious or secularist. It would be odd if one could not debate, from time to time at least, these foundational beliefs in the political arena, especially with regard to crucial matters (matters that could change society), such as abortion, marriage, the nature of the family, cloning, just-war doctrine, the goals of education and so on. Obviously, one could not exclude the beliefs of a worldview from politics just because one did not want to have this debate. But, as I have mentioned, one might avoid bringing the debate back to fundamental issues as much as possible for pragmatic reasons, although, crucially, one is still *motivated* by these issues (religious or secularist), and so the issue of their rationality is still a vitally important matter, wherever it is considered. One might *assume* some key arguments in politics and defend them in other places where an extended discussion is more conveniently carried out, such as academia. But the generally low level of public debate in the United States cannot be used as an excuse to exclude religious but not secularist arguments from politics.

Secularism Can Better Achieve Overall Agreement Among Worldviews

Proponents of secularism sometimes claim that their approach is better from the point of view of achieving overall agreement among worldviews, especially in a pluralist democracy. And so for this reason religion can be restricted in politics. Secularism is much better at accommodating different points of view in a state than traditional religion. In particular, it has a better chance of achieving an overlapping consensus, at least on many of the important issues, than any other religious approach. This is because traditional religions tend to be more rigid and exclusionary in their beliefs,[25] whereas secularism is more flexible and makes an attempt to accommodate those that profoundly disagree with them. For example, the secularist might claim that in the abortion discussion, the view that abortion should be legal is more accommodating and flexible than the view of traditional religion. This is because the secularist position accommodates both those who are for abortion and those who are against it, while the religious view cannot ac-

---

[25]Audi's view is that "religious people often tend to be, in a way that is rare in secular matters, highly and stubbornly passionate about the importance of everyone's acting in accordance with religious reasons" (*RC*, p. 102).

commodate those who are in favor of making abortion legal.

Let us elaborate the example of abortion to illustrate how this argument is supposed to work. Proponents of secularism begin with the view that abortion is a difficult moral issue about which reasonable people can disagree; they conclude that it should be legal so that individuals are free to choose on the issue. A number of reasons are given for this conclusion. First, *not everyone agrees* about the morality or otherwise of abortion; therefore one should not be able to impose one's moral views on others. One would be doing this if one were to make abortion illegal. Second, those who believe that abortion is immoral do not have to choose abortion, and obviously will not be forced to avail of abortion. This position, it is argued, is *neutral* as regards the question of the morality of abortion. It is not intended to promote the view that abortion is morally acceptable and that those who are against the practice of abortion are wrong. It is simply intended to facilitate both views on the question, and making it legal is the best way to do this. Thirdly, proponents of this view are not imposing their views on abortion on those who disagree with them, because they are not saying that abortion is moral nor that anyone must avail of abortion.

There are several problems with these arguments. In the first place, this view on abortion is not a neutral view. The secularist is in fact taking a stand on abortion. Usually, it is one of the following two stands: either abortion is moral, so we can legalize it, and if people think it's immoral they do not have to avail of it. If this is the reasoning of the secularist, then his position on abortion is that it is moral (and he wants this view placed in law). So this would not be a neutral view. The second option is to say that abortion is a difficult issue to which there is no clear answer, and so we will make it legal and allow people to make up their own minds on the question. If they decide in good conscience that it is immoral they do not have to avail of it. If the secularist follows this approach, his view of abortion is that there is no clear answer to the question, and so again he has a definite view of the issue, and is *not* neutral about it, as he originally claimed. The secularist wishes to impose his moral assessment about the abortion question on those who disagree with this assessment. By making it legal the secularist is forcing this position on those who disagree with him that abortion should be legal and who think that (as with slavery or prostitution or polygamy) it is immoral enough to make it illegal. So we can see that the secularist takes a position on abortion and tries to impose it by means of legislation on those who disagree.

Proponents of secularism might reply that in making the practice of abortion legal they are not forcing abortion on anyone since one does not have to choose it, but those who would make it illegal are denying the practice of abortion to others. However, this popular argument is again a confusion and is based on a misunderstanding of the views of most abortion opponents. The opponents of abortion do not just hold that abortion is immoral but are unclear, say, about what its legal status should be. Rather, just like the opponents of slavery, they believe that is it immoral and should be illegal. They do not want to live in a society where abortion is tolerated, just as the abolitionist did not want to live in a society where slavery was tolerated. So if the secularists win the argument and succeed in having their views on abortion established in law, they are forcing millions of people to live in a society where abortion is tolerated, and so they are forcing this key belief of secularism on those who disagree with it. It is true that the opponents of abortion are denying the practice of abortion. But it is simply disingenuous to claim that denying the practice of abortion involves imposing one's view on society but that permitting the practice of abortion is not imposing one's view on society.

We could give a similar analysis about a host of issues currently disputed in American society. And so secularism does not better promote an overlapping consensus than more religious views. We must also point out that the attempt to achieve an overlapping consensus in our modern pluralist society cannot fully succeed for the simple reason that, since many beliefs are often in conflict, not everyone can get what they want. People may be prepared to compromise on some questions, but will not be willing to compromise on all questions (e.g., abortion). So in a pluralist democracy in which there are different worldviews, there will inevitably be serious disagreements, and an overlapping consensus, though perhaps desirable, will be difficult—perhaps impossible—to attain.

The most serious problem with the claim that secularism accommodates more views than say, Christianity, is that this is a claim about the *content* of that worldview and not about its form or structure. Let us not forget that in order to exclude religion from politics what the secularist must argue is that secularism is formally superior to traditional religion. However, this particular argument is not about the form of the worldviews at all, but is really about the superior content of secularism. This leads the secularist into a serious problem. It is quite appropriate to argue that the content of your view is better than that of your opponents (on, for example, abortion). That is what the debate in a pluralist democracy is about. So the secularist is quite entitled to argue that his position on abortion is superior to the religious view, whether because it is more rational, is more practical, or for whatever reason. However, the important point is that if he attempts to argue on the basis of content he must allow the proponents of religious worldviews to do likewise. He cannot insist that he can argue for his view on abortion and try to persuade others of its truth, but that members of other worldviews with a different position cannot do this. In short, one must allow religion back into the public square if one takes this line of argument. But the whole point of the dispute we are discussing in this section is to keep religion out of the public debate. There is still no legitimate formal reason for discriminating against traditional religion. If you argue on the basis of content, then you must allow the religious believer to do the same. Of course, you still might believe that your content is superior, that legislation should be based on it, and that the religious view is wrong, but you must accept that the religious believer will argue just the opposite. And proponents of each view can then try to convince each other that *they* are right. One of the problems for the whole approach of the secularist is that he wants to appeal to the *form* of worldviews as a way of keeping religion out of politics, but as I have been showing in earlier chapters *any formal feature of religion is also possessed by secularism.*

We have considered some of the best-known arguments for excluding religious beliefs from politics and found them all wanting. It is not enough to claim that religious beliefs should be excluded because they are "religious," since, despite this restriction, it would not exclude religious beliefs that are based on reason and evidence. And some religious beliefs can be just as reasonable as some secularist beliefs (and some religious beliefs can be just as unreasonable as some secularist beliefs). Both Robert Audi and Michael Perry fail to appreciate the significance of this point, nor do they give due appreciation to the crucial fact today that secularism too is an influential worldview in our politics. We pointed out how no definition of "secular reason" can be used to discriminate against religious beliefs, and that sometimes "secular" or "neutral" reason really means secularism.

But there are still further reasons offered to justify discriminating against the religious worldview in a pluralist democracy. Let us now turn to consider a second set of interesting arguments for excluding religion from politics.

5

Keeping Religion Out of Politics II

We are beginning to see that many secularists are downright suspicious of religious beliefs and often regard religious believers as irrational, divisive or worse. Many secularists don't seem to regard the religious worldview as a reasonable worldview, even if they are understandably reluctant to put it this starkly very often. But many are suggestible to the view—and perhaps have made society at large suggestible to the view—that religious believers are not reasonable in some way that is hard to specify. This is more an impression conveyed by the secularist than a substantive view he could defend. This is why many religious believers sometimes find it hard to characterize this secularist attitude as anything more than a prejudice. Secularists are also quick to say that religious beliefs can be dangerous to society in a way that is rare for secularist beliefs. What they are getting at is that such beliefs are politically dangerous, and so should be restricted. This doesn't just mean that perhaps some religious cults or genuine religious fanatics are dangerous to society; this is supposed to be true of more mainstream religions as well. And once one begins to talk about mainstream religions, then impressions and attitudes will not be enough. It becomes imperative that we look in detail at the substance of these claims. In this chapter, we need to confront head-on criticisms that religious beliefs are stupid or irrational, and also that they are dangerous. There are two other arguments for keeping religious beliefs out of politics that we need to consider as well, arguments that appeal to the nature of law as nonsectarian, and to the U.S. Constitution. Along the way, I will say more about the reasonability of religious beliefs.

Most Religious Beliefs Are Higher-Order Beliefs, and So Should Be Kept Private

The secularist may try to establish a legitimate way for discriminating against religious views and in favor of secularist views by claiming that nearly all religious beliefs are what in chapter one I called higher-order beliefs, while by contrast the beliefs of secularists are lower-order beliefs. Recall that a higher-order belief is a belief that takes more faith to believe it; in this sense it "goes beyond the evidence." A lower-order belief is one that does not take as much faith to believe and is close to the evidence (i.e., it is a rational belief). So in general we can say that lower-order beliefs are more likely to be persuasive to reasonable people than higher-order ones. The secularist thinks that one can therefore legitimately employ many of the (lower-order) beliefs of secularism in the public square yet deny this opportunity to traditional religious belief.

The secularist will claim that *most* religious beliefs are higher order, and most secularist beliefs lower order, and so in practical terms this means that the secularist view should rule the political discussion. He might argue that when people appeal to religious beliefs to make public arguments most of these beliefs are very specific beliefs tied to a particular world religion and so they are higher-order beliefs. But the secularist appeals only to more general beliefs, many of which even a religious believer might accept. This is an interesting objection, and considering it will help us to tease out the secularist perspective more fully. The overall problem I see with this objection is that most of the traditional religious beliefs that might be appealed to in the public square are *not* higher order. Nor is it true that most secularist beliefs are lower order. Nor is it true that most secularist arguments involve more general beliefs. All of these claims are problematic, as I will try to show by discussing some specific examples.

We should note the issues that religious believers and secularists most disagree on, especially in contemporary U.S. society, questions that give rise to much of the dispute between religion and secularism over the role of religion in politics. These issues are abortion, euthanasia, sexual matters, changing concepts of the family, prayer in public schools, matters relating to free speech and censorship, the definition of marriage and so forth. (I will come back to some of these topics in chapter eight.) The debate in America is *not* about other matters that could arise in the dispute between traditional religion and secularism, such as whether everyone should believe in the resurrection of Christ, or whether eating certain foods is immoral, or whether the doctrine of the Trinity should be included in the Constitution, or whether public prayer should be mandatory each day for all citizens, or whether the state should be concerned with the salvation of citizens and so on. These matters are not at issue in U.S. politics or in the political debates of most Western cultures.

I argued above in chapter three that belief in God is a rational, lower-order belief and that it is therefore legitimate to appeal to this belief when debating in the political arena. The secularist contends that belief in the existence of God is a higher-order belief and so is based on a great deal of faith, and so it should not influence public policy. Belief in God might influence public policy in this way: a person might believe that God exists, that human life is a gift from God and has great value, that the fetus is a human life, and that abortion, therefore, is immoral and should be illegal. On this question, a secularist typically argues that since this view on abortion is based on a religious belief, it should not be allowed to influence public policy at all. I am suggesting that it is *rational* to believe in God, that life is a gift from God and has great value, and that abortion is immoral and should be illegal. The way a secularist might go about refuting this argument is to show that belief in God is not rational. And he is quite entitled to try to do this (and indeed to believe this). But I am arguing that his position is wrong; that he cannot show this by appeal to objective reason. He can reply that he does not hold my view. Or he could try to criticize some of the intermediate steps in the argument I mentioned, by, say, arguing that even though life is a gift from God, this might not rule out all abortions, etc. These are all perfectly good ways to argue. However, *they are not sufficient to rule religious beliefs out of politics.*

Let us briefly look at three other beliefs that are both a significant part of the religious worldview and the basis of some disputes with the secularist. The first of these is belief in human nature, a significant part of most religions, and a belief many religions have in common. Human nature might be defined as a set of characteristics and traits that all human beings share, that cannot be reduced to biology and that have special relevance for morality. These traits would include the capacity to reason, free will, moral virtues, moral responsibility, natural inclinations and so on. Human nature in turn can be traced back to the creative power of God. God gave us this nature. It guides us particularly in the identification of objective moral values, in discovering what is right and wrong. This belief in human nature is not, however, confined to traditional religious believers, for it was held by many pagan thinkers. Aristotle, the pagan Greek philosopher, who had an enormous influence on Western thinking, was one of the best exponents of this view.

It is one of the main beliefs of most forms of secularism that there is no such thing as human nature. And since there is no such thing as human nature, there is no special set of traits and characteristics that all human beings share. One implication of this is that moral values are now seen by many secularists as relative either to the individual or to the culture. Even if a secularist wishes to defend the objectivity of morality (such as Kai Nielsen[1]), this will now have to be done without appeal to human nature. But the rejection of human nature has been one of the main secularist arguments for the moral acceptability of homosexuality and premarital sex, for the rejection of marriage and for the changing definitions of the family.

My point is not that secularism is wrong on these matters, but that belief in human nature is a quite reasonable belief. Again, I cannot justify this here in any detail and I refer the reader to discussions in the philosophical and other literature.[2] But speaking generally the reason that people came to believe in human nature was because it was confirmed in their own experience: they recognized traits that all human beings had in common, all over the world and in history. They recognized that beneath all the different languages, cultures, beliefs and so on, we are all the same underneath. It was also supported by the argument that God designed the universe and has a plan for humanity. This belief in human nature cannot be proved, but it is a rational belief and, in my view, clearly a lower-order belief.

I would also argue that the belief that there is no human nature is not a rational belief, and so is a higher-order belief. I believe that all of the available evidence from studying how human beings behave, how they flourish, how they function well and so forth shows that certain types of behavior work better than others, and that these types of behavior have moral implications. But even if the secularist insists that his view *is* lower order—that both views are lower order—then this does not give him a good reason to

---

[1]See Kai Nielsen, *Ethics Without God*, rev. ed. (New York: Prometheus, 1990); see also his essay "An Examination of the Thomistic Theory of Natural Law," in *St. Thomas Aquinas on Politics and Ethics*, ed. Paul E. Sigmund (New York: Norton, 1988), pp. 211-17, along with the various other essays in this volume on the defense and critique of natural law and human nature.

[2]For a discussion of various approaches to human nature, see Leslie Stevenson, *Ten Theories of Human Nature* (New York: Oxford University Press, 1998); see also John Finnis, *Natural Law and Natural Rights* (Oxford: Oxford University Press, 1980); Robert George, *In Defense of Natural Law* (New York: Oxford University Press, 1999), esp. chap. 14; and Anthony J. Lisska, *Aquinas's Theory of Natural Law: An Analytic Reconstruction* (New York: Oxford University Press, 1996).

exclude the religious view from politics. It is possible for two opposing views to be both rational, and so lower order, if the evidence for both of them is somewhere in between, about evenly divided for and against, or is somewhat ambiguous. If a religious believer appeals to human nature to make a point about public policy matters, this is an argument based on lower-order beliefs, and so is rational and just as acceptable as any secularist counterargument.

Another lower-order, rational belief held by religious believers is the view that human beings are primarily social beings and not primarily individual beings. This means that it is part of the nature of a human being to live in a community with others (and this nature was created by God). It does not mean a human being has no individuality, but rather that human beings need to maintain a balance between their individual rights and the common good. This position would have implications when dealing with those matters where individual freedom clashes with the common good of society. Now this view is contrary to another main belief of secularism in its contemporary forms: that human beings are primarily individuals first and social beings second. This latter belief is the basis for much of modern political theory, which advocates the view that we are centers of rationality and autonomy, that we enter into society by *choice,* and not by *nature.* This results in a more selfish view of the human person, which has presaged the rise in "rights talk" in modern societies (but not talk of responsibilities), a view that almost deifies, absolutizes personal freedom at the expense of the common good.[3]

Again, my point is that the belief that human beings are primarily social beings is a lower-order, reasonable belief. It is more reasonable than the view that human beings are primarily individual beings. And so if a religious believer employs this belief in an argument in the public square, he is perfectly entitled to do so. For instance, one is entitled to argue that an individual has no right to euthanasia because the practice of euthanasia ignores the fact that we are social beings because of our nature (which is created by God), that our decision to commit suicide always concerns and affects other people.

Perhaps as a final example we can mention the many position statements that America's religious leaders and groups, including the Family Research

---

[3]For an insightful analysis of this phenomenon, see Mary Ann Glendon, *Rights Talk: The Impoverishment of Political Discourse* (New York: Free Press, 1991).

Council, the Conference of Catholic Bishops and the National Council of Churches have put out in recent decades on a variety of political and social issues, from abortion and stem cell research, to social welfare and Social Security, homelessness, the right to a just wage and racial injustice. Many of the views expressed in these documents are based on the religious beliefs of the various groups in question, especially the overarching belief that each human being is a child of God and has a fundamental dignity and integrity that should be respected and recognized as much as possible in our political, social and economic arrangements. Sixteen religious organizations, for example, representing different denominations, issued a joint statement of guiding principles in April 2005 concerning the debate over how to reform Social Security.[4] For each religion in question the arguments put forward in this document are grounded in their religious beliefs; they are also reasonable arguments and make a worthwhile, even profound, contribution to the public debate. For that reason they resonate with many members of our society, including law makers.

So we have seen that many of the religious beliefs appealed to in the public square are not higher-order beliefs. But we must also note that not all of the secularist beliefs are lower order.[5] I mentioned above the belief that there is no human nature as an example of a higher-order belief in the sense that it goes against the evidence; it takes a high degree of faith to accept this belief. Similarly, if the secularist believes that an individual can take drugs as long as one does not harm others, I would argue that this belief is not reasonable. This is because it is based on the view that harming yourself is a morally acceptable choice because one is primarily an individual being and has little responsibility to others. I reject this because I believe that in harming oneself, one also harms others because one is primarily a social being. Similarly, if a secularist argues that euthanasia should be permitted be-

---

[4]See *To Preserve and Strengthen Social Security: Religious Organization Statement of Principles,* April 26, 2005, released by the National Council of Churches, among other groups, posted at <http://www.ncccusa.org/news/050426SSPrinciples.html>.

[5]Beliefs that come under the heading "political correctness" contain many examples of higher-order beliefs. Many have argued that the phenomenon of political correctness is an example of a broadly secularist worldview run amok. One of the best documenters of this phenomenon in contemporary culture is *U.S. News & World Report* columnist John Leo, who regularly writes about the excesses of political correctness. See his *Two Steps Ahead of the Thought Police* (New York: Simon & Schuster, 1994), and *Incorrect Thoughts: Notes on Our Wayward Culture* (New York: Transaction, 2000). See also for a discussion of modern issues in U.S. politics, Jean Bethke Elshtain's insightful *Democracy on Trial* (New York: Basic Books, 1996).

cause self-determination is paramount and individuals should be able to decide how and when they die, I would reject this argument because it does not take into account the harm to the common good that euthanasia will bring.[6] I believe that this particular secularist argument for the legalization of euthanasia is based on a higher-order belief: that human beings are primarily individual beings. But my main point here is that whether the secularist view is higher or lower order, the traditional religious view *is* lower order, and so cannot be excluded from the public square.

Another way to express what I have been saying above is to point out that the argument for the lower-order nature of some significant religious beliefs is a *rational* argument based on an appeal to logic and evidence, and so one that all reasonable people can look at. It is not a narrow, simplistic, sectarian argument in any sense. By this I mean that the religious believer does not need to simply say, "euthanasia is immoral because my religion says so." Religious arguments will not rely simply on appeals to religious texts or religious authorities or traditions (as we saw above), but, in order to be considered reasonable, they must appeal to reasons that a reasonable person could accept. All of this holds for the secularist as well.

Of course, we can have a dispute about whether a particular belief is a higher- or a lower-order belief. And this is an important argument because it will affect the issue of whether or not the belief has influence in the public square. But even the disagreement about whether a belief is a lower-order or a higher-order belief *must itself be part of the public debate.* It is inevitable that people will disagree on whether various religious or secularist beliefs are rational, and this debate has gone on over the centuries. But the religious believer must be allowed to debate these questions; he cannot be excluded because he is "religious." This is because, as I already mentioned, the secularist view is also "religious," and secondly, because the

---

[6]This argument has been offered by Daniel Brock, James Rachels, Margaret Battin, Helga Kuhse and Ronald Dworkin, among many others. It is a fairly common liberal argument in the debate over euthanasia. See Daniel Brock, "Voluntary Active Euthanasia," in *Social Ethics: Morality and Social Policy*, ed. Thomas Mappes and Jane Zembaty, 5th ed. (New York: McGraw-Hill, 1997), pp. 70-73; James Rachels, *The End of Life* (New York: Oxford University Press, 1986), pp. 180-84; Margaret Battin, *The Least Worst Death: Essays in Bioethics and the End of Life* (New York: Oxford University Press, 1994), pp. 277-79; Helga Kuhse, *The Sanctity-of-Life Doctrine in Medicine: A Critique* (New York: Clarendon, 1987), p. 211; Ronald Dworkin, *Life's Dominion* (New York: Knopf, 1993). For an alternative view, see John Kavanaugh, S.J., *Who Count as Persons? Human Dignity and the Ethics of Persons* (Washington, D.C.: Georgetown University Press, 2001), esp. pp. 132-37.

claim that a belief of secularism is more rational than a belief of a religious worldview is a claim about the *justification* of the belief(s) in question. In short, it is a claim about the *content* of the respective worldviews, about whether or not this content can be adequately justified. And this is obviously a debate that all sides must be allowed to participate in. If members of worldview A believe that some of worldview B's beliefs are irrational, and B believes that some of A's are irrational, then both sides must be allowed to debate this matter between themselves. It is not acceptable for one side to arbitrarily rule the other side out of the debate, as I argued in chapter three.

People will continually disagree about the rationality of certain beliefs, especially on the three areas (reality, human person, moral and political values). This is why, as I mentioned in the previous chapter, members of various worldviews might adopt a pragmatic route on some issues that concern public policy. For a religious believer, this could sometimes involve offering a purely secular argument (i.e., an argument that makes no appeal to religious content) on a particular topic, such as abortion. Many thinkers (like the natural law theorists) hold that one can give a purely secular argument on many of the moral questions that are often the subject of controversy. While there no doubt is something to this claim, it carries with it the danger that "secular arguments" will become the presumptive way of deciding public policy issues and eventually lead to the marginalization of religion. This has already happened to some extent in the United States.

It is to be hoped that rational beliefs will rise to the top more often than not in a democracy. But this cannot be guaranteed. Nor can it be guaranteed that what the majority at any particular time agrees on will be *moral*. For although rationality and morality have been closely related in many ethical theories and in the history of much of our ethical practice, this cannot be guaranteed in the twenty-first century, dominated as it is by moral relativism, and even by an attack on reason itself.

The status of reason itself is very important. If one is an epistemological relativist (and perhaps a moral relativist), as so many secularists are, then one is hardly in a position to offer a persuasive argument criticizing the *rationality* of another worldview, especially with the intention of ruling that worldview out of place in political life![7]

---

[7]See the brief discussion on the relativity of reason in chap. 1.

Religion Is Dangerous; Secularism Is Benign

The secularist sometimes argues that religion is divisive and dangerous, and so it is important for maintaining public order that we find a mechanism for keeping disputes involving religious beliefs out of the public political arena. The claim that religious beliefs are divisive and dangerous means that the holders of these beliefs are more inclined to be dogmatic, perhaps more inclined to be fanatical, more likely to resort to violence to compel others to follow their beliefs. This is because religious beliefs are often tied to the existence of God and to the idea that one's salvation is at stake if one does not believe the right things or live in the right way. Given this conception, religious believers often see themselves as on a mission from God in the sense that they are trying to save souls. Robert Audi, John Rawls, Richard Rorty and Kent Greenawalt have all offered versions of the argument that religious beliefs are divisive.[8] Indeed, this is one of Greenawalt's main reasons for being worried about allowing religious beliefs a role in the public square. There is also historical evidence to back up this point, the secularist will argue, because we have had many religious wars in history, and still have religiously motivated violence today.

There is no doubt that religious beliefs and religious believers can be and often still are dangerous and divisive. However, as Nicholas Wolterstorff has pointed out, this is not a significant problem in the United States, where we have had a long period of peace between the various religions (and secularism).[9] So it is not convincing or realistic to argue that we should restrict religious beliefs in the public square because they will lead to violence. This is not an argument that can be taken seriously today in U.S. society.

Second, it is also the case that any belief can be regarded as dangerous— no matter which worldview it comes from, religious or secularist—as long as its proponents are prepared to use some kind of force to coerce others by law to live by or to practice the belief. As long as one is prepared to go this far, the issue of one's motivation for holding the belief is a secondary matter. Are secularists just as willing to coerce others (such as religious be-

---

[8]See Robert Audi, *Religious Commitment and Secular Reason* (Cambridge: Cambridge University Press, 2000), pp. 100-103; Kent Greenawalt, *Private Consciences and Public Reasons* (New York: Oxford University Press, 1995), p. 69; John Rawls's introduction to his *Political Liberalism,* paperback ed., with a new preface (New York: Columbia University Press, 1996); and Richard Rorty, "Religion as Conversation Stopper," in his *Philosophy and Social Hope* (New York: Penguin, 1999), pp. 168-74.

[9]See Nicholas Wolterstorff in *Religion in the Public Square,* by Robert Audi and Nicholas Wolterstorff (Lanham, Md.: Rowman & Littlefield, 1997), pp. 78-80.

lievers) to follow their beliefs on certain issues? The answer is obvious. They are even prepared to seriously restrict people's liberty, even to commit violence in order to promote their beliefs. This general point about promoting one's foundational beliefs is true, I think, of all worldviews.

Secularists (and liberals), for example, have shown much evidence of being willing to suppress their opponents and critics in recent culture. Robert Kraynak has noted that

> secularism is highly intrusive in the imposition of secular liberal values. It establishes public schools that systematically indoctrinate young people in secular humanism and prohibit the free expression of religion; it attempts to redefine masculinity and femininity by changing the culture of the family, the workplace, and the military; it launches its own versions of moral crusades, such as anti-smoking . . . in trying to restructure a private association like the Boy Scouts to diminish its moral opposition to homosexuality and to repudiate its religious roots [and so on].[10]

This activity has been especially evident in the media and in higher education, where alternative voices are routinely censored, suppressed or not represented. This is also true of liberal religious believers who favor the separation of church and state on the grounds that religious beliefs can be divisive. Liberal religious organizations have often censored more conservative voices, and liberal theology faculties have denied tenure to conservative theologians (in much the same way as they complain that conservative faculties have denied tenure to more liberal members).

It is interesting to try to imagine what human history would have been like if it had been dominated by secularist views. Perhaps we would have had just as much unrest as we actually had, perhaps we would have had the "wars of secularism." Indeed, in recent history we have had them—let us not forget Pol Pot and Stalin and Hitler, who were largely motivated by secularist outlooks. The philosopher David Hume once said that while the errors in religion are dangerous, the errors in philosophy are only ridiculous. If we understand philosophy here to include worldviews, then Hume was completely wrong. As Charles Taylor has noted, "The record of certain forms of militant atheism in this century is far from reassuring."[11] And if you are inclined to

---

[10]Robert Kraynak, *Christian Faith and Modern Democracy* (Notre Dame, Ind.: University of Notre Dame Press, 2001), p. 224.
[11]Charles Taylor, *A Catholic Modernity? Charles Taylor's Marianist Award Lecture*, ed. James L. Heft (New York: Oxford University Press, 1999), p. 17.

think that if the United States Supreme Court outlawed abortion tomorrow, this would lead to violence from those who could not accept this decision, then you should agree that some secularist beliefs *can* lead to violence!

Finally, we have seen violence several times in recent years at the various economic summit meetings of the world's largest industrial nations. This violence has been perpetrated mostly by Marxist and environmentalist groups, mainly motivated by a secularist agenda. Members of these groups were willing to use violence in an attempt to force people to accept their beliefs. There exists a continuum of believers in all worldviews, from placid believers to fanatics. And it is surely instructive that as secularism has become more and more influential in the United States, it has become more militant, and some might even say more fanatical (consider many of the court actions that the ACLU has supported as a case in point).[12] Much of this fanaticism has been motivated by an animus toward religion, evidence that secularism is just as capable of being divisive as traditional religion. Secularist groups can abuse their power in the way that religions (and especially the clergy) are often accused of doing. We only have to think about the wide use of power and influence we see in Hollywood, the mainstream media, the universities,[13] the National Education Association and the National Endowment for the Arts, to take only the most obvious examples, groups that not only promote a radical secularist agenda but are often tempted to suppress alternative views that challenge this agenda.

In short, religious beliefs are no more divisive than secularist beliefs, and in any case, in the United States, where there has been a long period of peace between the various worldviews, this is simply a nonstarter as a persuasive argument for keeping religious belief out of politics.[14]

---

[12]For a discussion of the left-wing agenda of the ACLU, see William Donohue, *The Politics of the American Civil Liberties Union* (New Brunswick, N.J.: Transaction Books, 1985); and for a sympathetic history of the organization, Samuel Walker, *In Defense of American Liberties: A History of the ACLU* (Carbondale: Southern Illinois University Press, 1999).

[13]Stephen L. Carter remarks, "On America's elite campuses, today, it is perfectly acceptable for professors to use their classrooms to attack religion, to mock it, to trivialize it, and to refer to those to whom faith truly matters as dupes, and dangerous fanatics on top of it. I have heard some of the wisest scholars in the country deride religious beliefs and religious believers in terms so full of stereotype and of—let us say the word—bigotry that we would be appalled were they to say similar things about just any other group" (*God's Name in Vain* [New York: Basic Books, 2000], p. 187).

[14]Michael Perry agrees that the argument that religious beliefs are divisive and dangerous is not persuasive for keeping religion out of public life; see his *Religion in Politics* (New York: Oxford University Press, 1997), p. 45.

Religious Beliefs Should Not Be Forced by Law on Those Who Do Not Think They Are True

A popular argument one hears everywhere today for keeping religion out of politics is that one cannot impose one's religious beliefs on others. No religion (or beliefs that are part of a religion), the argument goes, should be enshrined in law because it will be the case in a pluralist society that not everyone will accept that particular religion. In fact, many will reject it. What would happen to members of other religions if we were to take the beliefs of one religion and enshrine them in law? For example, if we took Muslim beliefs on mandatory prayer and made them the law of the land? Wouldn't this be an intolerable imposition on people from other worldviews, reasonable people who are trying to get by in a pluralist society just like anyone else? This would be to discriminate against most religions in favor of one religion, and this is unacceptable in our enlightened, pluralist state. Nobody should have to follow the belief of a traditional religion of which they are not a member. Laws, ideally, should be nonsectarian.

This argument has connotations of moral relativism about it, and I will come back to that issue in a later chapter. One might also suspect that it may be backed up by an appeal to the First Amendment of the U.S. Constitution, which would not be a good way to defend it, since it would not address the question of the justification of the moral reasoning behind this amendment. The problem I would like to identify with this interesting argument here is that it applies to *all* worldviews, not just traditional religions. It is true that, for *every* worldview, there will be people who do not accept that worldview and who subscribe to other worldviews. It doesn't matter which worldview you care to take, or which belief or value judgment of a worldview, there will always be somebody who rejects it. (There is always somebody in a free society protesting about something; as the Irish writer James Joyce put it, "there is always somebody screaming holy blue murder about bloody nothing!")

This is also true of secularism. As soon as the secularist asserts his beliefs and values on specific topics (e.g., on gay marriage), there will immediately be many who will reject these beliefs and who will not want them made the law of the land. So if traditional religion cannot be placed in law because not everyone accepts it, then by similar reasoning, secularism cannot be placed in law because not everyone accepts that view. To place a secularist position on a moral issue, such as abortion or euthanasia or smoking, into the law is to take a view that many people do not hold and to impose it on them. It is to promote a seculocracy, in short. But nobody should have to follow the beliefs of secularism if they are not a supporter of secularism. (By a secularist position, I mean a position on a particular question that the secularist believes to be true, whose opposite he believes is false, and which he wants to be made the law of the land.) But to do this for any of the beliefs mentioned, or for any of a host of other beliefs one might focus on, is to do what the secularist has just claimed cannot be done—it is to discriminate in favor of one worldview and against another. So this argument does not give us a good reason to discriminate against religious views and in favor of secularist views. It is either possible to impose the belief of a worldview on those who do not accept it, or it is not. If it is not, for the reason given in this section, then this applies to all worldviews, not just to the worldview of traditional religion.

However, we must remember that not only is it possible to impose a set of beliefs and values on the public, but that it is unavoidable. Nevertheless, I am not saying that we can just impose a belief *arbitrarily* on others. I have already argued that we should give reasons to support those beliefs we introduce into politics; I also rejected (in chapter three) the five problematic sources as a basis for introducing religious beliefs into politics. These restrictions also apply to the secularist. But as a matter of logic, any set of laws that is used to govern a people and that is enforced by military and police power, acting at and accountable to the will of the people, will be based on moral values, and those values will belong to some worldviews and will be rejected by others. Every value believed to be enshrined in the United States Constitution, for example, the value of equality, the right to free speech, the right to a fair trial, *excludes* its opposite, and by extension part of the worldviews of those who support these opposites.[15] Therefore the state and its laws are never neutral with regard to moral values, and those people who do not agree with the current laws in a particular state will be somewhat dissatisfied and may try to change those laws. If they succeed, they will

---

[15]In 1999, the Irish government set up a parliamentary committee to investigate how best to solve Ireland's abortion debate. Liberal groups who appeared before this committee spent a great deal of time arguing that, in a pluralist society, one cannot favor one view of the good, for example, the Catholic view on abortion, over other views. The absurdity of this claim should be obvious. The state cannot be neutral on the question of abortion, so whichever view prevails in the public debate will be favored in state law. This is true of liberal and secularist views no less than for religious views. See David Quinn, "Ireland's Abortion Impasse," *Human Life Review* 26 (fall 2000): 38-46.

leave those who support the current laws dissatisfied.

So, overall, while the argument under consideration in this section is an important part of popular rhetoric against religious arguments in politics, once one looks beneath the surface it is easy to see that it is a not a very convincing reason for discriminating against religious beliefs.

Religious Views Should Be Excluded According to the U.S. Constitution

This is a popular argument in contemporary U.S. society, especially among the establishment. It is an argument that unfortunately invites people to hide behind the U.S. Constitution and avoid debating the moral question of the proper role of religion in politics. The basic idea behind the distinction between religion and politics in U.S. society, and the view that religion should have no role in public life, is the idea that the state shall not establish a religion or deny freedom of religious expression. As the First Amendment to the Constitution puts it, "Congress shall make no law respecting an establishment of religion, or prohibiting the free exercise thereof." A number of important points need to be made concerning the *legal* question of the relationship between church and state in the United States.

First, the U.S. Founding Fathers were concerned with the issue of the state establishing a theocracy (understood here as a church established in some way by the state). Many of the peoples in the various colonies were of different religions, religions that sometimes disagreed strongly with each other, and it was a genuine fear on the part of many that the new Constitution would be used to promote a particular denominational religious view, to the exclusion of others, and that this might lead to social unrest. The Founding Fathers had a dilemma here. They recognized that any Constitution worthy of the name would have to satisfy two conditions: (1) it would have to be ultimately based on God's existence and on God's moral law and (2) it would have to include the core values of freedom, equality, justice and the common good, which many people believed in and had fought and died for. The Founding Fathers solved this problem in a very clever way, by adopting a deist position in the Constitution, and many of them may have been deists.[16]

---

[16]For a full discussion of deism among the Founding Fathers, see Kerry Walters, *The American Deists* (Lawrence: University of Kansas Press, 1992). See also Michael Novak, *On Two Wings: Humble Faith and Common Sense at the American Founding* (San Francisco: Encounter Books, 2002), who disputes the view that the founders were deists and argues that the documents are based on Judeo-Christian values.

Deism is the view that regards God as the intelligent Creator and designer of a law-abiding universe, but denies that God providentially guides the universe or intervenes in any way with its course or destiny. The American founders were attracted to deism because it allowed them to develop what we might call a rational core of religious truths, the values of which could form the basis of a system of government. They could then avoid disputes about higher-order doctrinal differences between religions. In this way, they could take what was rational and good from many different traditions, place it at the heart of the Constitution, and then later insert a clause forbidding the establishment of any particular religion and protecting religious freedom. This would preserve freedom of religion, and avoid public life getting bogged down in petty doctrinal disputes. In effect, their strategy was to place what I have called the lower-order beliefs, shared by many traditional religions, into the Constitution and to restrict the higher-order beliefs to a more private realm. Although I am not primarily concerned with the intentions of the Founding Fathers here, their intentions do lend historical support to the argument I am making in this book that religion has a role in politics in U.S. society. I also do not discount the theory that some of them, such as Thomas Jefferson, might have been antireligious.[17]

The second point is that there is an interesting current debate regarding the church-state relationship about what the "establishment clause" and the "free exercise clause" mean or can mean in the U.S. context. Many, many cases relating to these clauses have been decided over the years by the Supreme Court, some favorable to religion, some hostile to religion. A citizen interested in the legal question and where current law stands on this matter must study these cases, but it has to be acknowledged that one can make a case for both an "accommodationist" view, which allows some religious influence in public life, or a "separationist" view, which prohibits any religious influence in public life, depending on which cases one looks at. Many religious believers think that the long-term direction of the Supreme Court is away from religion having any role in politics, though this could change as the make-up of the Court changes. Perhaps recent appointments to the Court will change the general direction of the Court on this matter, and indeed there is a long history of cases that could be cited

---

[17]There is also debate about whether the Founding Fathers were primarily interested in establishing a Christian nation or just a religious nation. This debate, while fascinating in itself, is not one we can get into here.

as precedents in establishing a new direction for the Court.

Cases such as *Sherbert* v. *Verner* (1963), *Wisconsin* v. *Yoder* (1972), and *Rosenberger* v. *Rector and Visitors of the University of Virginia* (1995) do support accommodationist reasoning, and they establish important "free exercise" precedents. In the first case, the Court ruled in favor of a person's right to refuse to work on their Sabbath without losing unemployment benefits. The Wisconsin case gave religious groups such as the Amish the right not to have to send their children to public schools because it was against their religious beliefs, which rejects formal schooling after a certain age. The University of Virginia case is very interesting from the point of view of our arguments in this book because here the Court ruled that the university could not deny student activity funds to a Christian student newspaper on the basis of its religious content, especially as there was no prohibition on funding other student non-Christian worldviews, such as secularism or Marxism. It is hard to disagree with this reasoning, unless one can give nonarbitrary, nonpolitical reasons for why religion should be singled out for this kind of discrimination. I have been suggesting that there are no such arguments.

Two cases relating to the establishment clause should also be mentioned, *Zobrest* v. *Catalina Foothills School District* (1993) and *Zelman* v. *Simmons-Harris* (2002). These cases also support those who are more optimistic about the Court's progress toward accommodationist readings of the First Amendment. The first case concerned the parents of a deaf child who had switched from attending a public school to attend a parochial school. In the public school, the school district had provided a sign language interpreter for the child, but refused to do so in the parochial school on the grounds that it would violate the establishment clause and amount to the establishment of a religion by the state. The Supreme Court disagreed and ruled in favor of the parents. The Zelman case is a significant precedent because it concerns school vouchers, an ongoing political issue. Here the Court supported the Ohio "Pilot Project Scholarship Program," which allowed parents of children in the Cleveland School District to use public money to pay for tuition at private schools, most of which were religious schools.

While many religious believers are justifiably heartened by these "accommodationist" rulings, one always has to look at the reasoning behind the Court's decisions as a guide to how it might ultimately rule in the future. And the truth is that if one considers the scores of cases relating to these matters, there seems to be no consistent pattern to the reasoning![18] The reasoning in many recent cases seems, to this observer at least, at best inconsistent, even invented, sometimes, tortured—a situation that shakes one's confidence in the Court overall. The case of *Employment Division v. Smith* (1988), often referred to as the "peyote case," has troubled many, though admittedly the general issue at stake here is hard to decide. In this case the Supreme Court ruled that the right of the Native American Church to freedom of religion did not extend to the right to use the drug peyote at their religious services. This is a restriction on their religious freedom to be sure; yet at the same time one has to acknowledge, as I have argued, that there will have to be some restrictions on the practices of worldviews in any state. Whether this would extend to the use of peyote at a religious service is hard to decide. But some think that the logic of the Court's decision here must extend to prohibiting minors from receiving the Eucharistic blood at the Catholic Mass.[19] Yet if this case were ever brought, it is not hard to predict that the Court would *not* rule this way, and so it is hard to be sanguine about the impartiality and sound reasoning of the Court.

More troubling recent cases for religious believers involve those relating to the display of the Ten Commandments. In one case, *McCreary County v. American Civil Liberties Union* (2005), the justices ruled that framed copies of the Ten Commandments on display on the walls of two Kentucky court-houses were unconstitutional, but they upheld as constitutional a six-foot-high monument of the Commandments on the grounds of the Texas Capitol (*Van Orden v. Perry,* 2005). These two decisions, on any reasonable read-ing, seem inconsistent. The Court needed some rationalization for the con-flict between both judgments, which was provided by Justice Stephen Breyer, who wrote that the Texas monument was part of a "broader moral and historical message reflective of a cultural heritage," and so should not be seen as primarily religious. (Essentially the same rationale was used in

---

[18]See Francis Canavan, "The Impact of Recent Supreme Court Decisions on Religion," in his *The Pluralist Game* (Lanham, Md.: Rowman & Littlefield, 1995), pp. 27-44; also Perry, *Religion in Politics,* chap. 1. See also Thomas J. Curry, *Farewell to Christendom* (New York: Oxford Uni-versity Press, 2001), for a critique of modern interpretations of the First Amendment, including a review of recent court cases. For an excellent overview of the history of this subject, see Philip Hamburger, *Separation of Church and State* (Cambridge, Mass.: Harvard University Press, 2002); and John G. West, *The Politics of Revelation and Reason: Religion and Civic Life in the New Nation* (Lawrence: University Press of Kansas, 1996).
[19]See Kenneth Craycraft, *The American Myth of Religious Freedom* (Dallas: Spence, 1999), pp. 18-19.

recent rulings concerning the pledge of allegiance.) While this argument may salve the conscience of the Court for now, it is surely going to lead to more problems in the long run as we struggle with these issues at the legal level. Often in the United States, supreme court justices are our primary public philosophers. I do not find this encouraging, though this might change as the make-up of the Court changes. But eventually our thinking on these matters has to evolve to confront the arguments I have been making in this book. In short, the time is upon us when the legal question has to be informed by a more up-to-date analysis of the moral question.

The third point is that there is no doubt that various groups such as the ACLU have vigorously and aggressively promoted a new, radical interpretation of the establishment clause, an interpretation that aims to lessen the influence of religious arguments in politics. Rather than understanding it to mean that the higher-order beliefs of particular religious denominations should not be included in the law of the land, but that the law itself is based on a core of religious truth, from which it gets both its justification and its higher meaning, they now urge the interpretation that there should be no religion in public life at all. Thus even the basic core of religious truth must be removed or stripped of its meaning. This interpretation, however, is incorrect. It is one thing to claim that on the question of religion in public life, the U.S. Constitution is wrong and should be changed; it is quite another to claim that it does not mean what the founders intended it to mean—and what it was understood to mean for more than a hundred and fifty years. To adopt the first approach would be the correct way to go about arguing that religion should have no place (constitutionally) in public life, but, of course, from the point of view of getting your view adopted, it would be doomed to failure since it would be impossible to get majority support for this view. So the second way, although disingenuous and antidemocratic, is rightly thought to have more political expediency, especially if one has a majority of the supreme court justices on one's side.

The fourth and main point is that it is not acceptable to hide behind the Constitution on this matter in any case. Our concern in this book is with the philosophical (or moral) question of what role should one's worldview have in politics. We are only secondarily interested in the legal question of what role traditional religious belief can have in U.S. society, according to our Constitution. The philosophical question is obviously the main question, and ideally the answer to the legal question *depends* upon the answer to the philosophical question. So if one wishes to argue that religion should have no place in public life, one cannot simply appeal to the authority of a document to argue this controversial and far-reaching claim. This would be a kind of constitutional fundamentalism in which one appeals to the authority of a text but gives no thought to whether the values embodied in the text are *actually true* (or how they are *justified*). (Of course, I have just argued in this section that the appeal to the Constitution today by the secularist relies on an erroneous interpretation of that document.)

The secularist is obliged to defend the *philosophical position* that religion has no place in politics, and I have been arguing that the reasons usually offered to defend this claim are all very weak and unpersuasive. The discussion in the United States has been completely hampered by our focusing too much on the legal question and often deliberately ignoring the philosophical question. Given that secularism is now a fully fledged worldview, competing with religion in the public square, appealing to a particular interpretation of a document in order to exclude all religious views from public life should strike any fair-minded thinker as an exceedingly fishy case of special pleading! Constitutional fundamentalism, frequently appealed to by the mainstream media, is no more acceptable in politics than religious fundamentalism. Indeed, if my general approach in this book is right, eventually the First Amendment will have to be modified because, given that secularism is a major worldview in our culture, it can no longer be justified to only single out religious worldviews for special attention (and ultimately discrimination) in our laws.

Our survey and critique in this and the previous chapter of the various arguments for keeping religion out of politics brings us to an important conclusion: *the secularist is engaged in modern culture in an attempt to use the argument about the form of worldviews in order to win the debate about the content of worldviews.* This is a clever rhetorical strategy because it has several advantages for the secularist. If the secularist can keep the debate focused on the form of worldviews, arguing as she does that traditional religious worldviews are formally inferior to secularism and so should be denied a place in politics, then she is spared the difficult and dirty task of actually debating matters of content with the religious believer. She can simply argue that the antiabortion view, for example, should be excluded from political discussion because it is a religious view, and so she does not have to debate the religious believer on the *actual issue* of the morality of abortion. It is easy to see that this is a widely adopted strategy today. When was the last time you heard a public debate or discussion on the subject of abortion in which the issue of whether or not the fetus is a human being was actually discussed?

A second advantage of this strategy is that the secularist does not have to dignify the opposing view by actually debating it with its proponents. Over time this can have the spin-off rhetorical effect of stigmatizing religious views to the point where they are recognized as not being worthy of discussion, to the point where there is a cultural presumption against them. Religious believers become reluctant to bring up their views in public. Again, one can see that this has happened in certain circles in U.S. society (perhaps especially in educational institutions).

A third advantage, and one of the main motivations behind adopting this whole strategy in the first place, I believe, is that secularists actually wish to *avoid* the debates about content with religious believers. I see two important reasons for such avoidance: (1) They fear they cannot win these debates because traditional religious belief has very strong arguments on a host of different topics, from the existence of God to the immorality of abortion and euthanasia, but also (2) by far the majority of the American people are already persuaded of this fact (whether it is true or not). And so if the debate were to be engaged solely *in terms of content,* out in the open in the public square, the secularist would very likely lose. Whenever the debate comes down to content, the secularist faces defeat, so he needs an alternative strategy; therefore, it is no coincidence that some in public life (especially media commentators and opinion-makers) are tempted to keep the debate mostly at the level of rhetoric. And we must admit that the secularist has been remarkably successful, given the lack of public support for his main foundational beliefs. The secularist has hit upon a disingenuous, logically flawed but winning strategy for putting traditional religious belief on the defensive, which at the same time allows him to avoid debating the actual matter under discussion and having to defend his views.

Some argue that religious worldviews take a considerable risk if they become involved in public political debates. The risk is that they can end up compromising some of their key beliefs and values. Stephen Carter tellingly shows how this happened to the Christian Coalition when it strongly supported the "Contract with the American Family" in 1995, proposed by the Republican Party. Carter expresses the risk well: "Once a religious organization wants a role in determining the outcome of election contests, it will do what is needed to enhance and preserve that role. If purity of doctrine would weaken its influence, then doctrine is impurified in order to be influential."[20] Indeed, this is a version of St. Augustine's argument for keeping church and state separate. This argument is further strengthened by the recognition that power (and influence) often corrupts individuals and institutions no matter how idealistic they start out.

I agree that this is a very interesting, good argument that should give us pause. Yet I don't think it is sufficient to deny religion a role in public life, and indeed Carter would not go this far either, though some would. (It might, however, be an argument against forming Christian political parties, or secularist political parties or against explicitly endorsing particular political candidates.) While we must be careful to make sure that we do not compromise our religious beliefs and values when we enter the political arena, we must accept, I think, that some corruption is inevitable. But this is true of all worldviews, not just of religious worldviews. Moral purity is hard to maintain in the real world, even though all worldviews must be as careful as possible not to compromise their principles and values when they enter the arena of politics. But the price of staying out of politics to protect one's purity is too high. As I have pointed out, many religious beliefs have political implications, and you cede the public square to those from other worldviews who disagree with you about politics if you try to keep your view pure. It is also true that you compromise your integrity—as well as other principles and values—if you do not promote some of your beliefs in the political arena. This is especially true if you have a special talent for this but do not act on it. Consider what American society might be like even today if Martin Luther King Jr. had decided not to bother promoting his religious views in public.

Let me conclude this chapter with a few questions to which our analysis naturally gives rise. We need to ask, what are the implications of my arguments up to now for the place of religion in politics? This question can be approached in a general way and also in a specific way. More generally, the question considers whether the religious worldview requires a democratic

---

[20]Carter, *God's Name in Vain,* p. 56. C. S. Lewis originally made this type of argument against setting up a Christian political party in England. (Several European countries still have political parties called the Christian Democrats.) See C. S. Lewis, "Meditation on the Third Commandment," in his *God in the Dock,* ed. Walter Hooper (Grand Rapids: Eerdmans, 1970), pp. 196-99.

political system or if it would be more at home in some other political arrangement. How would one approach the question of the justification of a
particular political system, say democracy, as a religious person? The more
specific question asks which religious beliefs can one actually bring into
public political arguments? What limits might there be on which religious beliefs would be admitted? And indeed on secularist beliefs? How are the limits
decided? We now turn to these interesting questions in the next two chapters, as we look at the actual role that religious beliefs can play in politics.

6

Rawls, Religion and Democracy

If my analysis in the previous chapters is right, then we are presented with some intriguing questions about the role of religion in a democratic society. I have already argued in general that religious beliefs can be part of the public political discussion. But more needs to be said. One area we must consider is the relationship between religious belief in general as a worldview and the democratic form of government. Does the religious worldview require a democratic political system, or would some other political arrangement be more appropriate for religious belief? This question leads straight to another equally fascinating one: How should one defend one's political theory—from *within* one's worldview, as a part of one's worldview, or from some *independent* standpoint outside of one's worldview (and outside of everyone else's worldview as well)? More practical questions also arise. If I am right, for instance, that secularism is a worldview in itself and that all of the reasons offered for keeping religious belief out of public life are unconvincing, then which religious beliefs can one bring into public political discourse? What are the implications of my arguments for the actual practice of the public political debate between the various worldviews in a pluralist democracy (say among voters, politicians, judges, pastors, etc.)? Although I have touched upon these matters here and there throughout, we need to address them more specifically.

These questions are especially intriguing because secularism is also a religion, so when we ask which religious beliefs can be appropriately introduced into the public square we must also include in this question not just those worldviews that I have been calling "traditional religions" but also all secularist views. It is philosophically appropriate to ask of the secularist which of his (religious) beliefs can be legitimately brought into the public square, which beliefs might not be appropriate, and why. In this chapter, we will look at the more general questions; the next chapter will take up the more practical questions. We have two main concerns here: to consider the views of influential political philosopher John Rawls, whose approach to the relationship between religion and politics has become the standard way of dealing with the relationship in modern political theory. After our critical discussion of Rawls's view, we will consider some of the main issues that come into play when thinking about the relationship between the religious worldview and the democratic form of government.

Arguing from Within Our Worldview

It is essential to lead into our discussion of Rawls by emphasizing the point that when one approaches the question of what role religious beliefs should have in politics, one must approach this question from *within one's own worldview*. So when I take up this question from a more practical point of view (in the next chapter), I will be presenting my views of the appropriate role for religious belief in politics from within my own worldview (which is that of Christianity). This means that the views I will develop are part of my worldview and are justified insofar as my worldview is justified. This might seem an odd thing to say at first. For, from one point of view, it seems obvious that our position on an important matter like the role of religion in political life would have to be part of our worldview. From a straightforwardly logical point of view, it would seem that one holds one's worldview first, then one accepts a political theory (say democracy), which is justified from within or by appeal to the foundational principles of one's worldview. Then one proceeds to work out the role that one's worldview can play in politics (to work out the relationship between one's worldview and one's political theory). Further, one must also work out how to handle *other* worldviews with which one disagrees, and also what role *they* can have in politics. So it seems trivially true to point all of this out.

Yet from another point of view, namely, the culture of modern democratic pluralism, it might seem problematic to argue *from within our own worldview* for a way of dealing with or for a set of principles that will apply to all worldviews when they are engaged in public arguments. This is because the culture of modern democratic pluralism carries with it—sometimes explicitly, sometimes implicitly, but rarely carefully articulated—the connotation that all (or at least many) worldviews have a certain legitimacy and that the advocates of a particular worldview cannot impose their beliefs on those from another worldview. So from this point of view, modern political theorists, especially followers of Rawls, will be inclined to object to my approach to these matters, which is to argue from within my worldview for a set of principles that apply to all worldviews.

The argument for my approach is not just based on a critique of the alternative view offered by Rawls but also on my claim that it is not possible to argue *consistently* for a set of principles to regulate the discussion in public life from any position other than from within one's worldview. To put this point another way, an important part of any worldview will be its response to the beliefs, arguments and practices of *other* worldviews. Do the members of worldview A believe, for instance, that worldview B is false and also perhaps irrational? Do they believe that some of B's beliefs are worthy of inclusion in the public square but not others? Do they believe that B's beliefs are so false (or so odd) that they should not be expressed publicly? Does B feel the same way about A? And what does C think about A and B? *Each worldview will have as an essential part of its structure beliefs and principles about how to handle politically the beliefs, arguments and practices of other worldviews. This is particularly true for handling those beliefs that the members of the first worldview do not accept, especially if these beliefs might involve coercive legislation.* All players in the debate need to ask themselves this political question: how should I respond to beliefs and practices from another worldview that I strongly disagree with? Another way of putting this question, given our earlier distinctions, is to ask, how would I justify a principle of religious freedom toward other worldviews ("religious" understood to include secularist worldviews as well)?

I do hold that my worldview is objectively true, specifically that the foundational beliefs of my worldview are objectively true. Furthermore, I would be happy if everyone accepted these foundational beliefs. Most people adopt the same position with regard to their worldview (and if they do not, they need to think carefully about why, what this might imply about their worldview, and how they would justify their political theory). Yet I recognize that in a pluralist society I may not be able to convince a majority to accept the foundational beliefs of my particular worldview. I am also well aware that others will be in the same position with regard to *their* worldviews. The secularist also holds that the foundational beliefs of his view are objectively true. I will be proposing a rational way to conduct the debate in the public square given that different worldviews have conflicting views of the foundational beliefs.

Before we elaborate further on these points, we must consider another possible way of approaching them, one that is often offered by modern liberal political philosophers and that has become dominant in contemporary liberal political thinking. Indeed, it has become the standard approach to dealing with these matters. This is the argument that we can adopt a *neutral* set of procedures and values—a neutral political theory, if you will—that would then be employed to adjudicate worldview disputes and debates in a pluralist democracy. These procedures and values are agreed to by all worldviews simply by virtue of participating in a modern, pluralist society. They are therefore common to all worldviews, despite the differences among the worldviews on a variety of other matters. These procedures and values are used to regulate public arguments and debates, but they do not originate from within any particular worldview, so they do not favor any worldview over another. Thus, the public square is neutral in terms of its procedures and values, and therefore fair to all worldviews. This is the view presented by the philosopher John Rawls.

Rawls's position has influenced many. Kent Greenawalt's arguments for restricting religious beliefs in politics are significantly Rawlsian, although he is also critical of Rawls on some matters. Crucially, Greenawalt admits that *his* worldview *does* influence his choice of the values he believes should regulate the public square, though he does not acknowledge until the last two pages of his book the fact that if one holds a different worldview than his, or even weighs values differently, one will likely not accept his reasons for restricting religious beliefs in politics.[1] Robert Audi's and Phillip Quinn's[2] views are also very Rawlsian. It is fair to say that a Rawlsian spirit hovers over much of the debate today concerning political theory and concerning religion and politics; it is so ingrained in the way we look at politics that it prevents many from "thinking outside the box" on these matters. Political philosopher Robert Nozick has noted that after Rawls, political philosophers would either have to agree with Rawls and work within his political framework or else explain why they were not doing so. Others have suggested

---

[1]See Kent Greenawalt, *Private Consciences and Public Reasons* (New York: Oxford University Press, 1995), p. 133, for the first point, and pp. 180-81 for the overall conclusion of his book.
[2]See Phillip Quinn, "Political Liberalisms and Their Exclusion of the Religious," in *Religion and Contemporary Liberalism,* ed. Paul J. Weithman (Notre Dame, Ind.: University of Notre Dame Press, 1997), pp. 138-61.

that one of the appeals of his theory is that its essence is concerned with *protecting* the state from the influence of religious belief.[3]

So let us now turn to Rawls's very interesting theory.

John Rawls's Political Liberalism

In this section, I will briefly outline Rawls's position, and in the next section I will offer several reasons for why I reject it and do not believe it to be a workable theory.[4] Obviously I do not have the space to provide an exhaustive analysis of the various details of Rawls's theory, and in any case an analysis of this sort would take us away from our task in this chapter. I will therefore provide only an overview of Rawls's theory, called justice as fairness, with particular emphasis on those points most relevant for our arguments in this book. Rawls presents his theory of justice in two works, the much earlier *A Theory of Justice* (1971) and the more recent *Political Liberalism* (1993). This latter work is the one I shall be concerned with; it is Rawls's attempt to clarify and restate his main points in the light of the many years of discussion his earlier work had provoked.[5]

---

[3]See Daniel Dombrowski, *Rawls and Religion: The Case for Political Liberalism* (New York: SUNY, 2001); also Kenneth Craycraft, *The American Myth of Religious Freedom* (Dallas: Spence, 1999), pp. 8-10, 18; also Pierre Manent, *An Intellectual History of Liberalism* (Princeton, N.J.: Princeton University Press, 1994).

[4]For other discussions of Rawls's views on religion in public life, see Michael J. Perry, *Religion in Politics* (New York: Oxford University Press, 1997), pp. 54-61; Nicholas Wolterstorff, "The Role of Religion in Decision and Discussion of Political Issues," in *Religion in the Public Square,* by Robert Audi and Nicholas Wolterstorff (Lanham, Md.: Rowman & Littlefield, 1997), pp. 90-114; James Boettcher, "Public Reason and Religion," in *The Legacy of John Rawls,* ed. Thom Brooks and Fabian Freyenhagen (Bristol, U.K.: Thoemmes Continuum, 2005), pp. 124-51. See also J. L. A. Garcia, "Liberal Theory, Human Freedom and the Politics of Sexual Morality," in *Religion and Contemporary Liberalism,* ed. Paul J. Weithman (Notre Dame, Ind.: University of Notre Dame Press, 1997), pp. 218-52, for a very interesting discussion of Rawls's and Nagel's views on politics, society and religion. See also Paul Weithman, *Religion and the Obligations of Citizenship* (New York: Cambridge University Press, 2002), chap. 7. For a more general critique of Rawls's political theory, see John Kekes, *Against Liberalism* (New York: Cornell University Press, 1997), chap. 7; Joseph Raz, "Facing Diversity: The Case of Epistemic Abstinence," *Philosophy and Public Affairs* 19 (winter 1990): 3-46; and Jean Hampton, "The Common Faith of Liberalism," *Pacific Philosophical Quarterly* 75, nos. 3-4 (1994): 186-216.

[5]Rawls's view is often described as a view that gives priority to "the right over the good." This move comes from the Kantian tradition and is based on the attempt to defend an overall procedure for dealing with worldview disputes; the procedure is not supposed to give priority to the values of any one worldview—that is a party to the dispute—over the others. As will become clear in the rest of this chapter, I reject all priority of right-over-the-good theories because they fall into contradiction, since it is not possible to develop a *value-free* procedure for adjudicating between worldviews, and also because such views have the appearance of being dishonest in the sense that they subtly present themselves as neutral all the while sur-

Rawls begins by arguing that a free society inevitably gives rise to different and often irreconcilable comprehensive doctrines of the good (what I have been calling worldviews). Further, it is the case that many of these worldviews are *reasonable*. Given this fact of "reasonable pluralism," our task as political philosophers in a modern democratic state is to find some way of accommodating as many of the values of these worldviews in our public political and social institutions as we can in a way that we can all reasonably accept. We will need, in short, an agreed-upon structure or a procedure for regulating disputes over various issues in the public square. Rawls proposes an ingenious and clever way of arriving at this procedure. He argues that we can seek the principles for the regulation of public discourse among the various worldviews, not from within the worldviews themselves (what he calls the comprehensive conceptions), but from *within our (shared) political culture*. He believes that the political culture of a modern, democratic, pluralist state (such as the United States) has principles latent within it that most people accept and that carry implications for how the debate in the public square is to be conducted. These principles can be made explicit and are part of what he calls an "overlapping consensus." In this way, Rawls is trying to avoid basing his theory of justice on his *own* worldview (or comprehensive view of the good), thereby side-stepping the objection that he is attempting to impose the principles of his worldview (a kind of secular liberalism) on those who do not share this worldview, under the guise of neutrality.

Rawls argues that there is what he calls a "political conception of justice" latent in the culture; this political conception should regulate the basic structure of society: the background institutions that specify political and civil rights and determine entitlements to other socially regulated goods. So members of what he calls a "well-ordered society" could hold different and conflicting comprehensive worldviews, and yet, he believes, *still agree* to the political conception that is the foundation of the basic structure. But this political conception is not just a modus vivendi, a practical compromise that the members of the various worldviews might agree on for the sake of living in harmony in society, but which they are uneasy about and do not really support. No, the political conception reflects ideas implicit in the political

---

reptitiously privileging their own preferred values. For discussion and critique of right-over-the-good theories, see Michael Sandel, *Democracy's Discontent: America in Search of a Political Philosophy* (Cambridge, Mass.: Harvard University Press, 1996), chap. 1.

culture, specifically the key notions of the *freedom* and *equality* of citizens and a willingness to have *reasonable* standards of public discourse, consistent with freedom and equality.

The political conception, according to Rawls, is also "freestanding"—it is not presented as a part of nor derived from any worldview or comprehensive conception of the good (including Rawls's own). However, he believes that it could be justified by appeal to principles and values that are, as a matter of fact, part of many comprehensive doctrines. He goes on to suggest that when we appeal to the political conception when involved in a public-square political discussion we must offer "public reasons" in our arguments and not reasons that appeal to our comprehensive conceptions. Public reasons are reasons that we must sincerely believe all other citizens might reasonably accept. While this is obviously still extremely vague, it does lead to a core principle of liberal political philosophy: that public reason will normally *not* include religious reasons.

Rawls goes on to argue that a good way to arrive at the principles of justice in such a society is to posit what he calls the "original position," a kind of imaginary bargaining discussion in which all of the participants in society voluntarily place themselves behind a "veil of ignorance," and then engage in a conversation designed to arrive at the principles of justice which will then be used to govern and regulate society. That is to say, in the original position the participants do not know their talents and abilities, their social class or even their worldview (their comprehensive view of the good). Rawls believes this starting point is fair and just because one is more likely to agree to principles that benefit everyone and that everyone can regard as reasonable if one bargains from this position. In this way, the notions of freedom and equality, and of reasonableness, are latent in the original position, but that is okay because these values are also latent in the political culture. Under these circumstances, Rawls believes we would agree to two principles. First, that each person has an equal claim to a fully adequate scheme of equal basic liberties and rights, which is compatible with the same scheme for all (roughly corresponding to the scheme in the U.S. Bill of Rights). Second, social and economic inequalities would have to satisfy two conditions: one, they are to be attached to positions and offices open to all under conditions of fair equality of opportunity, and two, they are to be to the greatest benefit of the least advantaged members of society (this is called the difference principle). Rawls also develops a view of the person to accompany these principles; the main features of the person that he emphasizes are a capacity for a sense of justice and for a conception of the good. This is a broad sketch of how Rawls attempts to answer his central question of how is it possible for there to exist over time a just and stable society of free and equal citizens who remain profoundly divided by reasonable religious, philosophical and moral doctrines.

Although I have mentioned the principles of justice that Rawls believes would be arrived at from the original position, that part of his theory is not our main concern. I am only interested in the structure of the theory and how it differs from my views in this book. Most of the critical discussion of Rawls's theory in the United States has tended to focus more on the details of the theory (such as whether people would agree to the difference principle in the original position) and less on the *foundations* of the theory. Many commentators have tended to agree with the foundations of his view and to dispute only some of the details. Thus, while his theory has become dominant in contemporary political discussions, unfortunately there is little critical examination of its foundations. I want to suggest that the foundations of Rawls's theory do not stand up to critical scrutiny, and I will offer five main reasons for rejecting his view.

Problems with Rawls's Theory

The first problem concerns the issue of whether his procedure really is based on a neutral "political" conception of justice that does not involve his appealing covertly to his own comprehensive view of the good (a type of secular liberalism), his own worldview. I am not convinced that his procedure is or can be neutral, that one can set up a structure for the organization and regulation of political society without basing it on certain values. And these values will be part of a worldview and will have to be justified. For example, in Rawls's original position, a view of the person is clearly assumed: this is the view whose proponents hold that a person is primarily an individual, a center of autonomy and rationality, who should almost totally regulate his own life, including his community life, through his individualistic choices. This also carries with it an implication that freedom is the supreme value (a view emanating from liberal political tradition, especially the thought of John Stuart Mill). The problem here is that those who reject Rawls's view, who accept the more traditional Aristotelian/Thomistic view that human beings are primarily social beings by nature and not by choice, and that there has to be a balance between the community and the individual features of personhood, are at a disadvantage in the original position. They must commit to a beginning bargaining point that is closer to the worldview of liberalism than it is to their own worldview.

In fact, the more one considers Rawls's theory, one cannot help seeing it as a theory *designed* to exclude traditional religious views from the political arena. Rawls almost admits as much when he tries to state his concern more clearly in the introduction to *Political Liberalism:* "Thus, the question should be more sharply put this way: How is it possible for those affirming a religious doctrine that is based on religious authority, for example, the church or the Bible, also to hold a reasonable political conception that supports a just democratic regime?"[6] This suggests that the motivating force in his work is not so much how to establish a just society in a pluralist age, but how to deal with troublesome traditional religious views within an assumed liberal framework. "[It's] obvious that the parties in the original position are rational, *secular,* scientific men and women," as Robert Paul Wolff has observed.[7]

Another difficulty for the original position is that when one comes out of the original position there will be a serious tension between the values and principles of justice one agreed to behind the veil of ignorance and the worldview to which one subscribes, when the veil is lifted. It seems to me that it will be impossible to dissipate this tension and that it would be irrational to allow the political conception to trump one's own worldview or comprehensive conception. Rawls's approach also suggests a skepticism about the subject matter of worldviews in general, in that we must believe and live according to them (at least privately), and yet they can be trumped by the political conception. This skepticism represents paradoxically a position on the nature of the good life, and so it is not politically neutral. Also, we should be prepared at all times to suspend our worldview in the public square. But Rawls gives no attention to how it is possible to believe and practice one thing privately (in one's social circle) and another publicly (in the political arena), and even if this is possible, whether or not it is a *reasonable* thing to do. This is a crucial issue in the whole debate that he overlooks.

---

[6]John Rawls, *Political Liberalism,* paperback ed., with a new preface (New York: Columbia University Press, 1996), p. xxxix. (Hereafter referred to as *PL.*)

[7]Robert Paul Wolff, *Understanding Rawls: A Reconstruction and Critique of "A Theory of Justice"* (Princeton, N.J.: Princeton University Press, 1977), p. 127 (emphasis added).

My second problem with Rawls's theory is that if the theory is not based on a comprehensive view of the good, then it is not clear how it can avoid cultural relativism (the view that moral and political values are relative to and decisively shaped by one's culture). His theory appears to lead to cultural relativism because it is a theory based on ideas latent in our political structures right now, perhaps even ideas that most people would accept, yet the question of the truth of these ideas is postponed, even ignored. If the procedure he advocates really is neutral, then one can legitimately still ask if the conception of justice that emerges from our political culture is moral or true (or is immoral or false, or both). It is not adequate to reply to this objection by saying that one is only concerned with developing a theory that would be applicable in our society today but not for all time. For could not corrupt societies use the same type of *procedure* to justify their corruptions? The advantage of Rawls's strategy from his point of view is that if we talk only about a procedure, we can side-step the question of whether the values that undergird the procedure are true and morally better than others (and so must be part of someone's comprehensive conception or worldview). But the disadvantage is that we cannot comment on whether *the society as a whole* is moral or just, and our political theory is left somewhat vacuous. Rawls's theory also seems to flirt quite overtly with epistemological and moral skepticism because his overall approach suggests that we should not ask these questions, that there is no point in debating them because the issues are unknowable. We should simply try to get some kind of working consensus about democratic values and procedures, and ignore the question of truth. This is better, he seems to suggest, than holding out for truth and running into inevitable and sometimes bitter disagreements with members of different worldviews.[8]

A third problem is that the appeal to values latent in the political culture is really an appeal to our political *tradition*. This means that the justification for these values belongs to the first five sources discussed in chapter three. One of those sources, we recall, was religious tradition, and the secularist argued that it is illegitimate to introduce arguments based on tradition into the public-square debate because we cannot *reasonably* expect others to

---

[8]A good illustration of the real danger of cultural relativism that attaches to Rawls's view comes out quite clearly, I think, in Kent Greenawalt's defense of Rawls in his *Religious Convictions and Political Choice* (New York: Oxford University Press, 1988), pp. 49-84. Greenawalt's examples in this chapter mostly rely on an appeal to cultural values that most people accept; those who question the values are therefore outside the loop.

follow a tradition other than their own. The tradition is also usually supported by appeal to texts and authorities, which also belong to the first five sources. But if this is an illegitimate move for a religious believer to make, it must be similarly illegitimate for a secularist to make an appeal to tradition, backed up by authorities (such as Locke, Kant and Mill), or their texts. Superficial appeals to a tradition are likely to be rejected as unpersuasive by reasonable people as the basis for public arguments. A crucial part of Rawls's overall argument is based on an appeal to tradition—liberal political tradition—a tradition that many people reasonably reject, or, probably more accurately, they reject Rawls's version of liberal political tradition. Indeed, if we were to truly appeal to the values latent in our political tradition as a basis for democracy, many of these values would come from traditional religion and not liberal political theory. Let us not forget that both Locke's and Kant's arguments for liberal political theory were inspired by and ultimately justified by appeal to their religious beliefs, despite the attempts by later liberal political thinkers to ignore this crucial point.[9]

Our fourth problem with Rawls's view is that he has too superficial a view of traditional religious belief, and as a result he does not develop the similarities in form between comprehensive doctrines sufficiently. We saw in the quotation above that he seems to think that all traditional religious claims come from an authority or a text. He does not mention the possibility of rational religious beliefs. In fact, there is no discussion at all in his work of how a traditional religious believer might try to show that his beliefs are reasonable, from the point of view of introducing them into political debates, nor is there any discussion of how their rationality stacks up against the rationality of beliefs from secularist worldviews. Rawls in fact simply accepts that religious beliefs are in a different category, and so something will have to be done about them. He is simplistically assuming the inferiority of religious beliefs compared with the beliefs of liberal political theory. I think it is fair to say in general that one of the things that characterizes much of the debate about religion and politics in the United States among academics is a fairly profound ignorance of the nature of religious belief, manifested in a superficial knowledge of its major thinkers, themes, arguments and tradition.[10]

---

[9]See Jeremy Waldron, *God, Locke and Equality: Christian Foundations of Locke's Political Thought* (Cambridge: Cambridge University Press, 2002).
[10]This seems to me to be true of the views of Walter Berns on the American founding principles as expressed in his *Making Patriots* (Chicago: University of Chicago Press, 2001), pp. 23-46.

A fifth difficulty with Rawls's view is that the notion of public reason and the political conception of justice are problematic. His instinct is good here, I believe, because in general he wants views to be accepted in the public square only if all people can reasonably agree to them in a free and open society. I agree that this is a good principle, but I do not think it can spring from Rawls's political conception. One obvious problem with the political conception of justice is that it is a "freestanding" view, meaning that it is not supposed to be based on any comprehensive view of the good, but rather is based on intuitive ideas latent in our present political culture. My problem with this claim is that there is no agreement on what these ideas are, so any proposed set of them will always remain controversial and will probably have to be dogmatically imposed on those who do not accept them. Even if there were agreement, there would still be no agreement about the particular understanding, range and application of a value. We might all agree that freedom is a latent political value in our culture, for example, but not agree about how far it is to extend in the area of individual self-determination, for instance.

In the second place, it seems to me that it would be irrational for anyone to allow those values in the political conception of justice to trump the foundational beliefs of one's own particular worldview. Traditional religious believers simply could not accept this principle and retain the integrity of their position. It is true that traditional religious belief, I suggest in the next section, should accept the principles of democracy, but these principles are derived from the foundations of their worldview and are justified in terms of it. It would be irrational to then allow these principles to trump the foundations (i.e., in the sense that we would act as if the foundations were not true). Further, these principles could not have the content and logical con-

---

Among other things, Berns says that "with the free exercise of one's religion comes the requirement to obey the law regardless of one's religious beliefs" (p. 31), and "Whether a law is just or unjust is a judgment that belongs to no 'private man' [in Locke's phrase], however pious or learned or, as we say today, sincere he may be. This means that we are first of all citizens, and only secondarily Christians, Jews, Muslims, or of any other religious persuasion" (p. 31). (Why not also include in this list secularists or Marxists?) Berns recognizes that his views here are controversial. It seems to me that two other observations are appropriate: (1) Berns's position is a pretty good expression of what one has to do in order to fully support the conventional understanding of American pluralism—make one's worldview subordinate to American law (as interpreted by the courts in many cases). (2) No worldview—religious or secularist—could actually do this and retain its integrity. Berns does not see this because his view of religion is superficial, as reflected in his view that it can be easily relegated to a private sphere.

nection to the foundations to do this because then they could not be justified by appeal to the foundations nor derived from them. Rawls's view would have some purchase value if he could show that traditional religious believers were inconsistent in what they claimed in their foundations and in what they then affirmed in the political conception, but I do not think he can show this.

Rawls does suggest that one could justify the political conception of justice by appeal to one's comprehensive conception, but one need not. As I have said, however, it is problematic if the political conception can be justified in this way, because it is supposed to be able to trump the foundations in certain circumstances. Saying that one need not appeal to one's worldview to justify the political conception is also problematic, as we have seen, because it leads to cultural relativism. What all of this means in practice is that there is no overlapping consensus in modern political culture. Recall that an overlapping consensus is supposed to be a set of shared political values. And if there is no overlapping consensus, there is only one way that Rawls can arrive at a set of values to regulate the debate in the public square: by arbitrarily selecting them.

Let us turn briefly to consider more directly how Rawls's views apply to the question of introducing traditional religious arguments into the public square. Rawls holds the view that citizens can introduce religious arguments, but should be able to show that their views can be supported by public reasons, as I have noted.[11] Yet many religious believers will be suspicious of such a move because if one has to give public reasons, this may be really saying that there is no point in introducing religious arguments into the public square. But what does Rawls mean by "public reasons"? The idea of public reason does not just mean secular reasons, but also refers to the ideas latent in the political culture (i.e., those of political liberalism).

According to Rawls, public reason "presents how things might be, taking people as a *just and well-ordered* society would encourage them to be."[12]

---

[11]See *PL*, pp. 216-27. This is a problem for Robert Audi, who also argues for a Rawlsian position when he says that virtuous citizens will seek grounds of a kind that any rational adult citizen can endorse as sufficient for the purpose (Robert Audi and Nicholas Wolterstorff, *Religion in the Public Square* [Lanham, Md.: Rowman & Littlefield, 1997], p. 17). In his reply to this point, Wolterstorff points out that in contemporary society there is little agreement about anything, and that as soon as we assert a position, the one thing we can be certain of is that someone will immediately assert the opposite (see p. 95).

[12]*PL*, p. 213 (emphasis added).

To offer public reasons for one's view is to offer reasons that all people in a modern, democratic society *might* reasonably agree to, not necessarily that they would agree to them. This requirement would, therefore, exclude religious reasons. Public reason applies only to political advocacy-type arguments introduced into the public square, and only then on matters of "constitutional essentials" and questions of basic justice.[13] By constitutional essentials, Rawls means "fundamental principles that specify the general structure of government and the political process," roughly corresponding, as mentioned above, to the principles and values in the American constitutional documents. As also noted above, Rawls claims that the notion of public reasons will involve an appeal to political values inherent in our liberal conception of justice and that it does not assume the truth of any particular comprehensive conception of the good. Rawls received a great deal of criticism from religious thinkers for these views,[14] and in the 1996 paperback edition of *Political Liberalism* he allowed a slightly more permissive view by conceding that religious believers could appeal to their comprehensive views in the public square, but that eventually their arguments would have to be justified by appeal to the values latent in our political culture (in short, religious conclusions would eventually have to be justified by appeal to nonreligious premises). In this way, he took back with one hand what he appeared to have given with the other.[15]

This approach would, therefore, generally exclude traditional religious views from the public square. It excludes them because they are not based in "public reason" (which means that Rawls regards religious beliefs as unreasonable). I reject this, because—as I have already argued at length—arguments based on religious premises and conclusions can be reasonable and can be part of a public-square debate. Religious beliefs should also be excluded, according to Rawls, if they do not share a particular understanding of the values of political liberalism (which they do not for the most part). Philip Quinn has pointed out that Rawls's view would exclude comprehensive secularist doctrines as well if they do not accept the values of political liberalism.[16] However, the difference is that most secularist doctrines germane to the debate about pluralism in America do accept these values, and

---

[13]See ibid., p. 214.
[14]See Dombrowski, *Rawls and Religion,* chap. 2.
[15]*PL,* pp. li-lii.
[16]See Quinn, "Political Liberalisms and Their Exclusion of the Religious," p. 148.

so it is more accurate to note that Rawls's ideal of public reason excludes traditional religious views but includes most secularist worldviews. Moreover, Quinn has overlooked the fact that Rawls regards religious beliefs as "unreasonable" in a way that he thinks secularist beliefs are not. So in the absence of any proper justification of the "latent political values," it seems fair to say that his view is inherently and unjustifiably biased against traditional religious belief and in favor of secularism.

We can bring this point out most clearly by considering the example of abortion, which Rawls discusses in the following passage:

> Suppose first that the society in question is well-ordered and that we are dealing with the normal case of mature adult women. . . . Suppose further that we consider the question in terms of these three important political values: the due respect for human life, the ordered reproduction of political society over time, including the family in some form, and finally the equality of women as equal citizens. (There are of course other important political values besides these.) Now I believe any reasonable balance of these three values will give a woman a duly qualified right to decide whether on not to end her pregnancy during the first trimester. The reason for this is that at this early stage of pregnancy the political value of equality of women is overriding, and this right is required to give it substance and force. . . . A reasonable balance may allow her such a right beyond this, at least in certain circumstances. . . . any comprehensive doctrine that leads to a balance of political values excluding that duly qualified right in the first trimester is to that extent unreasonable; and depending on details and formulation, it may also be cruel and oppressive; for example, if it denied the right altogether except in the case of rape and incest. Thus, assuming that this question is either a constitutional essential or a matter of basic justice we would go against the idea of public reason if we voted from a comprehensive doctrine that denied this right. However, a comprehensive doctrine is not as such unreasonable because it leads to an unreasonable conclusion in one or even in several cases. It may still be reasonable most of the time.[17]

Several problems are obvious in this argument for *excluding* traditional religious arguments against abortion from the public square.[18] First, I think

---

[17]*PL*, pp. 243-44.

[18]In the introduction to the paperback edition of *Political Liberalism,* Rawls indicates that he did not mean this passage to suggest that he was giving an argument for abortion, though it was quite naturally interpreted in this way by most readers. He intended it only as an illustration of his point that comprehensive doctrines in the public square need to support a rea-

it is fair to say that the balancing of the values Rawls cites is not obvious, or nearly obvious; many people who would accept these values think it is obvious that the fetus's right to life outweighs a woman's freedom to end that life. Second, Rawls ignores the main issue in the abortion discussion in any case, which is whether the fetus is a human being or not. In the absence of a decision on this question, one cannot decide which way the three values are to be balanced without begging the question at issue. Rawls might object that if one decides that the fetus is a human being and then makes a judgment on the issue of balancing rights, then one is introducing one's own comprehensive view of the good, and that this is an illegitimate move. However, this objection is problematic because the same point is true if one decides that the fetus is not a human being. This is what Rawls has surely decided, which is revealed by his remark about the early stages of pregnancy. As Michael Perry puts it in his remarks on Rawls, "The path of public reason runs out before the 'pro-choice' position is reached."[19]

Third, if the values in the public square *did* allow us to decide this issue in a substantive way—that is, did pronounce on whether the fetus is a human being or not—this would confirm my point above that what we have here is a liberal comprehensive view of the good masquerading as a neutral view. If, in filling out what he means by public reasons, Rawls argues either that the fetus is not a human being or that we cannot know whether the fetus is a human being, isn't he surely bringing in his own comprehensive view of the good? I believe it is reasonable to read Rawls as subtly introducing his own comprehensive view on abortion but presenting it as a neutral (liberal) view.

Fourth, his last remark is a little condescending to religious belief, since it seems to be saying that although religious believers are generally wrong on this issue of abortion, they may not be wrong on everything, and their worldview may even be reasonable. It also shows a very poor understanding of religious belief in general, because if there is any belief of traditional religion that is persuasively reasonable it is surely the belief that the fetus is a human being and is worthy of protection in law. In fact, it is hard to un-

---

sonable balance of public reasons (see p. lvi of the paperback edition). Rawls does indicate that this passage expresses his opinion on abortion, but acknowledges that it is not an argument. However, since the balancing of public reasons mentioned in the passage is often presented as an argument for abortion in our culture, indeed represents one of the main forms of argument in support of abortion, I will consider it here as an example of an attempt to exclude traditional religious arguments on abortion from public life.

[19]Perry, *Religion in Politics,* p. 61.

derstand how a political philosopher could consider a belief like this and not see that it is reasonable, even if he himself does not adopt it.

For all these reasons, I do not accept Rawls's view; further I think one can plausibly regard it (whether he intended it or not) as an attempt to exclude traditional religious worldviews from public life, to place the values and beliefs of traditional religious worldviews in a subservient position to the values and beliefs of liberalism (which is a secularly inclined, if not a totally secularist, worldview).

Religion and Democracy

Given that we reject the Rawlsian approach on the role of religious worldviews within a democratic political system, it is important for us to reflect further on the relationship between one's religious worldview and the principles of democracy, including how we would approach a principle of religious freedom. Like most religious believers in the United States, I believe the general principles of liberal democracy are reasonable, and I adopt them as part of my Christian worldview. (It is because of this that many would say that everyone in the debate today subscribes to some version of liberalism, both liberals and conservatives, even if we don't always live up to the principles of democracy.) As I indicated in chapter three, this broadly means that because God exists and created all life, and because human beings are created in the image of God and so there is a human nature, one can extrapolate from all of this an account of human dignity and a scheme of human rights and responsibilities, which can become the basis for one's political structure. (This is roughly how the influential natural law tradition, exemplified in the work of St. Thomas Aquinas, proceeds, though Thomas himself was not a supporter of democracy.) Such a scheme must be justified on the view I have been developing from within one's worldview, and should consist of lower-order (rational) beliefs. In addition, I believe the religious worldview provides the best justification of this scheme of rights and values. While secularism also usually supports a scheme of rights, it cannot justify them adequately, cannot limit them sufficiently, cannot support responsibilities, and so often ends up for all practical purposes in moral relativism. This is in part why I think religious belief is more rational than secularism. So, unlike Rawls, I am arguing that the political values that are the basis of the state are arrived at from *within* my worldview. Rawls tried to avoid this move, and ended up either in cultural relativism or in sneaking in his own views under the guise of neutrality, as we have seen.[20] Francis Canavan has described this common liberal argument as "the pluralist game"—a confidence game by which certain groups press government into the service of their beliefs and goals under the pretense of preserving neutrality among all beliefs.[21]

The question arises as to whether I am suggesting that Christianity *necessarily* leads to democracy, as some have argued. Some have held that the notion of human dignity in Christianity naturally leads to democratic principles and a scheme of democratic values, such as freedom, equality, justice and so on.[22] While I am obviously quite sympathetic to this view, I am not insisting on it. All I am saying is that whatever political structure one favors, the values at the heart of this structure must be justified *from within one's worldview*. I accept that Christian values could very likely find expression in more than one type of political theory. Further, I accept the view, but cannot go into it here in any detail, that various worldviews might significantly agree on the basic values of democracy, *even though they might disagree about how to justify these values*. Their justification would come, though, from within their respective worldviews. I concur with Robert Audi's point that agreement, in moral practice especially, does not require agreement in moral theory.[23] So two people could agree on a moral position, but the position could be based on religious arguments for one but not for the other. The crucial point is that whenever there is a dispute about the principles and values of democracy, or (which is more likely) a dispute about how a particular value should be applied, this dispute will involve appeal to the foundational beliefs of one's worldview and will usually lead to a public debate in which all worldviews (morally) can participate (as long as they appeal to reason and evidence, as I have argued earlier, and not texts, authorities,

---

[20]Francis Fukuyama is another writer who suggests that democracy and religion are basically incompatible. What is interesting about Fukuyama's argument is that he fails to come to terms with the underlying philosophical questions his view invites, such as how the values of liberal democracy are themselves justified, and how democracies can avoid degenerating into relativism, despite alluding to these problems occasionally. See *The End of History and the Last Man* (New York: Free Press, 1992).

[21]See Francis Canavan, *The Pluralist Game* (Lanham, Md.: Rowman & Littlefield, 1995), p. 96.

[22]We need to keep the question of whether Christianity requires a particular political system distinct from the question of whether Christianity requires a particular economic system, though these are not always easily distinguishable in practice. Christian thinkers have held a variety of positions on both questions.

[23]See Robert Audi, *Religious Commitment and Secular Reason* (Cambridge: Cambridge University Press, 2000), p. 155.

etc.). It cannot be settled by appeal to some vague, arbitrary set of independent values or to an independent procedure that, as Rawls often puts it, "everybody nowadays accepts."

Robert Kraynak has argued that modern liberal democracy needs the Christian religion to support its basic moral claims, as we noted in chapter three. Michael Novak strongly agrees, and Charles Taylor appears to hold the same view. James W. Skillen has developed a very interesting and carefully nuanced case for how joining the concepts "Christian" and "democratic" can guide the pursuit of justice in a pluralist society. Richard John Neuhaus has written of "the Catholic moment"—that the Catholic Church, through the person and the philosophies of Pope John Paul II, is in a critical position to assume its role in the culture-forming task of constructing a religiously informed public philosophy for the American experiment in ordered liberty.[24] Neuhaus has emphasized that "the possibility of democracy's democratic self-destruction reminds us again that democracy requires more than the institutions of democracy. . . . Politics is in largest part the function of culture, and at the heart of culture is morality, and at the heart of morality is religion."[25] He believes that democracy is superior to other political orders because under the conditions of modernity it best accommodates the Christian understanding of human dignity. Novak argues, in a very interesting and provocative discussion, that "The moral reasoning behind natural rights . . . is based upon a special concept of human dignity: the dignity of having been created by God, called to be a friend of God, and being inalienably responsible to God for one's use of liberty,"[26] and later argues that Locke's views on freedom do not mainly come from observation, history, or philosophical argument, but from religion (from "a biblical metaphysic"). Novak goes on to discuss these claims in the context of the history of philosophy

---

[24]See James Skillen, *In Pursuit of Justice: Christian-Democratic Explorations* (Lanham, Md.: Rowman & Littlefield, 2004); Michael Novak, *On Two Wings: Humble Faith and Common Sense at the American Founding* (San Francisco: Encounter Books, 2002); Charles Taylor, *Sources of the Self* (Cambridge, Mass.: Harvard University Press, 1992), pp. 495-96, 498; also his *A Catholic Modernity?* ed. James L. Heft (New York: Oxford University Press, 1999). For Neuhaus's argument and for an excellent overview of the debate concerning Catholicism and American democracy, see part 5 of his *The Catholic Moment: The Paradox of the Church in the Modern World* (San Francisco: Harper & Row, 1987), pp. 233-88. See also Neuhaus's three-part series, "Proposing Democracy Anew," in *First Things*, October, November, December 1999 issues. See also David. T. Koyzis, *Political Visions and Illusions* (Downers Grove, Ill.: InterVarsity Press, 2003), chaps. 7 and 8.
[25]See Neuhaus "Proposing Democracy Anew—Part Two," *First Things*, November 1999, p. 90.
[26]Novak, *On Two Wings*, p. 78.

and theology, and argues for an even stronger thesis: that Christianity (specifically Catholicism) requires, and perhaps even makes possible, a political system based on democratic values.[27]

Paul Marshall illustrates how biblical Christianity, in particular, can support the democratic form of government and many of its values. While not going as far perhaps as either Neuhaus or Novak to say that democracy is the best political system for Christianity, he clearly supports democracy and argues that "believing that God is the ultimate source of political authority is perfectly compatible with what is generally called a democracy."[28] As Marshall astutely points out, the key questions for the Christian worldview "are whom God gives authority to, what that authority is, and what it is for."[29] He believes that the Founding Fathers intimately connected democracy and religion in their political vision. In the modern context, according to Marshall, Christian beliefs and values can serve as a moral check on our political decisions. Christianity can also provide a rational foundation for human rights, which are founded on the view that we are all created equal in the image of God. This mandates a political agenda because it means that governments cannot do whatever they like, nor can the electorate at large. Marshall acknowledges that there are fierce debates around the world about what constitutes human rights, even among Christians themselves, but his key point is that the Christian worldview can support the democratic form of government and that Christians have a responsibility to be involved in the political debate.

Kraynak and Marshall are not perhaps willing to go quite as far as Novak or Neuhaus, and neither am I. Although I hold that democracy needs Christianity, I would emphasize that this does not mean that Christianity requires democracy.[30] Kraynak believes that Christianity is not inherently a liberal or democratic religion nor a religion that offers a direct political message.[31] He surveys the history of Christian thinking on this matter in such thinkers as

---

[27]Ibid., p. 81. See pp. 78-85 for his discussion of Catholicism and the doctrine of natural rights, which is at the heart of the American founding documents.

[28]Paul Marshall, *God and the Constitution* (Lanham, Md.: Rowman & Littlefield, 2002), p. 67.

[29]Ibid.

[30]I am also not suggesting that secularism necessarily requires democracy or that democracy is by definition secularist, a view that has been proposed by some Christian thinkers. As indicated in chap. 1 in our description of two worldviews, secularism is compatible with several different political theories.

[31]See Robert Kraynak, *Christian Faith and Modern Democracy* (Notre Dame, Ind.: University of Notre Dame Press, 2001), p. 7.

St. Augustine, St. Thomas Aquinas, Martin Luther and John Calvin, and illustrates that none of these thinkers, nor many others, supported the democratic form of government.[32] It is also clear, I think, that none of them had a fully worked out position on the role of religion in politics. According to Kraynak, it is only with the work of the Spanish philosopher Francisco Suarez (1548-1617) that we see a move toward democracy, and it wasn't until the twentieth century that this position was argued for explicitly in the work of Catholic philosophers Jacques Maritain and John Courtney Murray.[33] It was not until the Second Vatican Council that the Catholic Church became quite sympathetic toward democratic values in its theology.[34]

One motivating factor behind the position of the Second Vatican Council and various Christian denominations that are sympathetic to and supportive of democracy is, as Kraynak points out, the straightforward argument that the notion of human dignity is political—it requires us to set up a political structure to promote and protect human dignity (as Marshall has also noted). Kraynak says this is why nations want the right to self-determination. Yet it is important to emphasize that it also requires us to promote dignity within our own nations, and so inevitably requires introducing our own worldviews into domestic politics. I am much impressed with Kraynak's analysis of the relationship between Christianity and democracy, and I agree with one of his major theses that modern liberal democracy requires the Christian religion to support its values. Secularism cannot provide this support, one of the reasons for its moral failures in contemporary society. We are probably both agreed that Christianity does not necessarily require democracy,

---

[32]See also on this matter a fine collection of essays edited by R. Bruce Douglass and David Hollenbach, *Catholicism and Liberalism* (Cambridge: Cambridge University Press, 1994).

[33]See Jacques Maritain, *Man and the State* (Washington, D.C.: Catholic University of America Press, 1998). See also John Courtney Murray, S.J., *We Hold These Truths: Catholic Reflections on the American Proposition* (New York: Sheed & Ward, 1960), pp. 97-123, for Murray's defense of the thesis "that only the theory of natural law is able to give an account of the public moral experience that is the public consensus" (p. 109). This consensus would include the principle of religious freedom. For a critical analysis of Murray's view and whether he comes close to the position of allowing American democratic values to trump Christian values, see the exchange between Michael Baxter, Michael Novak and David Schindler in the *Review of Politics* 60, no. 4 (fall 1998). In this regard, Pope John Paul II's famous remark that "the church proposes; she imposes nothing" would seem to imply a democratic political theory (see papal encyclical *Redemptoris Missio* [On the Permanent Validity of the Church's Missionary Mandate], 1990). This is because only if one's proposals are persuasive to a majority can they become law and influence society, and this would seem to presuppose a democratic political system.

[34]See the Vatican II document *Dignitatis Humanae* (Declaration on Religious Freedom).

though I am arguing that a democratic society would probably be the best form of government, as long as it can be influenced by, say, Christian values.

I also agree with Kraynak that religions other than Christianity should also influence the public-square debate insofar as they agree with Christianity on the issues in question, which they do for the most part. This is the only logical position to take on this matter, if one wishes to avoid the conclusion that traditional religions are basically irrational or to avoid moral and religious relativism. Other religions must logically take the same position with regard to the role of worldviews not their own in politics. Secularism too must adopt this position with regard to other worldviews. But although I would not want any view to have significant influence in the political arena if I believed it to be false, I would grant it the right to be expressed (subject to certain limits), allow it to attempt to influence the outcome of political debate, for the reasons I gave in chapter three.

One of the reasons religious believers might be suspicious of democracy is that, because of the general emphasis on freedom in a democratic state, it might happen that although political arguments can be influenced by, say, Christian values, they might not be. And in the United States, the general secular presumption is that one should not even try to introduce Christian values into the political arena. Religious believers run the risk in a democratic society that their religious beliefs will be rejected or will have little or no influence, and that other worldviews will dominate. Many Christian thinkers have lamented the fact that a true democracy would not include, as Kraynak eloquently puts it, "rights to abortion, free sex, homosexual marriage, disloyalty, pornography, or excessive capitalism. Distinctions such as these are supposed to keep liberal democracy from degenerating into immorality or vulgar self-expression or a consumer-worker society or soulless materialism."[35] A "true democracy" would be a democracy influenced by Christian values, according to Kraynak. Indeed, the issue of abortion is one of the best examples of the moral failure of secularism, because secularism conspicuously fails to limit human freedom in order to protect the right to life of the youngest members of the human family.

This is a risk the religious believer runs in a democratic society; indeed, it is a risk faced by every worldview. Perhaps it can be mitigated somewhat if in general the democratic state is inclined to allow a *significant amount*

---

[35]Kraynak, *Christian Faith and Modern Democracy*, p. 171.

of freedom for each worldview, so that members of the worldview can practice their worldview, can bring their children up in the worldview, even if it
has little influence in the culture, and even if the political arena is mostly
hostile to it. Although this would mitigate the problem, it obviously would
not relieve all the tensions because of the fact that some significant beliefs
in every worldview have a political dimension, and because, given that
worldviews conflict on some issues, this will inevitably lead to the state's rejection of the beliefs and values of some worldviews. This need both to allow the expression and practice of worldviews one does not fully agree
with, and at the same time to restrict these worldviews, at least on some matters, brings us to the principle of religious freedom.

The Principle of Religious Freedom

This focus on the interesting, even intriguing relationship between the religious worldview (or *any* worldview) and democracy prompts us to ask how
much freedom (as part of our democratic political theory) we would allow
for worldviews with which we disagree. Allowing a significant amount of
freedom is part of the essence of democracy, and we need to think about
the place and status of a principle of religious freedom within our respective
worldviews ("religious" understood to include secularism).

Walter Berns has argued, in the context of a discussion about the
founders of the United States, that the principle of religious freedom derives
from a nonreligious source—from a naturalistic account of the rights of man
originated in Locke and Hobbes.[36] While I do not think this is a correct account of the founders' understanding of the origin of natural rights, this is
not the most pressing issue. The deeper philosophical point is that the principle of religious freedom *must be justified from within one's worldview,* or
so I am arguing (for the religious believer, this will be from within the religious worldview).[37] Otherwise, we end up with the view that traditional religions are inferior in some way to secularist views, a position I have tried
to show is false, and we also end up with the view that religion should have
a greatly diminished role in politics. In addition, as Kraynak has argued, the
final result of a democracy based on a naturalistic account of rights is the

---

[36]See Walter Berns, "Religion and the Founding Principle," in *The Moral Foundations of the
American Republic,* ed. Robert H. Horowitz, 3rd ed. (Charlottesville: University Press of Virginia, 1986), p. 215.

[37]Murray discusses this matter in *We Hold These Truths,* pp. 61-63.

one that has been realized in the United States and is slowly spreading all over the Western world—one with deep moral problems, strongly under the influence of moral relativism and skepticism, one with little regard for moral responsibility and moral character, one dominated by crass capitalist consumerism, lowest-common-denominator media, increasingly corrupt business practices and so on.

The principle of religious freedom grants members of religions (worldviews) other than one's own the right to practice their religion in a democratic society. The philosophical question about religious freedom is how much freedom should members of religion A give to members of religion B, and vice versa (through agreed upon political structures)? The question, of course, has to be broadened to include secularism, to ask, in general, how much freedom should members of a worldview give to members of different worldviews—to not just express, but to practice their beliefs? It is clear from our earlier discussion that this is not an easy question to answer, and that the secularist view (exemplified in the work of Rawls) that religious believers should not bring their beliefs into politics is a restriction on religious freedom that must be rejected. I have already argued in chapter three that members of worldviews should give generous latitude to members of other worldviews to express and practice their beliefs, but obviously they cannot give total freedom, because whichever view gets established in law must of logical necessity exclude its opposite, as we have seen.

Many religions have modified their views on this question over the years. The Catholic Church, in particular, has significantly changed its position on this matter in the twentieth century, coming round to the view in the Second Vatican Council, expressed in the document *Dignitatis Humanae* (Declaration on Religious Freedom), argued for by John Courtney Murray, that the Church could support some of the basics of democracy as a political theory, including the view that other religions and worldviews should enjoy significant freedom of expression and practice. This gave rise to much debate within the Catholic Church in the United States in the attempt to accommodate, perhaps even reconcile, Catholic teaching with the principles of democracy, especially on freedom of religion.[38] The traditional view of the relationship between Catholicism and democracy before the Second Vatican Council had been more practical, holding that in principle significant reli-

---

[38]For the history of this debate, see John T. McGreevy, *Catholicism and American Freedom: A History* (New York: Norton, 2003).

gious freedom for other religions was not appropriate (since they were wrong on many issues), but recognizing that from a practical point of view one had to settle for less in a democratic society.

Although there has been much debate over this matter in both Protestant and Catholic literature, I think the main reasons in a nutshell for why various Christian denominations came round on this issue in the twentieth century are threefold: (1) there was gradual acceptance of the view, mentioned above, that the same (morally correct) values could be justified by different worldviews (and so these worldviews should have a certain amount of freedom because they were right on some matters); (2) a gradual acceptance that some theological claims belong to the realm of what I have called higher-order beliefs, especially claims about whether certain beliefs or behaviors would lead to eternal damnation (and so there is less pressing need to enshrine one's religious views in law); and (3) a growing emphasis on human dignity as including a significant amount of freedom.[39]

The main point is, however, that whatever degree of religious freedom one believes should be granted to members of other worldviews it must be defended from within one's own worldview and that all worldviews must address this question when it comes to the political arena, including the secularist worldview.

In this chapter, we have argued that the role one's religious beliefs should play in politics must be defended from within one's own worldview, not from some independent, neutral standpoint. We have looked at Rawls's alternative theory and offered some criticisms of it. We have also reflected more generally on the relationship between religious belief, specifically Christianity, and the democratic political system, including the significance of the principle of religious freedom, and how we should approach its philosophical defense. All of this lays the groundwork for us to now consider the actual practice of the public political debate between the various worldviews in a modern democratic society.

---

[39] I owe this point to Bill Stancil.

7

Religion in Politics

We turn to the practical but crucial question of what kinds of religious be-liefs one can actually bring into politics in a democratic society, according to the position I have been developing in this book. Our answer to this question, as we have just seen, must come from within our worldview and will be justified insofar as our worldview is justified. Similarly, any objections to our view will come from some *other* worldview and will have to be jus-tified as part of that worldview. (We should not forget that worldviews can overlap and agree on significant matters. I do not wish to imply any kind of relativism by saying that my arguments are part of my worldview, and ob-jections are part of other worldviews. I am also assuming that we all strive for our worldviews to be as rational as possible.) It would be helpful per-haps if we try to state more accurately our question. We are asking, what actual role can religious beliefs play in politics? However, I have argued that all substantive worldviews can be looked upon as "religions," so my ques-tion more precisely stated is: which beliefs of a worldview (be it a secularist or a traditional religious worldview) can be legitimately introduced into public political debates and which beliefs should not be introduced?

I will now try to lay out my answer to this question, and in doing so we will consider some concrete examples along the way. Later I will consider how my answer will affect our understanding of the relationship between church and state. It will also be helpful to illustrate my position with a fic-tional example. I will conclude the chapter with a discussion of the implica-tions of my view for the terminology of the religion-politics debate.

Introducing Lower-Order, Rational Beliefs into Public Arguments

My answer to the question of which beliefs of a worldview can form a legitimate part of a public argument will be closely tied to the exercise of reason and evidence. Recall that I have been defending the position that the reasonability of a worldview is essential, especially in public political debates. I also indicated that I accept the democratic political system as the one that best complements Christianity, without going so far as to say that Christianity requires democracy. But for the purposes of our position in this book, I am assuming that most religious believers would accept the democratic form of government. Given these points, I hold that only those beliefs that are *lower-order beliefs* can be introduced into public arguments. Recall that lower-order beliefs are those beliefs that are strongly based on evidence, that are justified by appeal to rational argument. Since the standards of reason and evidence must be brought to bear on every worldview, this seems to me a reasonable criterion for deciding what counts as a legitimate candidate for inclusion in public political, social and moral arguments. I regard this as a rational answer to the question of which beliefs a worldview can introduce into the public square.

Lower-order beliefs are more likely to be persuasive to others, or at least to be regarded as reasonable, even if not adopted by others. As an example, a member of the Jewish religion could introduce into the public debate about the legalization of marijuana the argument that this action would be subject to significant abuse, would lead to even greater dependence on and so create greater demand for even more dangerous drugs, and that the human misery this would lead to is immoral because it is against God's moral plan for humanity, and so marijuana should be illegal. This is a reasonable argument, and so his belief that marijuana should be illegal is a lower-order, rational belief. The fact that he can introduce the argument into the public square does not mean, of course, that it will eventually be adopted in law or even that it will influence legislation. The public may find other opposing arguments on the topic more persuasive.

It is also important to acknowledge that one might hold that some of one's beliefs are reasonable but still not want to force them on others through coercive legislation. There is a legitimate distinction, in other words, between holding that a belief is reasonable (in a strong sense) and so it can be introduced into the public square, and holding that another belief is reasonable (in a weaker sense) but should not be introduced into the public debate, at least as the basis for coercive legislation. The difference here is that one thinks the former belief is very reasonable, supported by good reasons, there are few good objections to it and so on. But one thinks the second belief, although reasonable, is not as well supported or that there are objections to it that give one pause. An example of the former type of belief might be that prostitution should be illegal, and of the latter type that smoking should not be illegal. If one does not make a distinction such as this, as Thomas Nagel has noted, all reasonable beliefs would have to be regarded as grounds for coercion, because one would have to hold that because the belief is reasonable, that anyone who rejected it is therefore unreasonable.[1] And this is to deny that the reasonableness of a belief can fall somewhere in the middle on the scale of reasonableness versus unreasonableness. Yet there will still be disputes between people who do not think their views fall into this middle ground. Sometimes a conflict of values cannot be avoided. But in a democracy we are supposed to accept the decision of the majority, even if we disagree with it. This is a rational requirement of the democratic form of government. As Nagel goes on to say, "legitimate government would be impossible if it were never legitimate to impose a policy on those who reasonably disagree with the values on which it was based."[2]

I would exclude higher-order beliefs from public arguments because they are not as closely tied to rational argument and evidence as lower-order beliefs (in the way I described in chapter one). This does not mean that they are irrational beliefs; but it does mean that it will be more difficult to expect people who are not members of our worldview to accept these beliefs, and to expect them to live in a society in which these beliefs would have the force of law (i.e., where these beliefs were the basis of coercive legislation). To put the matter in another way, it is reasonable to hold, I think, that one cannot reasonably expect people of one worldview to accept the higher-order beliefs of another worldview. But one *can* reasonably expect others to accept the lower-order (rational) beliefs of one's worldview. Of course, one may still not be able to *convince* others of the rationality of the lower-order beliefs of one's worldview, but at least these beliefs can be debated in the public square. In addition, one could be restricted from practicing the higher-order beliefs of one's view even in private, if enough citizens thought them sufficiently irrational or immoral to warrant outlawing them (e.g., laws outlawing polygamy). In short, dominant lower-order beliefs supported by a majority can be used to restrict not only public policy but also private prac-

---

[1]See Thomas Nagel, *Equality and Partiality* (New York: Oxford University Press, 1991), p. 161.
[2]Ibid., p. 163.

tice. (A reminder that almost any belief can be introduced into public arguments in an exercise of free speech; the argument here for which beliefs can and cannot be brought up is a *moral* argument.)

So, to illustrate with another example, I would not regard as appropriate introducing into a public discussion any argument that relied upon the resurrection of Jesus as one of its premises, although I believe the resurrection of Jesus to be an actual historical event. But I recognize that this is harder to establish by means of rationality and evidence than other beliefs of my worldview, that it takes more faith to believe it, and that members of other worldviews could reasonably reject this belief as a guide to public and social policy. This is a higher-order belief of my worldview, and so I do not think it is reasonable for me to think that others would easily accept this belief. This is not to say that no member of another worldview would be convinced by an argument for this belief or to say that it is not rational. But I acknowledge that in general it will be difficult to convince people to accept this belief who were not already seriously inclined toward Christianity, and that it would not be reasonable for me to force them to accept it.

The same conclusions can be drawn with regard to the secularist worldview. For instance, the secularist might argue that the belief that the legalization of euthanasia is a moral action because it leads to a reduction in human suffering is a rational belief, and so can be introduced into public arguments. I do not just mean that it is rational for a secularist to hold this belief; I am also saying that I would acknowledge from within my own worldview of Christianity that this is a reasonable belief, even though I do not hold it myself, or believe it to be true. So the secularist can legitimately introduce this belief into the public square, but he still has to convince others of its truth, enough (I will argue below) to gain majority support for it. In this way, his belief can guide public policy, perhaps even become established in law. I will suggest in a moment that it is antidemocratic to try to win political arguments, especially on serious, controversial issues, by appeal to the judicial system, rather than by appeal to the direct will of the people.

To take another example to contrast the difference between my Christian view on this matter and the secularist view, I suggested in chapter five that the secularist belief that there is no human nature is a higher-order belief because it is based on weak reasons and seems to ignore evidence to the contrary. Thus, I do not think this belief has any legitimate role to play in the public square. (This belief is often behind secularist arguments in favor of gay marriage.) So I hold, from the point of view of my world-view, that this belief should not be appealed to as support in public arguments. The secularist may disagree on this matter; he may hold that the belief that there is no human nature is a lower-order belief or even that my belief that there is a human nature is a higher-order belief. What do we do in cases where members of different worldviews do not agree on whether a particular belief is a lower-order or a higher-order belief? Whose view here prevails, and how do we decide? Again I suggest that each world-view must have an answer to this question as part of the worldview; that is to say, each worldview should have as part of its overall structure an answer to the question of how it is going to deal with disputes with other world-views concerning whether a belief is a lower-order or a higher-order belief.[3]

If there is a dispute about whether a belief is a lower-order or a higher-order belief—a dispute about whether a belief is quite sufficiently rational—then this dispute must be part of the debate in the public square, as I indicated in chapter three. I discussed four reasons for this view there, and so will only briefly recall them here. First, from a practical point of view, there is no way to deal with this matter other than to discuss it in the public square. It would be irrational for A to agree to not bring up his view just because B thinks it is irrational, and for B to defer to A if the situation were reversed. Therefore, discussion of whether the belief is lower-order or higher-order would have to be part of the *public* discussion. Second, it is also reasonable to air this kind of dispute publicly because one can benefit from the variety of perspectives that might be part of a vigorous public discussion. Third, there is also a reason of self-interest for adopting the conclusion that this kind of dispute should be a matter for the public square. One is sure of a hearing for one's *own* views if one adopts this principle, rather than if one agrees to submit to some authority, such as the courts, to settle the matter. Fourth, to settle the matter publicly is required by our adherence to democratic values. The actual debate in the public square on this matter

---

[3]This is a question Michael Perry does not consider. He rejects John Finnis's attempt at offering a secular argument against homosexual conduct, but does not address the issue of how the debate should proceed if, say, there were disagreement about the rationality of secular arguments on this matter. Perry simply concludes that his view on the rationality of the issue should prevail in the public square, and that Finnis's should be excluded. See Michael J. Perry, *Religion in Politics* (New York: Oxford University Press, 1997), pp. 82-96, and especially p. 96, for his concluding comments. But also see his later, more nuanced discussion in his *Under God: Religious Faith and Liberal Democracy* (New York: Cambridge University Press, 2003).

will consist of all parties explaining and defending their views and of trying to convince enough people that their view is reasonable. In this way, their beliefs, claims, views, values are put to the test of public justification and may gain enough public acceptance to have political influence and to guide public policy.

A Seculocracy for a Secularist People?

It is instructive to ask, do secularists want everyone else to become secularists? Do they want to establish a seculocracy? Or do Buddhists want everyone in the state to be Buddhists? Do they want a Buddhist theocracy? The answer to this question on the view I have been developing is that one does not normally want others to fully convert to one's worldview, but only to the practices (and perhaps the beliefs) of one's worldview *on certain matters*. For example, secularists might want everyone to accept their views about masculinity and femininity, or about the environment, or about smoking, or about drug taking, in the sense that they must live in a society shaped by these values. This is why secularists want their views placed in law, if possible, so that they can coerce people to follow them. Of course, getting people to *believe* that a practice is morally correct is another matter, but the secularist hopes that over time the belief will follow the practice. The religious believer wants the same thing. For instance, the religious believer might want his view on abortion to become law, so that abortion can no longer be practiced, and he hopes that over time belief in the immorality of abortion will become dominant in the culture.

One might not always wish for one's views to become the law of the land (at least directly), but simply want them to make a contribution to the public debate. One might, for instance, want hospitals to provide medical treatment for all, even though some might not have the ability to pay for treatment, because we are all equal creatures of God. One might want this view to influence the public debate on health care, while not necessarily wanting it to be part of health care legislation. One might exhort farmers, to take another case, to treat vermin humanely because we are called as creatures of God not to be unnecessarily cruel, but one might not want to place this view in law in order to restrict the ways in which farmers can get rid of vermin. (Or some worldviews might want their views on these matters made law.) Some types of behavior might be simply impractical to regulate. Laws against adultery or against ingratitude might fall into this category. Churches have spoken out in recent years on many issues, such as gambling, business practices, advertising, war, and the content of films and TV shows, in an attempt to influence the debate on these matters, without necessarily proposing or supporting legislative initiatives relating to them. There are also many topics about which one's worldview might have little to say or where one could not settle on a clear position, such as on matters relating to interest rate increases, interstate commerce, planning laws, littering and so forth. (Worldviews are not necessarily required to have positions on every topic.)

One reason the religious believer in particular does not necessarily want to convert others is because of the distinction between higher-order and lower-order beliefs. This distinction acknowledges that there is room for disagreement about some of the beliefs of one's worldview. So one acknowledges that one might not be able to convince others of one's views, that there could be a legitimate dispute over the rationality of higher-order beliefs, just as one would not be convinced oneself by higher-order beliefs from other worldviews. Another way to put this point is to say that one is usually trying to convert others to hold, and certainly to practice, *some of one's beliefs, but not all of them.*

For those who might be tempted to say that my view could be divisive in the sense that it would force coercive legislation concerning at least some moral values on those who do not share these values and would lead to contentious religious disputes in the political arena, I would point out that (1) coercive legislation is unavoidable in any society and (2) in U.S. society, coercive laws have already been implemented to force everyone to follow the secularist worldview on some matters. Coercive legislation is unavoidable because our laws must be based on some values, and those will exclude their opposites. Further, coercive legislation has already been enacted because millions of people are currently compelled to live in a society that permits practices they find abhorrent, for example, the practice of abortion. My view would not force *unreasonable* religious or secularist beliefs on people who do not subscribe to them, and that is the key issue. Most unreasonable beliefs would not survive the test of public justification.

Of course, I have already pointed out in chapter four that members of all worldviews might adopt a pragmatic position on some topics for the purposes of passing legislation favorable to their view. A traditional religious believer might even settle simply for order and stability in a state over truth and the promotion of the good life simply on pragmatic grounds, especially

if he thought the state in which he lived was corrupt or was so hostile to his
view that he should generally keep his head down.

I agree with Michael Perry that the actual debate in a liberal democracy
should be guided by certain attitudes and virtues, such as being fully informed, a willingness to probe arguments rather than to question motives,
honesty, sincerity and so on.[4] Two further values proposed by Perry are
more problematic: fallibility (recognizing one could be wrong) and pluralism (the existence of many views is a good thing). These two values are
problematic if they are understood in a relativistic sense. I have tried to
show that no worldview adopts fallibilism in the sense that it doubts *all* its
values (in such a way that its members would not want to *impose* those values on others in the state). Otherwise, one quickly falls into inconsistency,
as in Perry himself, since he is presumably *not* a fallibilist about the above
list of values (and indeed about many others also). To appreciate this point
it is helpful to distinguish today between two senses of fallibilism: fallibilism
about truth and fallibilism about allowing our views to shape the law. In the
first sense of fallibilism, one recognizes that one's views on a particular matter might not be true. In the second sense, one is not willing to impose one's
views on society through laws and coercive legislation. Regardless of the implications of the first sense for political debate, the key point is that nobody
is a *total* fallibilist in the second sense. In fact, increasingly today we see fal-
libilists (in the first sense) going around adamantly telling us all how to live,
trying to shape legislation according to their values!

Some Practical Applications

How will my position actually apply in certain areas where political decisions are often made in a democratic society? I will now attempt to illustrate
my view briefly by applying it to some of the main general areas where public discussion is carried out. It is important to keep distinct the legal question
on these matters (especially as regards the United States) from the moral
question of what is the correct way to handle these matters in a state operating with the principles I have argued for above. I am mainly interested in
the moral question in this chapter.

Minority rights. On the question of minority rights, raised by John Stu-

---

[4]See Michael Perry, *Love and Power* (New York: Oxford University Press, 1992), p. 101. Robert
Audi disagrees. His principle of secular motivation is a way to test a *traditional religious person's* motives.

art Mill in his *On Liberty* (1860), we first need to get clear about what we mean by this concept. If the concept refers to rights that only the members of a particular minority group have then there really is no such thing as minority rights in a democratic society. Because any rights granted by the state would normally apply to all people who live in the state (e.g., the right to be treated equally in job applications applies to all people). If the concept refers to giving minority groups a right to practice a behavior, say, that the majority finds morally objectionable, then it is more controversial. The concept is usually used today in this sense—to refer to the general right of minorities to practice or live differently in some ways than the majority. In a democratic state, minority rights are granted by the majority (but even here we must be careful to note that it is not only the minority that has this right, but all citizens; it is simply that a minority choose to exercise it).

Mill worried that citizens in a modern democracy might impose what he called a "tyranny of the majority" on the minority. This means that they might impose their views on the minority, who disagree with these views. Yet this is a too simplistic way of putting the matter. For in a democratic state it is the majority that must decide whether it would be tyrannical, that is, *irrational or immoral,* to impose its dislike of a practice or behavior on those who disagree. After all, many laws in a state are tyrannical in Mill's sense because they are *imposed* on all citizens (e.g., laws prohibiting speeding or drug use, tax laws, residential property laws, laws against polygamy, etc.). My view requires that matters that arise with respect to minority rights must be handled by rational debate in the public arena, and the most persuasive view (in the eyes of *the majority,* let us not forget) must prevail. This is more reasonable and more fair than allowing a minority to decide which view should prevail.

A democratic state might not want to deal with these matters every time they come up. So a long-term way of dealing with many of the questions that arise in a democratic society might be for the majority to set out in law *a specific area of personal freedom* in which the majority will not normally interfere. It would have to be spelled out what this area of freedom includes and does not include. For example, it might include the right to (heterosexual) marriage, the right to bear arms, to publish seditious material, to practice homosexuality, to form certain types of interest groups, but it might not include the right to practice bigamy, polygamy or gay marriage. But this specific area will still have to be defined by the majority (in the ideal state). It will be monitored by the courts, of course, but it should not be substantially altered by the courts, nor should it be initially established by or defined by the courts. It should not be primarily the study of legal precedent and the history of various court cases that decides what is permitted and not permitted. This would give too much power to the courts and would lead to contentious disputes between the various worldviews. This is the current position in the United States with regard to a number of issues, and it is one of the reasons why the United States has a wider area of personal freedom than most Western democratic countries. Many issues that would be settled in these countries by the legislature and the people are settled in the United States by judges, lawyers and interest groups.[5]

I believe that this is the fairest and most rational way to settle these public disputes. They should not be settled by the courts because it is too difficult to ensure—especially in a pluralist society—that the courts reflect the will of the people. On controversial issues, issues about which people strongly disagree, the will of the people should be sought directly. I would even say that controversial issues should not always be settled by appeal to the laws of the land (the Constitution, for example) because again there may be prior questions about what the Constitution means, of whether one's worldview agrees with certain interpretations of the Constitution, or whether it is still appropriate for our changing times. It is much more reasonable to seek the will of the people directly on these matters in a referendum than to have a handful of people deciding what the moral outcome should be (as, for example, on abortion).

Voting. The practical effect of the position I have been defending would be that, on the issue of voting in elections, a citizen can appeal to her religious beliefs (secularist or traditional religion) as long as she sincerely thinks these beliefs *are lower-order (rational) beliefs.* As I have argued, it is reasonable to introduce such beliefs into politics. A traditional religious believer does not have to leave her worldview at the door of the polling booth, no more than the secularist does. People can also appeal to their religious beliefs when it comes to influencing people on how to vote on election matters. Indeed, perhaps in the modern state there should be some *formal* mechanism for various worldviews to make their views known on the issues

---

[5]Stephen Carter has pointed out something that we are inclined to forget: that the courts are part of the government (i.e., part of the state), not a check on the power of the state, as current rhetoric often likes to put it. In this sense, many of their judgments do not protect our liberties but restrict them, especially if we do not agree with the court's judgments. See Carter, *The Dissent of the Governed* (Cambridge, Mass.: Harvard University Press, 1998), p. 105.

of the day both to the electorate and especially to the government.[6]

So a religious believer could vote against gay marriage because she is persuaded that it goes against the natural order, a natural order established by God. The argument would have to be filled out in more detail than this, of course, but she would not have to do this herself. It is sufficient that she knows there is such an argument available (and that it be an argument based on lower-order beliefs). She might find such an argument in a policy statement on this topic from her church. Not everyone is required (as I pointed out in chapter three) to be able to present these arguments in the public square. It is enough that some representatives of the view in question engage in the public arguments and that these arguments be generally available for everyone to consider. Ideally, a vigorous (not necessarily public) discussion should precede one's judgment that one's argument is a reasonable argument. This is also why it is crucial to participate in a discussion where all the major views are given a fair chance to be heard, something that is not always practiced in our media or even in our academic debates.

Hiring. On the matter of hiring for employment, could an employer ask an applicant about his religious beliefs, on my position? The answer to this interesting question is no, as long as these beliefs are not relevant for the job in question and that nothing has been mentioned about the applicant's religion in the job advertisement. An employer should not normally ask a job applicant which worldview he is a member of, what foundational beliefs he holds, whether he practices them and so on. This is not an easy line to draw, though, and many employers (e.g., public universities) cross it all the time. Some employers are in the odd position, especially in U.S. society, of hiring applicants according to their worldview, though officially they are not supposed to be doing this; indeed, it is often illegal to do this.

But keep in mind that applicants are always asked questions at job interviews about their religious beliefs, despite our pretensions to the contrary! For as soon as one asks candidates if they accept certain moral values that are part of many business practices, such as treating all customers equally, or doing an honest day's work, or about the matter of providing a service that people badly need and so forth, one is asking them about their worldview. And if they were to answer in an unsatisfactory way on any of these matters, they would not be hired. Employees must subscribe to at least some

---

[6]The opposite view—where the state not just influences but has some formal control over religions—is known as Erastianism, after the Swiss religious thinker Erastus (1524-1583).

of the values of their employers. We do not need to explore this interesting matter here, but it is noteworthy because it emphasizes again that once one begins to look at the pluralist debate *in terms of the more general category of worldviews* then one clearly sees that discriminating against traditional religious worldviews is arbitrary.

Judges. On the issue of judicial decision-making, my view entails that judges should not appeal to their religious beliefs but must rely on applying the law as it is written. They must try to do this as much as possible, yet we must acknowledge that it is probably impossible for judges to completely ignore their various worldviews on every issue that might come before the courts. The decisions of judges, though, carry a presumption of independence from their own worldviews because they are operating with a set of written laws or principles that have come (ideally) from the people, to which they are supposed to appeal when making their decisions.

But the matter is not as simple as all that. In many cases it will be sufficient for judges to simply appeal to the law as written, and to ordinary reasoning, to make a judgment on an issue before the courts. Further, discussion and debate among the various judges on the court and an appeal to legal history may help in arriving at a judgment. But when a new issue is before the court, one on which there is no legal history (e.g., abortion or euthanasia), then judges may have to go beyond ordinary reasoning and appeal to their own worldviews. The issue may come down, as some judicial decisions surely do, to the personal beliefs of the judges. Could a judge who finds herself in this kind of situation appeal to her traditional religious beliefs? (There seems little doubt that in modern societies she could appeal to her secularist beliefs if she were a secularist.) My answer is yes, as long as she sincerely believes her religious beliefs are rational and supports them with reasons and evidence. She could even refer to her religion directly in her judgments. Although, in this particular situation, a judge might be tempted to adopt the pragmatic approach referred to earlier in the sense that she would not explicitly appeal to the foundational beliefs of her worldview, or to her worldview by name, whether it be religious *or* secularist (yet another reason why it is essential today to appreciate that secularism is a worldview). Judges should probably always give the appearance of being neutral, even if it some cases it is impossible to be so. (It is clearly a sham to claim that judges can always be neutral between competing worldviews in a pluralist democracy.)

Politicians. Politicians can appeal to their religious beliefs, again as long as they are lower-order, rational beliefs. Since these are rational beliefs that can be legitimately introduced into public debates, it is entirely appropriate to appeal to them when running for office, when formulating policy or when voting on policy. (Indeed, they may have been elected on some of these beliefs.) Again, it is just as appropriate for a traditional religious believer to do this as it is for a secularist or a Marxist.

The example of President Kennedy being elected as the first Catholic president of the United States is often discussed in this context. One of the worries some people raised about his possible election was that he would follow his Catholic religion (and therefore the pope) whenever it clashed with U.S. law or with the wishes of the American people (one of the issues people were concerned about was Kennedy's opposition to racial segregation). But this scenario just raises the question of which values will a politician appeal to or regard as primary whenever he or she makes a decision, especially concerning coercive legislation. These values will surely come from his worldview (unless he specifically campaigned on certain values already adopted in law, and surely these will also be part of his worldview). Further, his worldview should be reasonable and freely adopted. (To deny that religious believers can do this, especially in free America in the twenty-first century, is to say that they are basically stupid and easily led.) A politician, like many members of a worldview, might look to his "church" for guidance, or to an authority, or interest group, or political party, as indicated in chapter one, but must decide whether to follow this guidance or not (e.g., a secularist politician might look to the work of secularist philosophers for guidance on abortion or capital punishment, but still has to decide whether to follow this guidance or not). This applies no matter which value one is concerned with that might be the subject of a contentious debate in a democratic society. In addition, politicians are restricted, as I have said, to introducing only lower-order beliefs into public arguments.[7]

Churches and pastors. It is appropriate on my view for churches and pastors to introduce lower-order (rational) beliefs into the public-square debate, for instance, on proposed legislation concerning such new moral areas as human cloning. Indeed, churches and pastors have a vital role here, be-

---

[7]For a discussion of Kent Greenawalt's views on some of these matters, including why politicians and judges should restrict their appeal to religious arguments, see *Private Consciences and Public Reasons* (New York: Oxford University Press, 1995), chap. 14.

cause it will surely be the case that many ordinary members of a worldview will not have the time to, or may be unwilling or be unable to, articulate their views in a public forum. This is where representatives of their worldview can help them. One might say that pastors are professionals part of whose job is to help explore, explain, defend and promote the worldview in question, not just privately in their communities but also publicly, especially on momentous issues. Churches therefore play an absolutely essential role in helping people articulate their worldviews *politically*. As I suggested above, perhaps there should be some *formal* mechanism for various worldviews to make their views known on the issues of the day to the electorate and the government. Of course, churches and pastors too might adopt a pragmatic approach, if it was appropriate.

Our discussion of churches and pastors brings us naturally to the question of the relationship between church and state.

The Relationship Between Church and State

It is obvious that the typical understanding (the conventional wisdom) of the relationship between church and state in modern democracies will have to be rethought in the light of our analysis so far. This relationship should not be confused with the more general issue of religion in public life. Church and state refers to the relationship between those groups that broadly represent worldviews, and those institutions, public bodies, agencies of the state, including the government itself, that make up the state.

In the first place, all worldviews either have or can have churches, that is, institutions that serve to promote the worldview in various ways. Usually, the bigger a worldview (in terms of membership) the greater the likelihood that it will have a fairly significant church, which exists to nurture, explain, defend, promote and propagate the worldview in question. Therefore, the usual meaning of the phrase "church and state" will no longer be useful, for the term *church* in the traditional phrase referred only to a set of particular worldviews, that of traditional religions, as in statements like "separation of church and state" or "we need a closer relationship between church and state" or "the churches are opposed to the state on the issue of divorce" and so forth. But if the arguments of this book are correct, we now need a term that encompasses *all* worldviews that may come into relationship with the state. An appropriate phrase might be "worldviews and the state" because this captures the fact that *all* of the various worldviews have to be considered in their relationship to the state; it does not restrict the worldviews to be considered in their relationship to the state to the subset of traditional religions. The important question then is not, what should the relationship be of traditional religious worldviews to the state, but rather, what should the relationship be of *all* worldviews to the state, secularist views as well as traditional religions? Before we can explore this question, we need to elaborate briefly on what we mean by the state.

Briefly put, by the state we mean the government, government institutions and the laws of the land. In a democratic society, with which we are primarily concerned in this book, the government is directly elected by the people and is accountable to the people. In this way, the laws express the will of the people. The laws are also backed by police and military power, which again is approved by and is accountable to the people. In addition, many of the laws of the state are based on moral values, and again these moral values are accepted by and approved by the people and can be changed by the people at any time. Yet it is not quite as simple as this; but this is where we must begin. One factor that complicates this matter in modern democracies generally and in the United States in particular is that the current debate on these matters is carried on *within a context* of an existing Constitution and Bill of Rights, both of which are supposed to guide us on these questions. We cannot, much as we might like, discuss these issues as if the Constitution, for example, did not exist. But for philosophical purposes, we can do this if our aim is to discuss how these matters should be handled ideally (or philosophically). For now, we will look at these matters mostly from the philosophical perspective, but in the last chapter we will look at them with an eye to how they are handled currently in the United States. In short, we should always keep two questions clearly distinct in our minds: (1) On what values ideally should the laws of the land be based, especially concerning the rules and procedures for regulating public political discourse, and how are these values justified? (2) What are our present (constitutional) values for regulating public political discourse, and how did we arrive at them? Although the second question—the constitutional or legal question—is crucial in any understanding of U.S. society, it is the first question—the philosophical or moral question—with which I am concerned.

We hope at least that the main values underlying a democratic society, say U.S. society, are lower-order values, and that they are values most democratically minded people can accept. ("Democratically minded" means that people accept many of the principles of democracy in general outline as a serious part of their particular worldview; it does not mean that the principles of democracy trump their worldview, as we have seen in our discussion of Rawls above.) Of course, we know that many people at any one time in a democratic state will not agree with all of the values behind the law. Perhaps some will not agree with an interpretation of the Constitution or with a particular way a value might be implemented. But usually people, despite their disagreements, agree to abide by the laws. They also have the option of attempting to change the laws in a variety of (peaceful) ways.

This brings us in our discussion of the proper relationship between church and state to the question of whether the state is neutral between worldviews and promotes no worldview itself, as liberal political philosophers claim. It should be obvious that the state is not neutral and cannot be neutral.[8] This is because many of the laws of the state embody moral values, and these moral values enshrine in law key beliefs that are held by various worldviews (e.g., beliefs about justice, equality, peace, freedom, the common good). These examples clearly appeal to the three areas that form the substance of a worldview—the nature of reality, the nature of the human person and the nature of moral and political values—and they are among the foundational beliefs of various worldviews. In addition, those who do not agree with these values are excluded from *practicing* their worldview on these matters by the state. For instance, those who believe that some people are not equal to others cannot practice this view in hiring for a job. As Richard John Neuhaus has put it, "the public square will not and cannot remain naked. If it is not clothed with the 'meanings' borne by religion, new 'meanings' will be imposed by virtue of the ambitions of the modern state."[9] And, indeed, as Robert George has noted, "the claim that the law ought to be morally neutral about marriage or anything else is itself a moral claim. As

---

[8]Charles Taylor has also criticized liberal political philosophers for obfuscating their metaphysical and ethical assumptions about the nature of the person and the good society. See his *Philosophical Arguments* (Cambridge, Mass.: Harvard University Press, 1995), pp. 236-37. For more on the issue of whether the liberal state is neutral, see Greenawalt, *Private Consciences,* chap. 6; and Francis Canavan, *The Pluralist Game* (Lanham, Md.: Rowman & Littlefield, 1995).

[9]Richard John Neuhaus, *The Naked Public Square* (Grand Rapids: Eerdmans, 1984), p. ix. Later he says that "when recognizable religion is excluded, the vacuum will be filled by *ersatz* religion, by religion bootlegged into public space under other names" (p. 80). And in "Proposing Democracy Anew [Part Three]," *First Things,* December 1999, he puts it this way: "The state should not confess a faith. It does this, however, when, in hostility to the faith confessed by its people, it confesses the ersatz religion of militant secularism" (p. 71).

such, *it* is not morally neutral, nor can it rest on an appeal to moral neutrality."[10] So, for example, any state that bases its laws regarding marriage on this subtle moral claim is imposing this view on those who believe the state should not be morally neutral about the nature of marriage.

Charles Larmore struggles with this matter in his attempt to argue for a neutral justification of political neutrality, as does Bruce Ackerman. Both end up begging the question.[11] Larmore confirms George's criticism by admitting that the liberal state "does not aim at *complete* moral neutrality. It tends to be neutral only with regard to controversial conceptions of the good life and *not to all values or norms whatsoever.*"[12] The problem is that those norms and values it is not neutral toward will be used to *restrict* various versions of the good life that the liberal political philosopher does not approve of, as we saw in our consideration of Rawls's view, and so Larmore's analysis begs the very question at issue. In short, the liberal political philosopher is never totally neutral toward key values in the philosophical, moral and political debate concerning how society should be organized politically; there are always some values that are not doubted, and which are used to restrict other views. Even if the democratic values are sometimes doubted (i.e., if one doubts the democratic process), it is often within the context of a particular group not getting what it wants politically, and this frustration still implies that this particular group thinks its view is better than the alternatives.

It is a key claim of my view that *coercion is always going on in political society,* and it is impossible to find an individual or worldview not trying to impose at least some beliefs on others. Some worldviews, however, may be

---

[10]Robert George, *The Clash of Orthodoxies: Law, Religion and Morality in Crisis* (Wilmington, Del.: ISI Books, 2001), p. 75.

[11]Ackerman's attempt to defend a principle of neutrality for a liberal state is self-contradictory because he would force his principle on others who do not agree with it. That is to say, it is not a value-free principle, as he seems to think. His discussion on the application of the principle fails to bring this out, primarily because in illustrating how it would be applied he appeals to the example of the distribution of material goods rather than the much deeper philosophical issue of establishing laws based on our moral values. See pp. 10-14 of *Social Justice in the Liberal State* (New Haven, Conn.: Yale University Press, 1980). Ackerman's discussion of abortion is especially weak; see pp. 127-28.

[12]Charles Larmore, *Patterns of Moral Complexity* (New York: Cambridge University Press, 1987), p. 55 (emphasis added). Larmore's discussion is rather superficial in that he never directly addresses the questions of whether the political "procedure" is really neutral or of what values are inherent in public discourse, and he does not illustrate his position with any concrete examples.

more coercive than others. The amount and types of coercion can be hard to judge; views that are subtly coercive can be more successful (and perhaps more dangerous) than overtly coercive views because they might be able to transform society very gradually against the wishes of the majority or unbeknownst to the majority or in a way that the majority is powerless to prevent. Some would argue that such is the case today with the worldview of secularism.

To say that the state is always coercive is also to say that the state promotes a particular worldview in the sense that one could extrapolate from its various laws, regulations, ordinances and practices its foundational beliefs on the three areas, as well as the way the government believes people should be allowed to live. This does not mean that the worldview is complete, fully articulated or officially promoted by the state. This worldview may not be a worldview that any particular member of society adheres to, though it is likely that many people who grow up in the society would accept the worldview promoted by the state almost in toto. Let us not forget that, although the state is accountable to the people, this does not necessarily mean that it is the people who always lead. The state—in terms of ideas—can lead the people too. And many will surely accept the values promulgated by the state completely (this can also become intertwined with the notions of patriotism and civic responsibility, especially in U.S. society—concepts that are taught to school children from an early age). One of the problems of modern democracies is the increasing gap between the people and those with political power.

Other worldviews may concur with the view that is at the foundation of the state on some matters but not on other matters. We might echo a point made by the philosopher Jacques Maritain, that the state can promote particular values without being officially committed to any particular theory of the justification of these values.[13] This means that different worldviews can agree on some values at least and can arrive at a kind of "overlapping consensus" among the worldviews. This phenomenon is well exemplified in the United Nations declaration on human rights (a declaration on which Maritain had some influence). We might say that as an ideal, in a modern pluralist, democratic society, the state tries to adopt a worldview that is as broad as possible so as to accommodate as many beliefs from as many different

---

[13]See Jacques Maritain, *Man and the State* (Washington, D.C.: Catholic University of America Press, 1998).

worldviews as possible. (When we say that the "state" tries to do this, we mean that the various worldviews within the state try to do this, within certain limits.) This way the beliefs of as many people as possible can find a place in public arguments.

However, the state must also recognize that not all views can be accommodated simply as a matter of logic, and so some people will be profoundly disappointed and disgruntled. This disagreement must be handled with the utmost care. One of the reasons debates in modern democratic states have become more contentious is that, as more worldviews gain prominence, many of which conflict with one another, a difficult transition has been required from a monolithic leaning society to a pluralist one. This transition has not been handled well, and has often been directed by one particular view—secularism—to the exclusion of others. The result is an increasing polarization of worldviews and a growing belief that reasonable disagreement is no longer possible on some questions. This can lead to a tendency to regard one's opponent as morally wrong, even as morally evil, leading to a tendency to vilify him or demonize him.

So our main conclusion is that the members of all churches can bring the beliefs of their worldview to bear on the issues of public life as long as these beliefs are lower-order beliefs. For example, the Catholic cardinal of New York can bring arguments from his religious worldview into the debate concerning the moral rights of workers and the treatment of the homeless. The secularist can bring arguments from his secularist worldview into the debate concerning the same issues. On the other hand, the cardinal should not bring his belief in the Eucharist into the public square because this is a higher-order belief. Similarly, those who advance the secularist argument that "abortion should be legal because those who are against it are attempting to deny women the power to make their own decisions" should not bring this belief into the public square because it is a higher-order belief.[14] If there is a dispute about whether a particular belief is higher order or lower order, this also is a matter for the public square, as I indicated earlier. So the phrase "separation of church and state" now means that higher-order beliefs only must be excluded from the public square. Higher-order beliefs might concern such matters as forcing people to pray publicly, preventing people from praying in schools, forcing doctors to learn how to perform abortions

---

[14]The Pulitzer Prize-winning columnist Anna Quindlen made this argument in *Newsweek* in a 2000 column.

and so on. Though what it includes and excludes will itself be part of the debate in the public square.

Indeed, it is necessary to have a full and open public discussion about the beliefs that various worldviews might introduce into the political arena with a view to influencing public policy. This would circumvent the danger of people pretending that their beliefs are lower order when deep down they know that they are really higher order. A secularist might argue, for instance, as if he believes that his view on abortion is really a lower-order belief when deep down he suspects it is actually a higher-order belief. A full public discussion should hopefully bring this pretence to the surface. Our general hope is for reason to prevail in the discussion as much as possible.

A Fictional Example: Form and Content

It might be helpful to consider a fairly detailed example involving an imaginary state in order to show how my arguments above would affect the course of the discussion in the political arena. Let us suppose there exists a state, call it Tran, that is run according to the principles of democracy. It is a state where ninety percent of the population follow a religion called Olim ("religion" in my sense of this term). The situation in this state is that the principles of Olim are the basis of the Constitution, according to the wishes of the majority, on a variety of moral and political issues. For example, in the state of Tran abortion is legal, no prayer is allowed in public places, it is morally obligatory to assist the poor, businesses are carefully regulated, racism is regarded as immoral and is illegal, smoking is illegal, and vegetarianism is mandatory. And so on. There are a few minority groups, corresponding roughly to the other ten percent of the population, who are very upset by the fact that Olim has the advantage in the state of Tran. (A minority group is any group that does not support the beliefs of the majority, especially on those values that have guided public policy and law.) One minority group, in particular, the Coalationists, frequently argue, according to the U.S. model, that one should not be able to enshrine one's religion into the law of the land, and that it is immoral of the Olims to impose their religion on minorities through coercive legislation, some of whom are traditional religious believers, and some of whom follow other religions (i.e., worldviews).

An objection to my position in this book might be that this kind of situation is undesirable and is a good argument against my view because it shows what happens if you allow religion into politics and try to settle matters of public dispute by appeal to a majority vote. Just to take two particular issues in Tran: in the schools, no pupils are allowed to pray to the God of their traditional religion, and all students are taught that homosexual behavior is moral. Isn't this an intolerable situation where the religion of Olim is being imposed on those who disagree with it? Wouldn't it be far better if the state of Tran had a separation of church and state where this could not occur?

One of the main points of my position so far is that one cannot object to the situation in Tran on the grounds that the *form* of the worldview of Olim makes its entry into the public square unacceptable. We have seen that all substantive worldviews have the same form, and so any singling out of a particular religious worldview would be purely arbitrary. The worldview of Olim has played the game entirely fairly here (let us stipulate). They sincerely believe that all of the beliefs they have introduced into the public square are lower-order, rational beliefs; they have debated the issues publicly, in competition with all other substantive worldviews in the state of Tran. They have made every effort to show those who disagree with them that they are reasonable, even if they cannot convince everyone. They have emerged victorious in the public-square debate (in this example, let us also stipulate that they have not appealed to the courts). This is because the majority of people in the state of Tran are convinced that these lower-order beliefs of Olim are correct and good for society. Let us also stipulate that they have granted to those people who do not belong to Olim a substantial realm of personal freedom (e.g., freedom to teach and practice many of their worldview beliefs), within limits. Tran follows democratic principles and is not an oppressive state.

Yet it is possible to make an objection to the beliefs of Olim being placed in the constitution of Tran on the basis of the *content* of those beliefs, and not on the basis of the *form* of the worldview itself. In other words, it is quite acceptable to take issue with one or more of the specific beliefs of Olim and to offer arguments for why it is not appropriate to make those beliefs the basis of coercive legislation. This objection, however, differs from the earlier one because it is not aimed at singling out that worldview as a whole for criticism because of a problem with its form. The objection based on content *politically requires* that one recognize that the worldview of Olim is a legitimate worldview, just as legitimate as any other view, and is therefore entitled to a voice in the debate. So it is appropriate to disagree with a specific belief of Olim and to offer arguments against this belief, but one must recognize that the proponents of Olim are entitled to enter the debate and to argue against the objections.

This is a very significant difference from the original point of the objection, which, being aimed at the form of the view and not the content of its beliefs, *was designed to keep the worldview as a whole out of the debate*. It was suggesting that the worldview of Olim was not an appropriate worldview for entry into political debate. In short, the objection was aimed at achieving a dishonest result. It was aimed at winning the argument about content by simply raising an issue about the form of the worldview. This gives the opponents of the worldview the rhetorical high ground in all areas: they can claim that they have nothing against Olim, it is just that it does not have the right form (but one is free to practice Olim in private); it enables them to keep the beliefs of Olim out of the public square *without* having to debate specific beliefs; it enables them over time to create the impression that bringing beliefs into the public square from a worldview that does not have the right form is inappropriate and even perhaps irrational; and lastly, it enables them to create the impression *among the members of Olim themselves* that their own beliefs are second class and should only be practiced privately. Yet we have seen that this is not a legitimate move and must be rejected by the believers of Olim.

On what grounds could one object to a belief of Olim based on content? One might think, for instance, that a belief of Olim was morally wrong, such as their belief that vegetarianism should be mandatory, something their majority has ensured has happened in Tran. One could object to this on the grounds that vegetarianism is immoral, or that one should at least have a choice about the matter, etc. But one would have to engage the debate in the public square and to persuade the majority of the members of Olim to change their minds on this issue. One could not argue that the view of Olim was a religious view, and that one's own view was not, and so should govern the political arena. It is obvious from all we have said above that any argument like this is deeply flawed.

One could also argue not that a particular belief of the religion of Olim was immoral, but that it was a higher-order belief, according to our understanding of this term in chapter one. This would mean that one was convinced that this particular belief of Olim was based on too much faith for the members of that religion to *reasonably expect* other people to follow this belief. One might feel, depending on how the religion of Olim argues its case, that it might be similar to the Catholic religion placing a belief in the Trinity into the U.S. Constitution. On an objective view of rationality, which we are committed to in this book, I believe this would be a very good argument against putting a particular belief of Olim into the constitution (if it is a higher-order belief). But one would still have to convince the members of Olim that one should not put this belief into the constitution—one would have to convince them that the belief in question *was* a higher-order belief and not a lower-order belief. This, of course, might not be an easy task, but might be doable if the members of Olim were generally reasonable people. As I mentioned earlier, although one's view might be correct from the standpoint of objective rationality and morality, the majority in a democracy will have to decide these issues, and the majority do not always decide correctly. But this is the most rational way to proceed. It is more rational than either excluding a view because of its form or allowing a minority position to regulate the behavior of the majority. (Let us recall that a minority position here is not only a position that a minority of people hold, it is also a position that the majority believes to be unreasonable in some sense.)

A practical problem can arise for any minority view in any democratic state: its members may be forced to live under beliefs and practices they find deeply objectionable. This can occur because the majority adopts laws that some minorities reject (or because the courts, as in the United States, interpret laws to introduce values that many reject and on which they did not have a say).[15] The minority in a case like this may try to change the law, and must hope that citizens are committed to the basic principles of democracy and to the task of trying to show that their views are reasonable to those who disagree with them (the minority, too, must accept these conditions). A state committed to these principles ideally will not impose higher-order beliefs on the minorities. (Of course, it does not always work out this cleanly in practice, but this will be a problem that will affect all worldviews.) So in Tran, ideally, the advocates of Olim in particular, but also the advocates of all other worldviews, would be guided in voting only by lower-order beliefs; judges would not appeal to Olim in their decisions, but only to the law (which is based on lower-order beliefs); and job applicants would not be asked about their religious beliefs. But what absolutely should not happen

---

[15]Except in the United States, of course, it is often the majority, not the minority, that has to live under many controversial laws they find objectionable, as on the matter of prayer in public schools.

is what I have been arguing in this book: *no minority (or majority) view can be excluded simply because its worldview does not have the right "form."*

Another point is worth mentioning before we move on to consider how all of this might affect the terminology of the religion-politics debate. It is theoretically possible for one to object to a particular substantive worldview on the grounds that *all* of its beliefs are higher-order beliefs. All of its beliefs, in other words, require too much faith to make it acceptable to include them in the public square. This initially sounds like one is objecting to a worldview on the basis of its form. Yet it is not. This is because the argument for this objection will have to consist of taking the beliefs of the worldview one by one and showing why each is a higher-order belief, and, of course, one will have to engage the members of the worldview in debate when one is doing this. In short, the objection is not to a particular feature concerning the form of the worldview as a whole, but just to the content of each belief of the worldview, and so it is still an objection based on content.

The reader will have noticed throughout this present section that Olim is a *secularist religion* in the state of Tran. I chose a secularist example deliberately in order to illustrate how problematic it is to discriminate against a particular substantive worldview on the basis of its form alone, and also to further encourage us to think outside the box about religion and politics. It is obvious that Olim closely parallels in some important respects contemporary American secularism and that the arguments for excluding it from the public square are not good arguments. However, *mutatis mutandis,* the arguments for rejecting traditional religious belief from public life are similarly afflicted. One can reread the fictional example again and substitute other worldviews for Olim (for example, the worldview of traditional religion) and other specific beliefs from various worldviews in place of the initial examples in order to illustrate the startling similarity between the forms of worldviews.

As a final example, let us consider a state based primarily on traditional religious principles, where traditional religion is the default view, where secularism is privatized, marginalized, looked upon by many with suspicion, perhaps as inferior, and where secularists have been shamed into restricting their beliefs in political discussion. Let us also suppose that this state has a "freedom of secularism" clause in its constitution that says, "Congress shall make no law respecting an establishment of secularism, or prohibiting the free exercise thereof." Imagine also that many books are published in this state on the topic of "secularism and politics," some arguing that secularism has a role in politics, but most arguing that it does not.

This example shows two things: (1) that traditional religion is the dominant view in this state, and so secularism has to fight for its place in the debate, and (2) that secularism has a legitimate place in the debate unless religious believers can show that secularism is *formally* inferior to religious belief. Secularists will argue that it cannot do this, and so the singling out of secularism in the constitution for special mention (i.e., discrimination) cannot be justified. Similarly, in our current situation today, the reverse is true, of course: secularism is the dominant political view, and traditional religious belief has to fight for its place. But the singling out of traditional religious belief for special discrimination in our democratic society is similarly unjustifiable.

It is appropriate at this point to conclude by looking at the terminology and the language of the whole debate anew and to consider how we might revise many terms and phrases to reflect our new position on the role of religion in politics.

Looking at the World Upside Down: On Revising Our Terminology

There is obviously a well-used set of terms, phrases and concepts to which we continually appeal when talking about religion and politics: *secular, religious, worldview, church, ritual, proselytizing, church and state* and so on. The widespread use of these terms is a good example of the prevalence of this language in our cultural debate about issues of religion, pluralism and worldviews. Yet it should be clear that, in the light of my arguments, we will have to take a careful look at our terminology. In the light of my view that all worldviews can be described as religions and that there are no legitimate reasons for putting traditional religions into a separate category for the purposes of keeping them out of the public debate, it might become necessary to abandon traditional terminology altogether because it only adds to the confusion. Alternatively, we could retain the terminology but redefine it somewhat. There are advantages and disadvantages to both approaches.

In what follows, I will offer suggestions for how we might look at the various terms, concepts and language of the religion-politics debate anew. Let me emphasize that my proposal is only a suggestion, a thought experiment. I am not advocating that we start trying to implement lots of new terminology —the subject of religion and politics in already confusing enough. But one advantage of looking carefully at the terminology and engaging in this thought experiment is that it does help us to think outside the box on religion and politics, and hopefully to further appreciate the arguments of this book. Imagining how our terminology might be changed allows us to look at the beliefs and actions of secularists in the same way that we are all used to looking at the beliefs and actions of religious believers. And this helps us to see clearly the similar structure of both views.

The main advantage to changing some of the traditional terminology is that it would allow us to minimize the confusion this terminology undoubtedly generates, especially in the light of my arguments. Thus, for example, it would be better to replace the word *religion* with the word *worldview*, because this latter term is more neutral. It also enables us to recognize that if a set of beliefs comprises a substantive worldview, then this worldview cannot be arbitrarily discriminated against and treated as if it somehow does not belong to the category of legitimate worldviews. Even leaving the main arguments of this book aside for a moment, it would be advantageous to replace *religion* with *worldview* in many of our discussions today because it would significantly lessen, I believe, the rhetorical force of the attacks on traditional religious belief made in contemporary U.S. society by secularists. For example, instead of the *New York Times* reporting that "the couple is opposed to abortion because of their religion," they could say "the couple is opposed to abortion because of their worldview."

A disadvantage, though, to changing our current terminology is that not only does it have a long tradition and is well established, even entrenched, but by retaining at least some of it and redefining it (as I have been doing) one can more easily see that any formal distinction between religion and secularism is an arbitrary one. One can see that any attempt to isolate traditional religious belief is unacceptable. One can see this if one calls Protestantism a religion and also calls Marxism a religion. Given that they are both religions, one cannot say that federal money, for example, can be used to fund the Marxist religion (say at universities), but not the Protestant religion (say for theology majors or student publications), unless one can show that Marxism is superior in some way that would allow it such preferential treatment. And I have being arguing that one cannot show this.

I am suggesting that perhaps we could retain the terminology but redefine it, and this will help us further illustrate the arbitrary discrimination against the traditional religious worldview that we have seen in the United

States in the last fifty years. This last reason is my main reason for suggesting this approach to the terminology. I will briefly indicate how some of the main terms might be redefined and indicate, where appropriate, how useful our redefinitions will be for illustrating my main arguments in this book. The reader can redefine other terms of interest in a similar fashion. (Perhaps in the long term we could gradually introduce new terminology.)

The obvious terms for redefinition have already been mentioned. The term *religion* refers to any substantive worldview that satisfies the definition in chapter one. Hence, evangelical Protestantism, Marxism, Catholicism, Judaism, Islam and Secularism are all religions. A "church" will now refer to any group that promotes a particular worldview. The group can be somewhat loosely defined and need not be long established or well organized, though many churches will have these features. On the new definition, the cardinals, bishops and priests of the Catholic Church, the leaders of the Communist Party of America, the leaders of the Christian Coalition, the editorial writers of the *New York Times*,[16] the members of the Executive Committee of the ACLU, and the philosophers, scientists and psychologists mentioned in chapter two, would all be part of "churches." Churches in many different worldviews might promote similar beliefs on a particular issue (e.g., that the state should provide substantial support for the homeless), but this should not lead to confusion about the meaning of the word *church*.

The term *priests* might now describe individuals whose main job is to promote a particular worldview or who are regarded as spokespersons or special authorities for a particular worldview; many of these, though not all, will belong to churches. So, Pope Benedict, Billy Graham, the editorial board of the *New York Times,* the late naturalist Carl Sagan, the executive director of the ACLU, and secularists Steven Pinker, Richard Dawkins and Thomas Nagel are all priests in the crucial sense that they significantly promote a particular worldview. The specific ways in which they do this are not important at this point. Nor is it important whether they want to convince people to adopt their worldview, to follow part of their worldview, to merely tolerate their worldview, to vote according to their worldview, or to legislate on the basis of their worldview. I have discussed most of these points above, but the crucial matter is that priests are people who promote their particular

---

[16]For an overview of the worldview of the *New York Times,* see William Proctor, *The Gospel According to The New York Times: How the World's Most Powerful News Organization Shapes Your Mind and Values* (Nashville: Broadman & Holman, 2000).

worldview in some significant way. The word *proselytize* will also have to be redefined somewhat. Although it is not a word that is used exclusively of religion, it is used mainly of religion, often in a pejorative sense. When we say that someone is proselytizing we generally are making an accusation, implicitly criticizing their actions. This word might now refer to anyone advancing a worldview with passion and commitment aimed at bringing in new converts, an approach that would justify describing it as proselytizing and not simply as promoting the religion in question (indeed today this word is beginning to have this more general application).

To describe a person as "very religious" would mean that he was very committed in thought and action to his worldview. A "holy Joe" (or a "holy Mary"), a pejorative phrase, is used in my home country, Ireland, to describe a member of a traditional religion who is overly pious in a somewhat naive, strict way! This could now be extended to describe anyone who holds and practices a religion in this way. Thus we might describe a person who has an overly pious, strict way of practicing secularism, or who is excessively politically correct, as a "holy Joe"! Indeed, offending against political correctness is now the secularist version of blasphemy. The word *ritual* will also have to be extended, as I indicated in chapter one, to include the practices of not only traditional religions, but of all religions. Thus, some secularist rituals might include candlelight vigils (instead of prayer vigils), enjoying the *New York Times* editorial page as a source of spiritual edification, celebrating Darwin Day,[17] listening to various types of music, sending solstice cards at morally and politically significant times of the year, watching certain TV shows, attending monthly meetings of various secularist societies, contemplating the majesty and beauty of the universe, perhaps even eating and drinking certain types of food.

The meaning of the word *secular* could also be revised. Its original meaning intended to describe a worldview that was not religious; then it came to refer to affairs of the world. More recently it has been used to implicitly distinguish secularism from traditional religions *in terms of their form*. But there is no distinction between traditional religion and other religions in terms of form, and so the word *secular* will now simply refer to the religion of secularism. The terms *secularism* and *secularist* will be understood in the same

---

[17]Although officially, Darwin Day, February 12 (Darwin's birthday), is not intended to promote atheism or secularism and is not perhaps aimed at criticizing religion, it is undoubtedly used for both of these purposes by many of those who celebrate it.

way. Perhaps, as I suggested in chapter two, it would simply be better to replace *secular* with *secularist*. "Secularist believers" would obviously be an accurate, timely new term. In the future we might also come to identify some as devout or as strict secularists. (Perhaps we will even see secularist names for children, such as Atheist Smith and Secularist Jones, just as we got Liberal in the nineteenth century, a Kansas town—founded for atheists— where many streets are named after atheists and secularists!)

We might refer to some of our major universities or media outlets (accurately) as "the secularist belt," and no doubt some professors would be "secularist fanatics," on a crusade promoting (irrational) secularist dogmas! (This language is regularly used to describe religious believers.) A host of other terms could be redefined in the same way. We could redefine the phrase "religious bigotry" to include bigotry against any worldview, or "sectarian" to describe the stance of any worldview. We should also distinguish between academic secularism (the study of secularism) and confessional secularism (the advocacy of secularism) in the way that we distinguish between academic religion and confessional religion. This distinction is long overdue given the tendency of secular organizations, especially universities, toward political and moral advocacy. We might also usefully refer to any state that is based on a secularist ideology as a "seculocracy," as suggested in chapter two, just as we sometimes call a state based on a religious ideology a theocracy.

Several newspapers reported on unrest in India in March 2002 under headlines like "Religious Rioting Shakes India." This might give rise to similar headlines about secularism, such as "Secularist Rioting Shakes Seattle" (in reports on the violence surrounding the summit meetings of the large industrial nations there a few years ago[18]), or perhaps "Secularist Rioting a Feature of Antiwar Protests." We could also rewrite the phrase "he got religion" or questions like "does your family always talk about religion?" a line spoken by Charles Ryder in Evelyn Waugh's novel *Brideshead Revisited*. In fact, reading *Brideshead Revisited* (or any work that deals with matters of traditional religion, or with religious and secularist worldviews side by side) in terms of the issues of this book and substituting the word *worldview* for the word *religion* in various passages and making other appropriate terminological substitutions would be highly instructive in terms of the theses of this book.

---

[18]We did get the headline "Edinburgh Braced for Violence as Anarchists Come Flooding In" as groups of anarchists ran amok through the streets of Edinburgh, Scotland, during the summer 2005 G8 economic summit. See *The Times* (London), July 4, 2005.

I hope I have said enough to illustrate that the redefinition of terminology is suggestive, illuminating and intriguing!

We have looked from a more practical point of view at the question of which religious beliefs can be introduced into politics, according to the views I have been arguing for in earlier chapters. We have considered the implications of my position for the various areas in which public arguments are often presented, and looked in particular at the relationship between church and state. We found it helpful also to look at how my arguments would work in a fictional state, Tran, before finally giving the terminology of the debate a closer look in its own right. We must now move on to consider some specific topics relating to worldview debates in the political arena in U.S. society.

8

Pluralism, Relativism and Religious Debates

American Style

It is now time to look at the relationship between religion and politics in a particular society, time to apply our ideas to some often contentious topics that come up in American society. This will help us to see how the views expressed in earlier chapters would apply in an actual society on some specific issues. We have answered the moral question concerning the relationship between religion and politics in a democracy, as it were, so now we can apply our conclusions to some concrete cases in which we have a special interest, including school prayer, euthanasia and other moral issues, the display of traditional religious symbols in public places, and the significant presence of moral relativism in American culture. Before doing that, however, we need to briefly describe the particular form of political society in contemporary America. Many would see American political society as secular, liberal, pluralist and democratic. I will therefore begin with a critical overview of these concepts as they define the form of pluralism that has shaped American society and will briefly comment on how these concepts will have to be adjusted to satisfy our earlier arguments.

In my description of American pluralism, I am thinking mainly of the conventional wisdom regarding pluralism—the dominant way of thinking about pluralism in the United States. How does U.S. society understand itself as a pluralist society? In chapters four and five, I looked at philosophical arguments for keeping religion out of politics in a democratic society. In what follows, I am interested primarily in how the legal question *should* be an-

swered (not how it is currently answered) in a democratic society in the light
of our earlier answer to the philosophical question.

American Pluralism

Some people would say that although the American people are quite religious, America is nevertheless a thoroughly secular society, especially in the
establishment classes, its government, public institutions, intelligentsia, media, judiciary and so forth. As sociologist Peter Berger famously put it, if India is the most religious nation in the world, and Sweden is the most secular,
then the United States is a nation of Indians ruled by a nation of Swedes!
But what does it mean to describe American society as a secular society? Perhaps a number of points are intended. One is that American society is not a
theocracy—it does not promote a state-established traditional religion. A
second point conveyed is that political figures do not usually run for office
(at least overtly) on a traditional religious agenda but on a secular agenda.
The president and members of Congress are often described as "secular officials." The third point conveyed is that religion should play little or no role
in public life, in debates and analyses concerning public policies, social programs, moral issues and social problems.

From the point of view of my perspective in this book, one can see that
these points are problematic and will have to be modified if my arguments
are accepted. First off, it is not quite true to say that American society is not
a theocracy, if my analysis in this book is correct. To be a theocracy, a state
has to promote one particular religious view over others; it has to favor one
particular view in its institutions, laws, policies, etc. If one says that America
is not a theocracy and one means by this that we at least aspire to the position that no particular beliefs, views or values of a traditional religion are
favored in public life over others, then it is true that America is not a theocracy. But this is not all there is to say about the matter. American society
aspires—at least historically—to a kind of consensus religion or worldview
based on as wide an agreement as possible about the lower-order beliefs of
many different worldviews, and it is perhaps possible to describe *this* view,
upon which the state is founded, as a worldview in itself, or at least *as a set
of values that the state promotes.*[1] But the word *theocracy* is one of those

---

[1]Alasdair MacIntyre, *Whose Justice? Which Rationality?* (Notre Dame, Ind.: University of Notre
 Dame Press, 1988), pp. 326-48, has developed the view that liberalism can be looked upon
 as a tradition that shapes society.

words that we will have to think of defining more broadly; perhaps it should now refer to the promotion of a part of a worldview (any worldview) in law or in the conventional practice of the state at the expense of or in preference to other worldviews. Since American society (and indeed any state, by definition almost) does this, it could be described as a theocracy in the sense that the values it promotes are *established*. The state is always promoting some values at the expense of others, and so can always be described as a "theocracy," no matter which worldview is being promoted (or established). But since the word has explicit theological origins and reference, it might be better to dispense with it altogether for now, at least when talking about American society. As mentioned earlier, we can refer to a state where it is primarily secularism that is established in law as a "seculocracy." Some may deny that the state establishes some values at the expense of others by arguing that the state is really neutral between worldviews and values, but I have shown in earlier chapters that such arguments are not plausible.

Another significant feature of American society is that it is a pluralist democracy, meaning that there are several different worldviews in the state: traditional religions, secularist religions, various cultures, ethnic groups, political ideologies, many of which overlap in important ways. There are often disagreements and conflicts among the separate worldviews on certain matters. On the view I have been developing in this book, we must be careful to keep in mind the distinction between lower- and higher-order beliefs when talking about pluralism. In particular, we need to ask, where should a *particular* worldview, worldview A, stand on the issue of pluralism itself on my analysis? Would the proponents of worldview A welcome pluralism, be a supporter of it, or would they be suspicious of pluralism? I think that proponents of worldview A should welcome pluralism. They should welcome a diversity of views in the discussion, especially concerning the truth status of lower-order (rational) beliefs. This is because they value, *as part of their worldview*, free speech, rational, open discussion and debate, and the search for truth and understanding. And, as John Stuart Mill noted, even if one strongly believes one's view is true, it can still be strengthened and invigorated in the clash with error. So for these reasons the members of worldview A should welcome a plurality of views in the debate. Sometimes vigorous public debate can lead one to new insights and perhaps to even change one's position or values on a particular question, or even to convert to another worldview. We should at least recognize that many worldviews have some good insights, even if wrong in important respects, and even if we could not finally adopt them.

It is worth emphasizing a point that is clear from our discussion above, that pluralism *itself* is not a worldview, but beliefs about pluralism are a *part* of one's worldview. How significant a part depends on the nature of the worldview in question. To say that one is a pluralist is just to say that the values relating to pluralism (the existence of, tolerance of and healthy debate between worldviews) are part of one's worldview. If one gives considerable weight to pluralist values in one's worldview, one is more likely to be sympathetic toward other worldviews that are flexible themselves and critical of worldviews that are not flexible. How much weight one should give to pluralist values is obviously a crucial question for each worldview. One popular argument for giving strong weight to these values in contemporary political theory, as we have seen in our discussion of Rawls, is a general skepticism about knowledge (Perry's "fallibilism," mentioned in the previous chapter). This particular argument for religious pluralism is unlikely to be acceptable to most people outside the intellectual classes. This is not just because most people have little time for skepticism, but because those who advocate this skepticism usually go on to contradict themselves, like Perry and Rawls.[2]

The fact that pluralist values are just a part of one's worldview explains why one may be a strong supporter of pluralism yet still hold that certain worldviews *cannot* be pursued in a free society. This is because the values that pluralists advocate concerning how the debate between various worldviews is to be conducted are put forward as objectively true values, and if one disagrees with them, then one is wrong, and, according to the supporter of pluralism, there is no place for one's dissenting values in the debate. The pluralist advocate will also hold that some of his own moral beliefs should

---

[2]As I pointed out in earlier chapters, there is a skeptical, relativistic tendency in those attracted to liberal political theory, manifested in the paradox of denying that it is possible to achieve objective knowledge on the one hand and then going on to regulate the public-square debate according to (their own) privileged values. Here is a passage representative of this approach from Kent Greenawalt: "In actual life, disentangling realist arguments from arguments based on shared social principles is largely impossible. People in any society lack the self-transcendence to understand which arguments are grounded only in shared assumptions and which are grounded in the nature of things and are true, independent of what most people at that time and place happen to think is right" (*Private Consciences and Public Reasons* [New York: Oxford University Press, 1995], p. 29). Notice that Greenawalt himself in this passage seems to achieve the self-transcendence that he thinks is largely impossible! He is able to do something that he thinks most people can't do: transcend his own social situation to discover objective knowledge!

be established in law. So, for instance, if an advocate of pluralism holds that there should be freedom of religion in a state then the position that there should be no freedom of religion is not welcome in that state because it contradicts one of the values of liberal pluralism and so must be rejected (though it can be expressed, of course). Similarly, if he holds that drug taking should be illegal, then the view that drug taking should not be illegal must be rejected. And so, despite rhetoric to the contrary, supporters of pluralism do not tolerate *all* views. In our discussion of Rawls's political theory, we saw how he develops his theory to attempt to impose *the values of liberal pluralism itself* (which are a part of his own worldview) on those who disagree with them *without arguing for those values,* and without allowing all worldviews (especially religious worldviews) an equal voice in the debate. Further, Rawls's *version* of these values (which is what many reject today who disagree with him, rather than the values themselves) prejudices the outcome of the discussion, especially concerning the role of religion in politics, as we have seen.

American society is democratic because its political leaders and president are freely elected by the people and are accountable to and answerable to the people. The notion of democracy carries with it the implication that the voices of as many people as possible should be heard, especially in public debates over political, social and legal topics. We have noted that the majority can make a mistake in a democracy and vote for the wrong laws, for laws that are immoral or irrational or both. This is one of the risks in a democracy. The great virtue of a democracy is that the majority get to vote on the most important issues; that way we do not have a minority deciding what is good for the majority. For if the majority can be wrong, so can the minority. It is also a virtue of democracy that the minority gets to try to persuade the majority of the rightness of their views, can attempt to get the majority to adopt their views and to make them the basis of the law. As noted in chapter seven, democracies have tended to handle the issue of minority rights by setting out in law a specific area of personal freedom within which the state (i.e., the majority) will not normally interfere.

American pluralism is liberal in the sense that it tends to place great emphasis on values associated with democracy: freedom, equality and justice. It places emphasis on the civil and political rights of the individual, and consequently supports a substantial realm of personal freedom for the individual, such as freedom of speech, freedom of association and freedom of traditional religion.[3] The conventional liberal position is that the state cannot interfere in these areas of personal preference, except to prevent one from harming others. When an action can be said to harm others has been interpreted narrowly by the U.S. courts. In debates about TV violence, changing sexual morality, whether the Internet should be censored, liberals usually side with the individual engaged in controversial activities and not with the person allegedly being harmed by them. Perhaps a defining feature of American liberalism, in the debate between the freedom of the individual and the common good, at least as it pertains to moral issues, is that the liberal sides completely (and often loudly) with the individual, and often at the expense of the common good. This general tendency is evident in John Rawls's political liberalism and dominates much of contemporary political thinking. It has influenced the work of thinkers such as Ronald Dworkin, Isaiah Berlin and others, and versions of it can be traced back to John Locke.[4]

This liberal approach now dominates modern societies, not just modern American society. Indeed, most of us would accept some version of these values as part of our own worldview. Yet we must note that there is a strand of liberal thinking whose proponents hold more extreme views on freedom, pluralism and relativism, and it is fair, I believe, to say that those who identify with this strand see themselves as enlightened about politics and society. When I use the term *enlightened* I do not simply mean that *opponents* of the extreme version of pluralism describe its proponents as enlightened (in a pejorative sense), a charge that might flatter the proponents, and that they could easily shrug off as a cheap shot from a disaffected adversary. No, I mean to draw attention to the fact that many proponents of modern pluralism *describe themselves* as enlightened; they see themselves as holding the progressive, modern, tolerant, forward-looking view on politics and society (they are more uncomfortable with using the word *true* to describe their views, for obvious reasons). They also regard their opponents as backward-looking, old-fashioned, intolerant and out of touch with the needs of our changing times, and frequently portray them as such. In fact, a quite significant part of the contemporary argument for liberal pluralism involves a mostly rhetorical appeal to what an enlightened view it is. It is fair, I think,

---

[3]Of course, most Western societies support a similar realm of freedom, which might come as a surprise to at least some American politicians who often talk as if the United States were the only country in the world that supports freedom!

[4]For an overview of this position and its difficulties, see the various essays in Michael Sandel, ed., *Liberalism and its Critics* (New York: New York University Press, 1984).

to therefore include this point in our brief description of liberal pluralism. To regard oneself as holding the enlightened view on momentous matters of politics, law and religion, however, carries with it a danger. One may be tempted toward intolerance (even fanaticism), to regard one's opponent's views as inferior or as not worthy of debate. This can lead to the desire to promote a seculocracy—one may try to impose one's "enlightened" views on others by means of coercive legislation, without giving those who deny these views due regard or a fair hearing.

Another feature of American society I wish to mention here but will analyze later in detail is a pervasive *relativism* in American life. Moral relativism is the view that moral values are not absolute in themselves but are relative either to the society or to the individual. Relativism has taken a great hold on the contemporary American mind. The view that the individual chooses his or her own moral values, based upon whatever criteria he/she likes—feeling, emotion, peer pressure—and that nobody else can say one is wrong, nobody can impose one's moral values on another, forms an influential part of many people's current approach to moral questions. Although relativism is fraught with serious problems, it plays an increasingly significant role in our religious, moral and political life, so much so that I will focus on its various attractions, strategies and problems in the last sections of the chapter. For now I simply want to emphasize that the public debate in America is often conducted *against a background of moral relativism,* and so an understanding of the phenomenon of relativism will help us to understand—from a more practical point of view—the dynamics of current public-square debates in modern liberal societies.

Given this general background set of reflections on U.S. society, we must now consider some specific issues that are often the subject of contentious public debate to see how the arguments of this book might apply to them.

School Prayer

Let us first take the issue of prayer in the public schools. The subject of controversy has been over whether or not some form of organized prayer should be allowed in public schools where many of the children come from different worldviews and where the school itself (and the state) is not supposed to be advocating any particular worldview, though it clearly does advocate values that are part of various worldviews (and that exclude their opposites).

Organized prayer has not been allowed in public schools in the United States since the 1960s, when the atheist Madalyn Murray O'Hair, founder of the political advocacy group American Atheists, brought a federal court case (*Murray* v. *Curlett,* 1963) against school prayer and found a sympathetic judiciary. The Supreme Court's decision to ban organized prayer in public schools was and continues to be controversial, with many traditional religious believers baffled by it and only going along with it reluctantly. Indeed, polls show that a good majority of the American people support prayer in public schools. Yet it is true that over the past forty years or so many religious believers have come round to accepting the court decision. Perhaps the overt motivation behind O'Hair's lawsuit was the First Amendment to the U.S. Constitution, which prohibits a theocracy. The covert motivation was surely her atheism; she did not want any view contrary to her own being openly expressed in public schools. After her successful court challenge, the First Amendment no-establishment clause increasingly came to be interpreted to mean that allowing a prayer in school, even a nondenominational, voluntary prayer, would amount to an establishment of religion by the state, something the Constitution forbids. Following a succession of court cases,[5] this gradually mushroomed into the view that religion has little or no place, not just in public schools, but in politics. We have moved from "freedom of religion" to a position that some have been tempted to call "freedom from religion"!

Supporters of prayer in public schools usually argue that allowing a prayer would not represent the establishment of a religion by the state, but simply the state's facilitation of a specific ritual of traditional religious worldviews. Opponents of school prayer offer a second argument against it as well, in addition to O'Hair's constitutional argument. This is the more philosophical argument that if school prayer is allowed it would amount to allowing a traditional religious view to impose its beliefs on others who are not of that religion, and that this is immoral. Supporters reply that the prayer would be nondenominational, voluntary and so on, that nobody would be coerced to say the prayer. Opponents of school prayer are against school prayer even in those cases where everyone in a class (or a school) is a member of the same traditional religion (including even the teacher).

Before we analyze this issue in the light of the view I have been defending in this book, we need to remind ourselves that we are not interested in

---

[5]See Stephen L. Carter, *God's Name in Vain* (New York: Basic Books, 2000), p. 224.

the question of the proper interpretation of the U.S. Constitution. I am interested in the (moral) question of whether some form of *organized, voluntary* prayer should be allowed in public schools (and in other areas of public life) in a democratic, pluralist society. The traditional distinction between church and state is too simplistic, as I have shown, and would now be best revised to mean the separation of "worldviews and state." Therefore, to claim that traditional religions cannot be promoted in public places, including schools, because they are "religious" is to discriminate against traditional religion arbitrarily. The argument that organized, voluntary prayer should not be allowed in public schools puts traditional religious worldviews in one category and secularist views in a different category, and it suggests that the latter are superior to the former. I have argued at length that this kind of move is logically flawed.

Secularists cannot consistently claim that their view is neutral, that they are not really advocating any worldview or set of values, but are merely saying that they are treating all traditional religions equally and neither discriminating against any of them nor promoting their own view. This is because establishing a classroom where prayer is not allowed (and by extension a school where religion is greatly diminished), for all practical purposes advances the view of secularism.[6] The practical result of the elimination of prayer from the schoolroom is to advance the worldview in which prayer plays no role, namely, secularism. As John Courtney Murray said in commenting on the earlier *McCollum* v. *Board of Education* (1948) supreme court decision that went against school prayer, "In what direction will this decision press and push and move American society, especially the institution of the school? And I answer: In the direction of secularism."[7] Francis Canavan has pointed out that "when the state teaches only secular subjects from a secular point of view in its schools, it willy-nilly favors those of its citizens who regard religion as irrelevant to life and believe that all human problems have purely human and secular answers."[8]

---

[6]Kent Greenawalt struggles with this point in his defense of no prayer in public schools. See his *Religious Convictions and Political Choice* (New York: Oxford University Press, 1988), p. 197-202.

[7]John Courtney Murray, "A Common Enemy, A Common Cause," (published posthumously) in *First Things,* 26, October 1992, p. 34.

[8]Francis Canavan, *The Pluralist Game* (Lanham, Md.: Rowman & Littlefield, 1995), p. 2; see also pp. 17-25 for an insightful discussion of supreme court decisions on school prayer and classroom Bible reading.

Banning organized school prayer is to turn schools into secularist zones, or zones where the secularist approach to reality is the presumptive worldview. One cannot claim that the presence of a ritual of a worldview (prayer) has political significance but that the absence of this ritual has no political significance. *This is because the absence of this ritual represents a significant action of a particular worldview in the same culture, namely, secularism.* In U.S. society, not saying a prayer in certain contexts carries just as much significance as saying a prayer, because it is revelatory about a person's worldview in an ideological (not just an informative) sense, and has *political significance.* Let us not forget that secularists often have as one of their key beliefs that "thou shalt not promote your religious values in public arenas."[9] In this sense, a school that is in effect a religion-free zone sends the message that traditional religion can be relegated to a private realm and that secularism should be the presumptive view.

A school in which religion is diminished advances the worldview of secularism and is not neutral, as I have said, but it can do so in a number of ways. It might not advance secularism in an overt way. That is to say, the teacher will not usually actively promote secularism in the classroom (except by forbidding prayer), or denigrate religion openly (though one might recall the ACLU lawsuit that forced a high school teacher to remove his personal Bible from his desk in case the students would see it).[10] Indeed, many of the teachers will be members of a traditional religion and will simply be following the law, a law they might not agree with. Forbidding school prayer may well advance secularism in a covert way, either intentionally or unintentionally. While the secularist does not require overt teaching of secularism in forbidding school prayer, he still promotes the view that religious beliefs have no place in the public arena, a key belief of his worldview and a belief that, if generally adopted by society, *would automatically promote secularism.* In addition, as we saw in our discussion of secular reason in chapter four, to create an environment in which religious arguments can play no role (such as in a newspaper editorial page or in a public school

---

[9]I owe this way of formulating the point to Fr. Bill LaCroix, S.J.

[10]See Stephen L. Carter, *The Culture of Disbelief: How American Law and Politics Trivialize Religious Devotion* (New York: Doubleday, 1993), pp. 11-12. The school was also forced to remove books on Christianity that the teacher had given to the school library, despite the fact that the library had books on other religions. See Carter's book for an excellent overview of the discrimination against religion in American politics, including discussion of current controversies.

classroom) is to advance the secularist worldview. And this is to discriminate against traditional religious views without good reason. It is to promote the view that there is something odd or inferior about traditional religion.

Of course, it is essential to point out that it would be quite appropriate and legitimate for a secularist to object to the school prayer on the basis of its *content*. As we have seen in the case of Tran in chapter seven, a secularist could object to a particular prayer or to any form of prayer in school, as long as he attempted to give specific arguments explaining why the content of the prayer was inappropriate. But it is not appropriate to argue against school prayer on the basis of the form of that worldview of which prayer is a part; one cannot simply object to prayer in school because it is religious, as we have seen. However, a secularist might, for instance, object to a particular prayer because he believed it to be irrational, or because he believed it to involve primarily higher-order beliefs, or because it was a denominational prayer in a school class of many denominations. These points might form the basis for legitimate objections. Yet the key issue about them is that the secularist must allow his opponents to be *a part of the debate as well*. Indeed the religious believer might well insist that a voluntary, nondenominational form of prayer is best in schools, and agree with the secularist argument that nonvoluntary prayers would be an *unreasonable imposition* (just as religious believers think that forbidding prayer altogether is an unreasonable imposition). But this question would have to be part of the public debate; it should not be decided in advance on the grounds that there is something wrong with religious beliefs. The whole point of the legal church and state distinction, especially the way it is used today in American society, is to avoid any discussion over content by restricting traditional religious views on the basis of their form.

Display of Traditional Religious Symbols in Public Places

Let us now turn to the question of the display of traditional religious symbols in public places, and more generally to the question of displaying symbols from any worldview in public places. Let us take the case of a town where the people decided at a meeting of the town council to display a Christian cross in the middle of the town square, according to the wishes of the majority who live in the town. Some will argue that this is unacceptable because the state is being used to promote one particular traditional religion over all of the others, and this violates the Constitution. I have pointed out that the interpretation of the U.S. Constitution is a secondary matter and that we are mainly looking at the philosophical question (or to put the issue another way: we are looking at the moral point that *should* be driving the constitutional point). Yet the secularist's *philosophical (or moral)* argument against displaying the crosses is an interesting one: that it is wrong because it marginalizes the members of some worldviews; it suggests that one worldview is better than the others. Some will also argue that if the cross is removed, this simply means that the state is *neutral* between different worldviews, and should not be interpreted to mean that the state is endorsing a *different* worldview.

We have seen above that the state, by definition, cannot be neutral between worldviews but must always endorse some of the beliefs of particular worldviews, by virtue of the fact that it enshrines a set of values in its laws, which are then imposed on all citizens. This is not altered by the fact that the state may seek to reach a consensus position on as many of these values as possible, because the values will still be promulgated *in law*. But on the matter of not allowing the display of a cross in the town square, the state is really advocating a position, as in the school prayer case above. The state really indicates that it endorses the belief that traditional religious views in general cannot be promoted publicly, and that view will be reflected in the prohibition of symbols of traditional religious views in public. This is tantamount to promoting a key belief of the secularist worldview in the laws of the land and to forcing this belief on others through coercive legislation in the crucial sense that they will have to live according to it. So it is not a neutral view.

In short, one cannot consistently claim that to display a Christian cross publicly is to promote a part of a worldview in law, but that not to display any cross is not to promote a part of a worldview, especially since the *absence* of the cross indicates a particular worldview in our culture (viz. secularism), as I pointed out in the above section on school prayer. (Imagine if all the members of the town council were secularists and passed a law to ban all crosses in the town; or imagine if a particular group of atheists petitioned a court to ban crosses and won.) Such an argument is simply a case of special pleading by the proponents of secularism for the superiority of their worldview. It is really an attempt to promote their worldview at the expense of traditional religious belief, without offering any argument in support of it. Of course, there may well be religious believers on the town council, but if they vote to ban the display of religious symbols they are allowing a secularist belief to trump their religious beliefs whenever the two clash. (Let us remind ourselves that, for the sake of avoiding unnecessary tediousness, I am using the secularist's arguments as representative of all arguments for excluding religious beliefs from politics, including those of some religious believers.)

If the absence of crosses or other traditional religious symbols in general in a state is part of a significant worldview in that state, then if one succeeds in passing laws banning such displays, one is inevitably promoting secularism. It is interesting to compare our situation on this matter today with the situation a couple of centuries ago. At that time, secularism was not a significant worldview in the sense that it had very few adherents, no public voice and little influence on politics and society. In that kind of cultural environment one perhaps could make a case for the conclusion that if the government decided to ban the public display of overt, recognizable symbols of *all* worldviews, this might not be understood as the promotion of secularism at the expense of all traditional religions. But today in our society where secularism is a significant worldview with a strong and dominant voice in the public square and much influence on matters of law and politics, it is surely the case that if a major symbol of this worldview is made the law of the land the practical effect is to promote this worldview at the expense of all the others. (And let us not overlook the point that secularism may well have *positive* symbols in the future, such as, for example, using the seasonal greeting "Happy Holidays" instead of "Happy Christmas!")

We also need to emphasize that if one insists that when the state prohibits the public display of the symbols of traditional religions, that we should not interpret this to mean that the state is promoting the worldview of secularism, but rather that the state is neutral, that this argument can be turned around. One could plausibly argue that the state could allow the promotion of traditional religious symbols, as long as the state *makes it widely known* (say in court judgments or in congressional legislation) that this does not mean that the state endorses symbols of different worldviews. This would also apply to cases of displaying the Ten Commandments. The state could allow such displays as long as it was somehow made clear that this does not mean the state is necessarily endorsing the worldview of which the display is a part. It does not follow from this that the state would have to allow the display of all such symbols. Symbols that have much public support, or perhaps that were very influential in the establishment of the state, or that express many of the values widely held in the state might inevitably receive some preference. But only in the sense that they can be displayed, not necessarily that they are endorsed by the state.

A secularist might reply by saying there is an advantage in prohibiting a display that is lost by allowing a display. Since there will always be someone in a town who does not support the worldview whose symbol might be on display in the town square, the banning of all such displays will forestall the suggestion that the state supports a view that some do not hold. I think an effective reply to this objection is that, first, the state could make it clear that it supports *none* of these worldviews (as a whole), and, second, that by not allowing any displays one is forcing a key belief of a particular worldview upon those who do not agree with it. In this case, one is forcing a key belief of a minority view, secularism, on a majority who disagree with it. This is complicated in U.S. society by the fact that many religious believers allow their thinking on this question to be decided by appeal to recent court interpretations of the Constitution and not on the philosophical or moral issues involved. In fact, many allow their thinking on the constitutional question to *dictate* their thinking on the philosophical question, therefore putting the cart before the horse.

As in the case of school prayer, one can always object to a *particular* display of symbols in public places on the grounds that their content is unacceptable, for a variety of reasons. One could claim that the display is morally offensive, irrational or unsuitable for some other reason. But as already pointed out one must be prepared to debate this point with the proponents of the display and not try to rule their view out of order arbitrarily. Thus one could object to a display of a Christian cross in a public square because the town contains many Muslims. This might be a good objection, since the cross is a clear symbol of the Christian religion and since it might give offense to many Muslims, who might think their religion was second class in the town. One would have to consider the cultural context in the town and whether it was reasonable for Muslims to think that their view was second class, and one would have to find out if there were *actual* objections to the display (rather than, say, outside, secularist, ACLU-led, legally based objections).

One could extend this argument to cover cases where everyone in the town belonged to a particular religion, but where many of the thousands of visitors to the town each year did not and so forth. But even this type of argument *would have to take account of the culture in question*. It could be that many people would like to see evidence of religious belief in public, even if it is not their own religion. One might try to persuade the majority in the town to forbid public displays of religious symbols on some of these grounds. But note that this would not prevent all the worldviews from agreeing that a nondenominational or even multidenominational religious symbol could be placed in the town square. The second issue is that it would not prevent a town where everyone was a member of a certain worldview from displaying the symbols of that view publicly. Again the argument about content is appropriate, but it cannot be used to ban traditional religion *in general* from the public square.

Yet the issue is still more complicated than this, as arguments concerning religion and politics always are. If one argues on the basis of content that it is unfair or morally offensive or unsuitable for some other reason for the majority to display a prominent religious symbol in a town where there is a significant minority with a different view, one will have to convince the majority of the truth of one's content-based argument. This will involve convincing them that the cross will make people feel uncomfortable, or perhaps that the public display of the cross might involve higher-order beliefs of their religion. It will also involve convincing them that this particular kind of discomfort is something they should be concerned about enough to prevent them from displaying publicly symbols of their worldview. (After all, many other laws and displays in the town make some citizens uncomfortable, for instance, the toll-road fee, the law allowing smoking in restaurants, the law against abortion, laws requiring that all people be treated equally in business practices, residential property laws, adverts promoting safe sex, etc.) The secularist can raise many reasonable points on these matters, and the strength of the arguments will depend on the exact nature of the cases involved. But the main point is that the secularist cannot rule any worldview (here the traditional religious worldview) out of order *arbitrarily* because of its form. The secularist must debate all of the issues on the basis of their content, and must respect the majority decision on these issues (even if he thinks it's wrong, which, of course, it could be).

Perhaps we can illustrate this last point more clearly with an example. Suppose we had a town that had a majority of Ku Klux Klan members, and the majority voted to put a symbol of the Klan in the town square. In addition, suppose that a significant minority in the town are fundamentally opposed to the worldview of the Ku Klux Klan. This is an interesting case to consider not just because it seems morally repugnant to allow the display of the symbol, but also because the KKK is *not* a traditional religious worldview. It might seem that in this case, according to my view, the minority must try to persuade the majority of its views, and that until it succeeds, the KKK can display its symbols. However this is not the case, as I illustrated in chapter seven. On the view that I have been arguing for, the KKK belief that some people are superior to others is morally wrong. I believe my view on this matter should be enshrined in the law of the nation. I hold that this is a lower-order belief of my worldview, and therefore I can introduce it into public arguments and try to get it adopted as the law of the land (and so would apply to this particular town as well). In this way, I would ban the KKK from acting on this belief in any public situation in their town. I would be inclined not to ban them from *expressing* their view at least in some types of public expression for the reasons I gave in a previous chapter. Of course, I could still lose this argument in the sense of not being able to convince a majority in the nation as a whole of its truth (though this is very unlikely), but that is a price of democracy.

Religion and Moral Issues: The Euthanasia Debate in Oregon

We turn now to consider the relationship between traditional religion and moral issues in public-square debates in a democratic society. I will briefly consider the case of the euthanasia debate in Oregon in 1997 as an example of a debate in U.S. society where the traditional religious worldview played a role. In this debate, the pro-euthanasia side consistently portrayed the anti-euthanasia view as being a traditional religious view, and they appealed to the constitutional argument that one should not try to impose one's religious beliefs on everyone else. Of course, there were other arguments too, but this was one of the main arguments. It also had great rhetorical power, so much so that the Catholic Church in particular, but also other churches, took something of a back seat in the debate and did not present the arguments against euthanasia from a position of strength and confidence. We often see the same strategy used throughout the country in the debates concerning abortion and gay marriage, to mention just two other examples. In short, the arguments against euthanasia, abortion and gay marriage are frequently portrayed as religious arguments, and the arguments in favor of these practices are portrayed as secular, neutral arguments. The traditional religious arguments are then ruled out of order because of the legal separation of church and state, so the secularist side claims the rhetorical high ground on the issue of *form* without having to significantly engage the argument about the actual *content* of the questions under discussion. However, one does not have to be a philosopher to see that there is something fishy about the pro-euthanasia tactic—that the main argument for euthanasia is legitimate, but the main argument against it is illegitimate!

It should be obvious on my view that this strategy is seriously flawed, misleading, and it discriminates against religious views. Since I have already discussed the reasons in detail above, I will simply summarize them here and in the examples that follow. First, *all* arguments on these matters are "religious," in the sense that they are based on faith, are part of a worldview and are not held by everyone. Therefore, in arguing in favor of euthanasia, pro-euthanasia groups are trying to force their religious (and ethical) views on those who hold other worldviews (and who are opposed to euthanasia). This is yet another attempt to win the argument by appealing to form or structure, and thereby avoiding the debate about content. The rhetorical force of this move, given that it has a lot of respect historically in America (even though it is deeply flawed), is obvious—it is clearly a great advantage if one has an effective strategy to win a public debate on an important ethical issue by appealing to some flaw in the overall *form* of your opponent's worldview, without having to engage the actual substantive questions on the basis of *content*.

Second, the religious argument against euthanasia is an argument that appeals to lower-order (rational) beliefs, and so it is a legitimate argument to introduce into the public square. This argument could take several forms. For example, an anti-euthanasia argument might take this form: human life is of supreme, fundamental value because it is created by God; any action that compromises this value is morally wrong; euthanasia is such an action; and it is therefore morally wrong. One will note that no appeal is made to higher-order beliefs in this argument. The argument makes no appeal to traditional religious traditions, doctrines or texts, to *justify* its main theses. Its main premises will be justified by rational argument. In addition, the view that human life is supremely valuable because it is created by God is not a controversial claim; it has been held throughout history by people of many different cultures and political backgrounds. In any case, any dispute about whether it is a reasonable argument or not will also have to be played out in the public square.

The arguments of this section apply, *mutatis mutandis,* to the issues of abortion, gay marriage and other similar matters.

Moral Relativism in American Culture

One of the issues that has been lurking in the background—and that often lurks in the background in any contemporary discussion concerning democratic pluralism and matters of religion and politics and related moral disputes—is the theory of *moral relativism*. Moral relativism is the view that moral values are not absolute in themselves but are relative to some other guide or standard, such as one's individual preferences or one's culture. One seldom hears a debate today on any of the questions of this book without hearing some appeal to the view that moral values are all really relative anyway, and that one should not impose one's morality on others. We need to consider the significance of this approach for the topic of religion and politics before bringing our arguments to a close.

One effect of the widespread relativism in American life is to promote pluralism; at the same time relativism is reinforced by pluralism. Relativism encourages the view not only that each person is entitled to hold his or her own worldview, but that each worldview is legitimate in itself, and that there are considerable problems about criticizing the worldview of another. On the other hand, the presence of a number of different worldviews in a society gives credence to the idea that each worldview has a certain legitimacy to it and has just as much right to contribute to society as any other view. So relativism is both a cause of pluralism and a consequence of it.

A climate of relativism has great cultural significance, however, because relativistic claims play an important role in the way that the secularist, in particular, argues his position, and in his general attempt to denigrate religious belief. I am not saying that secularism is necessarily relativistic; nevertheless it often is relativistic. It is fair to say that it is closer to relativism than is the traditional religious worldview. As we saw in earlier chapters, the secularist often approaches many of the topics in dispute in U.S. society mainly from a relativistic perspective, while proponents of the religious worldview approach them from a more objective moral perspective. Most important, secularists often appeal in U.S. society to what I like to call "the rhetoric of relativism." This rhetoric is used in an attempt to keep traditional religious beliefs and values out of public arguments and debates, while at the same time avoiding a substantive debate about these beliefs and values.

In these last sections of the book, I would like to analyze and illustrate this phenomenon in detail because I think it plays a central role in the general debate between religion and secularism in modern liberal democracies, a role that is not fully appreciated by either worldview. A discussion of this issue will make the whole matter of the debate between worldviews in a pluralist, democratic society much easier to navigate, I believe, and give us a kind of practical guide in how to handle complex, confusing debating strategies concerning issues relating to religion, morality and politics, especially in U.S. society.

As we saw earlier, relativism is the view that moral values are not absolute in themselves, but are relative either to the society or to the individual. The first type of relativism is called cultural relativism, and the second type is called extreme relativism (or subjectivism). Extreme relativism, which is more common in U.S. society than cultural relativism, is the view that the individual chooses his or her own moral values, that nobody else can say one is wrong, nobody can impose one's moral values on another. So one cannot consistently criticize the moral values of other people, nor can they criticize yours. So A might hold that if he thinks extramarital sex is moral, then it is moral for him, and if B thinks it is immoral, then it is immoral for B. But B cannot impose his moral views on A, because everyone has the right to choose their own moral values. Nor can A criticize the moral views of B. This kind of approach is obviously very common today. Before we look more closely at moral relativism, and its problems, it is worth briefly contrasting moral relativism with its counterpart—moral objectivism.

Moral objectivism is the thesis that moral values are objectively true and absolute and apply always and everywhere, whether people accept the values or not. The moral objectivist might hold, for example, that kindness is an objective moral value and that everyone therefore morally ought to be kind, whether they agree or not (though people might still disagree on which actions exemplified kindness in particular cases). The objectivist also might hold that slavery is immoral and that it should be illegal everywhere whether people agree with this or not. In answer to the question, to whom do moral values *apply?* the objectivist answers *everyone* (not just to me or to my culture). Moral relativism and moral objectivism are theories about the *applicability* of moral values, not, as some mistakenly believe, theories about which values are moral.

Although moral objectivists hold that moral values are absolute, they do allow for exceptions. But the exceptions are also absolute in the sense that they apply to everyone in the exceptional circumstances. For instance, an objectivist might hold that in normal circumstances it is always wrong to steal. Yet she might allow that in unusual circumstances, such as when a person's family is genuinely starving, it is morally okay to steal. But she would hold that it is always okay to steal in this unusual circumstance. So she does allow for an exception, but the exception also applies objectively. In this way, moral objectivism is not rigid and can allow for legitimate exceptions.

Finally, objectivists do not always agree with each other about what the correct moral values are. For example, on the issues of capital punishment and abortion, both those for and against these practices are objectivists but disagree with each other about the correct moral position to take on these matters. In addition, on both of the topics mentioned the objectivists on both sides feel so strongly about the morality of their position that not only are they *advocating* their view, but they are also trying to get their view *enshrined in law,* so that everyone in the country will have to follow it. All sides have formed advocacy groups to try to bring about this goal. This is the strongest way one can promote one's view in a democracy—by trying to get it adopted as the law of the land.

The Problems with Relativism

Moral relativism is an impossible thesis to actually live by. It is not an accident that one will search in vain for a genuine relativist—someone who really believes that all moral values are relative and who *lives* accordingly. The problems facing relativism broadly fall into two categories, logical and practical. Let us first look at the logical problems.

Relativism often falls into a logical contradiction immediately. This is because the relativist is usually quick to criticize objectivists and to accuse them of wanting to impose their moral values on everyone else. For example, a relativist might argue that those who are against abortion are trying to impose their moral values on the rest of society. However, what the relativist is usually saying here is that it is wrong to impose your values on everyone else because there are no objective moral values. This position, however, involves a contradiction, because the word *wrong* in the statement means *morally* wrong! So what they are actually saying is that it is objectively morally wrong to impose one's values on others because there are no objective moral values. Stated this way their position is obviously contradictory because they are saying on the one hand that there are no objective moral values, but on the other hand they are making an objective moral judgment. This contradiction is at the heart of moral relativism today. It most often comes out in the relativist's recommendation of tolerance toward others, or to put it in the negative, in their moral criticism of others for being intolerant. Again, for relativists to criticize others in this way is to make an objective moral judgment, and so contradict themselves. I like to call this problem the "sin" of relativism: one commits this sin if one claims that there are no objective moral values and then goes on to make objective moral claims oneself. So a relativist today who is full of moral indignation at some particular grievance is being inconsistent in the crassest way possible.

A more practical problem with relativism is that it is simply impossible to live without making objective moral judgments. If one were a true relativist, one could not criticize a car thief when he robs your car, could not criticize the bank for overcharging you, could not condemn racism, could not condemn murder. A genuine relativist would have to respond in the case of, say, being discriminated against on the basis of race, that the racist is just practicing his own values and that, while he (the relativist) disapproves of them, they are not *morally* wrong! For nobody can impose his or her values on another, and so the racist is right to practice whatever values he chooses to practice. It is no wonder that there are few genuine relativists around.

Another obvious problem for relativism is that there can be no moral progress on this view of ethics; all that can happen is that cultures and individuals can *change* their beliefs for various reasons from time to time. So if a culture changes its position from the practice of slavery to the abolition of slavery this is not because they came to recognize that slavery was immoral —for that would be to make the objective judgment that slavery is immoral. Moral reformers are similarly anathema to relativism; people like Socrates, Jesus, Gandhi, Sojourner Truth, Martin Luther King and Mother Teresa are misguided because they made the mistake of thinking that there are objective moral values that can be known and of trying to impose specific objective values on societies that had not been practicing them up to now.

If relativism has so many problems, why are so many people attracted to it? People may be attracted to the language of relativism simply because it sounds better than the language of objectivism. It sounds more tolerant, open-minded and, above all, nonjudgmental. A high premium is put on sounding this way today. Even people who know they are making objective judgments and who agree that such judgments are totally appropriate will sometimes attempt to dress these judgments in relativistic-sounding language or at least to move the language in which their judgment is expressed as close as possible to that normally used by a moral relativist.[11] Second, people are attracted to relativism because it allows them to avoid responsibility for their moral judgments; they can hide behind the language of relativism. This is all the easier to do if it is a commonly accepted strategy in society, which it is in ours. People may hide behind the language of relativism because it is easier for most people to tell themselves that values are really relative, and that *this* is why they are changing their moral position, than it is to tell themselves they are being immoral. It is easier to say, for instance, that no one can impose their views about extramarital sex on others than to argue that extramarital sex is moral. Third, an extension of the previous point is that relativism allows people to avoid moral conflict, at least in a general sense; it fosters the illusion that we can agree to disagree and that *we are all correct.* Fourth, people are often seduced by relativism because they are not confident of their own views on moral questions, and the rhetoric of relativism gives them a way of believing what they like, even if many others, whom they respect, do not agree with them. It can be unsettling for one's moral beliefs to be challenged, and relativism can be a way of dealing with or avoiding this. Extending this a little further, people may be drawn to relativism because they are simply confused about their moral values or about the justification of morality in general. This is surely why large numbers of people are drawn to it in our society (and so they unintentionally, rather than intentionally, fall into the serious logical and practical problems facing relativism).

There are two valuable points to be learned from moral relativism, even if we do not adopt the thesis.[12] One is that moral relativism teaches us to be careful about claiming that all of our cultural practices are absolute (consider eating or burial practices), and we have much to learn from other cultures.

---

[11]Here is a good example of this from a statement by the United Church of Christ supporting the legalization of euthanasia: "The church affirms individual freedom and responsibility. It doesn't claim that euthanasia is the Christian position, but the right to choose is a legitimate Christian decision. Government shouldn't close options that belong to individuals and families." As quoted in *The Oregonian*, October 16, 1997; also view at <www.deathwithdignity.org/historyfacts/religion.asp>.

[12]I owe these points to James Rachels, *The Elements of Moral Philosophy* (New York: Random House, 1986), pp. 22-24.

Moral relativism also teaches us to have an open mind when engaging in moral debates; this is a productive way to approach moral debates. Ironically, moral relativism teaches us these points while we come to see at the same time we should not become moral relativists! This is akin to the way in which many people who are not pacifists welcome the presence of that position in the debate during times of war because it cautions those who support war not to be too hasty or aggressive. In short, its opponents recognize that it can teach an important lesson even though they believe that it is fundamentally wrong (and perhaps even immoral).

The Rhetoric of Relativism

There is a major feature of contemporary relativism at work in our society that has been very influential but has not been identified up to now or given any attention in the discussion concerning religion, morality and politics. I am talking about the distinction between relativism as a philosophical thesis about morality and the rhetoric of relativism. The rhetoric of relativism describes that position where an individual does not hold relativism as a moral theory but frequently appeals to the rhetoric (or language) of relativism. The rhetoric of relativism includes such phrases as "nobody can impose his/her values on anybody else," "who's to say what is right or wrong?" "who are you to judge others?" "I have my values and you have yours," or more generally, "your worldview is only one perspective on reality," and so on. These phrases are appealed to solely for their rhetorical power in a society that is already in large measure seduced by such language, is under the influence of such language. However, the moral theory behind the rhetoric is not actually held by those who appeal to the rhetoric of relativism. People like the *language* of relativism because it can be very influential in moral and political debates in a society in which this kind of language has significant rhetorical power.

The main reason for appealing to the rhetoric of relativism is that it is a significant aid in getting one's values accepted without having to argue about the content of those values and without having to consider seriously the views of those who disagree with one about these values. We can identify the following five steps involved in the appeal to the rhetoric of relativism as we consider a few specific examples.

Example 1. A is involved in a moral debate with B on the subject of extramarital sex. A thinks extramarital sex is moral, and B thinks it's immoral. A might proceed this way:

Step 1: A begins by sounding like he is attacking moral knowledge *in general* and advocating the view that we cannot know the truth about any moral issue, that moral values are relative, that A has his values and B has her values, and so nobody can impose his or her views on anyone else. He might put this by saying that nobody can claim to have the truth or the right answer on this matter. That is to say, A sounds just like a relativist.

Step 2: A argues (usually implicitly) that since there is no moral knowledge in general, each person is therefore free to make up his or her own mind on the question of extramarital sex, and nobody can force his or her view on anyone else. This move puts the unsuspecting objectivist B on the defensive, and she backs off in the debate. This is because she appears to want to force her view on A, but A does not want to force his view on B. So A appears to have the moral high ground.

Step 3: A then gets to *advocate* his view, usually in a subtle way, that extramarital sex is moral without having argued for it specifically and without engaging the contrary arguments of B.

Step 4: A then asserts or, more accurately, acts as if extramarital sex is *objectively moral*. And it also becomes clear from his moral discourse that he holds many other objective moral values (thereby contradicting step 1).

Step 5: B smells a rat, but is not sure how to proceed!

The effect of this powerful rhetorical strategy is that A succeeds in occupying the moral high ground, in advocating his position, although he has not actually given specific arguments in favor of it and has not debated B at all. In short, he has managed to use a general, unargued-for claim about *the relativity of moral knowledge* to define the terms of the debate. From B's point of view, she has lost the debate without having engaged the issues of the specific subject matter at all, and she is often not sure just why she lost! Let us illustrate this strategy with an even more specific example.

Example 2. Abortion discussion on Tran Radio:

Announcer: Today we are considering whether the practice of abortion is moral and whether it should be legalized in Tran. We have Smith and Jones arguing opposite sides of the issue. We begin with Smith, who supports the proposed amendment to Tran's constitution, an amendment that would legalize abortion. Smith, why do you support the amendment?

Smith: Because it is time for the state of Tran to catch up with the rest of the world. Abortion is legal in every other civilized country. Women should have the right to an abortion; it is a right women in other countries have. Why not here? The decision to have an abortion is a very private, perhaps painful one, and it should be left up to the woman and her doctor. Why should we be able to tell women what to do?

Announcer: Jones, what is wrong with that argument?

Jones: Well, abortion should not be legal because it is immoral. It is the killing of an innocent human being. Killing innocent human beings is wrong. Just because other societies engage in this practice does not mean we have to accept it. I do not believe those societies are civilized—they have a way to go yet.

Smith: My problem with that argument is that it's just your view. And this is a free country. You are entitled to your view, but why should you feel that you can impose it on others? People should be able to decide for themselves on this question. Who are you to impose your view about a very controversial issue on everyone? Nobody has the right answer on this question. If you do not like abortion, you do not have to support it. But don't deny it to others.

Jones: I believe abortion is immoral because it is the taking of an innocent human life. That is wrong, and so abortion should be illegal.

Smith: Yes, but you are trying to impose your view on abortion on all those who believe abortion should be legal; I am not trying to impose my view on you.

Jones: You are trying to impose your view on me, because you are trying to force the legalization of abortion on me, trying to shape society according to your moral views.

Smith: I am simply saying let us make abortion legal in Tran, so people can make up their own minds on whether to avail of it, support it and so on. What is wrong with that? I respect your moral views, Jones, but I do not want to be forced to follow them.

(Biased!) Announcer: Jones, are you not being dogmatic and presumptuous in forcing your views on others . . . ?

In the first example above, what is really going on is that A supports extramarital sex, thinks it's moral, but does not wish to argue this explicitly, so he appeals to an abstract statement of relativism to carry the argument for him. Of course, he is not a relativist at all, but this *device* allows him to win the debate without having to debate the actual questions. Those who use the rhetoric of relativism do not subscribe to moral relativism as a philosophical thesis about moral knowledge, but they need their opponents to believe that they are advocating moral relativism (or at least to be very confused about what is going on), otherwise their debating strategy will not work.

In the second example, A believes abortion is moral but does not want to argue for this. Or maybe he does not think it is a sufficiently immoral practice to make it illegal, but does not want to argue for this. Why? Perhaps because he is not sure that it is moral at all? But also because his rhetorical strategy will not work if he asserts it openly—he wants to make it look like he is not taking a position on abortion and that B is so that he can claim the moral high ground and win the discussion without actually debating *the specific issue* of abortion. Acknowledging that he does actually hold a position on abortion would defeat this aim. (I do not mean to say that all arguments for or against abortion are of this form, but many of them are.)

A final example. Examples of the use of this strategy abound in our contemporary culture. Here is a last example (loosely) based on a real event. A pro-abortion speaker was invited to speak on the campus of a Christian university. But the administration intervened and dis-invited her because her views were against the mission of the university. Some people criticized the administration's action, using this argument: "She should be allowed to speak because all views in the debate should be heard." Here we have a general argument for her speaking rather than an argument that her views *on this particular topic* might have some merit. This argument allows one to support her speaking, but does not require one to give any credence to her views. Now this strategy would be alright if one really believed the principle that the main views on a topic should be heard and was prepared to apply it *consistently.* However, I am assuming that if the speaker was defending a view most of the faculty disagreed with, the abolition of affirmative action, for example, this principle would *not* be used to invite such speakers (at least at many campuses). If one does not promote the principle consistently then one is more likely to be using it only *as a rhetorical device,* and that it is not one's real reason for wanting to permit the speaker to give a lecture.

Why proceed this way? First, because the principle has real rhetorical power when used on unsuspecting opponents—after all, who wants to be accused of being against free speech? But second, it also allows the opponent of the university administration's decision to support the speaker's appearance *without appearing to support her arguments*. The real reason they want to support the speaker is because they do support her specific arguments or think they have some merit, yet they do not want to come right out and say this for reasons of political expediency. The strategy outlined in this example is commonly used today at institutions of higher learning for inviting and rejecting speakers.

A few brief qualifications will help further clarify the strategy of those using the rhetoric of relativism. First, let us remember that this is a rhetorical strategy, and so it would never be laid out as clearly as I have laid it out here. The whole point of the strategy is to get one's opponent to back off without having to actually debate the issues. This is obviously a problematic approach so it is important that the person whose moral views one disagrees with does not realize what is going on, otherwise the strategy loses its rhetorical purchase value, and A (as in the above case) would lose the moral high ground. Second, this strategy only works with an unsuspecting moral objectivist (which is most of us); it will not work against anyone well versed in the logic of moral arguments. Third, I am not saying that the person using the rhetoric of relativism is necessarily being invidious here; he or she may not know the actual logical moves of the argument, may not be aware of the confusions and logical problems with the strategy, but may simply know that this kind of talk *works*. This is why relativism is usually presented in the form of a *question*—"who are you to impose your values?"—rather than as a positive thesis, "I hold that there are no objective moral values," a thesis one would then have to defend. In our culture, the *question* can be enough to put one's opponents on the defensive (test this out for yourself!). But if the "relativist" presented his position as a positive thesis and then tried to argue for it, the rhetorical value would disappear and the positive thesis would be rejected, even by the "relativist" himself.

The rhetoric of relativism is used, in short, to mask the contradictions in A's argument in his debate with B. Here is another way to illustrate his strategy. Suppose as before, (1) A claims (or more likely, suggests) that there are no objective moral values. So (2) B's claim that extramarital sex is objectively immoral is incorrect. However, (3) A also believes that racism is objectively immoral. In this case (3) contradicts (1). *This contradiction destroys A's refutation of B in (2).* However, at this point A appeals to the rhetoric of relativism *to mask the contradiction.* In a society where this rhetoric has a lot of force, this obfuscation can be very effective. Its effect is to undermine B's position—often to force B out of the discussion (or at least to cause whole groups of people in a society to not take B seriously)—without actually arguing the points at issue at all. Nowadays, we can even identify a phenomenon we might call "in your face relativism." This is where the contradictions facing relativism are acknowledged and then brushed aside as if this is all that is necessary. But the contradictions cannot be resolved, thereby relativism must be rejected.

The rhetoric of relativism is employed by many in contemporary American culture in debates concerning religion and politics. It is a device aimed at removing religious arguments from politics, just as the rhetoric of church-state separation is often used as such as device. It is a favorite device of the secularist believer who frequently accuses the religious believer of being an objectivist, of being dogmatic, exclusionary and so on. The secularist then goes on to advocate his own objectively held moral values in an attempt to establish a seculocracy.

Tolerance: Traditional and Contemporary Meanings

Before bringing our discussion to a close, let us take a brief look at the special virtue of tolerance. It is championed today in America and is often presented as the hallmark of pluralism. Tolerance is frequently urged by both secularists and liberals (and relativists) as the proper response to the religious, moral and political beliefs of others. The secularist recommends tolerance because this is the most effective, practical way of accommodating the differing worldviews in a pluralist society. If one has several different, competing worldviews, the secularist argues, then it is much more desirable that they get along with one another than that they be at each other's throats. In addition, given that the secularist usually advocates a more relativistic view in ethics and politics, he needs to call for tolerance since he is inclined toward the view that there is no absolute truth on a host of moral and political questions. A frequent criticism by the secularist of the proponents of traditional religious worldviews is that the latter are intolerant. The charge of intolerance has much force today; it would be no exaggeration to say that it is an important part of the arsenal of the rhetoric of relativism. You might get the impression from all of this that secularists and liberals are very tolerant themselves and refrain from judging people. But everyone knows that you would be wrong in this impression, for often the secularist is quite intolerant and dogmatic; not only does he judge people, but it is often a badge of honor to severely judge certain people on certain issues (this is called political correctness). Indeed, one indication that members of a worldview might be inconsistent or insincere or otherwise dissembling in an attempt to impose their own agenda is if *they urge principles on others that they do not follow themselves* (for instance, if they appeal for tolerance but are intolerant themselves). This is evidence that these proponents do not believe the principles but simply use them as handy rhetorical devices for advancing their political agenda.[13]

In order to clarify further the special virtue of tolerance, it is necessary to distinguish between two meanings of the word: the *traditional* meaning and the more *contemporary* meaning. *Tolerance* of a view (or a person) in the traditional sense means one is willing to consider the view, to discuss it, to engage in debate with its advocates, but in the end one might not accept that the view is true. But one agrees to put up with it to a greater or lesser extent depending on the issue in question (e.g., compare disagreeing with racism to disagreeing with vegetarianism). This view of tolerance is tied to the notion of truth and would make no sense without it. For only if you believe in truth, specifically that a particular view or position is true, can you be tolerant of other positions with which you disagree. It is only in this sense that tolerance can be a virtue—it is virtuous to be tolerant of something that you yourself believe to be wrong (depending on the issue and to what extent, of course). Tolerance is a virtue with a limit to it; if one goes over the limit one is in the area of approval, and if one goes too far over the limit, one can even be accused of advocating the position oneself. (Compare par-

---

[13]This may also explain why secularists generally treat smaller, more marginal religions with great respect; in fact, secularists positively encourage marginal religions as a way of undermining mainstream ones. A marginal religion is a religion with few supporters compared to the major world religions and whose beliefs and values are not major players on the cultural scene. By occasionally emphasizing the essential equality of all religions, secularists covertly strengthen the argument for separation of church and state, and they also try to weaken the influence of major religions on the culture. This move is important because the major religions represent a powerful philosophical and moral challenge to their view, while the minor religions do not. It is no accident that secularists are very "nice" to marginal religions and generally critical of and hostile to major religions. This is often because the marginal religions are not a threat to their view, and the major religions are.

ents who are very intolerant of their teenage kids' behavior, parents who are quite strict, parents who are tolerant, and parents who are excessively tolerant.) As one of my students succinctly put it in a term paper a few years ago: "If you become excessively tolerant, you slip to the point of condoning the action you intended only to tolerate."[14] The reason it is good to tolerate some matters that we believe to be wrong, especially in a pluralist society, is that moral practice rarely runs completely smoothly. Also, we can't have laws against everything. Therefore, we will all be called upon from time to time to be tolerant of some matters we believe to be wrong. The degree of tolerance we should exercise, of course, depends on the topic in question.

The more contemporary meaning of tolerance asks one to be tolerant of a view in the sense that one accepts that the view is *philosophically justified,* that the view is somehow morally correct. This is what is meant today when we are asked to be tolerant of abortion, for example. This is nothing other than a code name for moral relativism—for if one's position is pro-life then one can only be tolerant of abortion in this second sense *if one is a moral relativist!* It is not acceptable, according to advocates of the second meaning of tolerance, to be tolerant of something in the sense of just putting up with it, to a greater or lesser extent, although one disagrees with it. In our society today we are seeing a gradual shift from the traditional meaning of tolerance to the more contemporary meaning. Of course, those who advocate the second meaning of tolerance are not themselves consistent for they are not really relativists (as we have seen) and are quite intolerant of many views and of the advocates of those views.

We need to appreciate that when the secularist advocates tolerance, it is often the second form of tolerance that he has in mind. And when he accuses others—usually religious believers—of being intolerant, he means intolerant in the second sense. The reason the secularist advocates the second form of tolerance is obvious. Again, it is an attempt to get his views accepted by appealing to the rhetoric of relativism (this time in a different, yet still well-established form), but without having to actually debate the moral issues under dispute. Thus he wants to put opponents of extramarital sex on the retreat by arguing that they are intolerant in the second sense. In this way, he does not actually have to argue the merits *of the issue itself.* And he wants to avoid this argument for two important reasons: one, he knows that

---

[14]I owe this formulation to former Rockhurst student Lisa Daley.

he could very likely lose it, in the sense that most people will reject his argument. But, second, he would have to acknowledge that the argument that extramarital sex is immoral is now a *legitimate* argument in the debate and deserves a place at the table. And the very essence of his view depends on not granting this point.

The overall confusion is exacerbated in American society by the fact that the distinction between these two forms of tolerance is hardly ever clearly made, and so when the secularist appeals to the second form of tolerance, many believe he is appealing to the first form. They then almost inevitably become defensive about their views because they agree that being excessively intolerant in the first form is mostly not desirable. In fact, American society is engaged in a wholesale shift from the first meaning of tolerance to the second meaning, without an appreciation of the real moral issues at stake. The result is at least a partial diminishing of our overall respect for the virtue of tolerance. This is all the more unfortunate because tolerance is an important virtue in a pluralist society, and it is a pity to see it hijacked in a relativistic sense and insidiously pressed into the promotion of particular moral and political causes.

Finally, we must acknowledge that religious believers themselves have made mistakes in how they have responded to the challenge of relativism and secularism in American life. The first mistake, mentioned in a previous chapter, was to project the view too often that religious belief is purely a matter of faith and that it should not be judged by the standards of reason. This position came to have the unfortunate effect of contributing to the view that religion has something to hide. It also had the effect of marginalizing religion because the secularist argued that any view so marginal in terms of reason must also be marginal in terms of its political influence. As a result the public-private distinction became prevalent. This has been a dominant theme in American religions; it thus became a dominant theme in American culture and eventually began to affect how religious believers in many different democracies regarded their beliefs.

Another mistake that traditional religious believers made in the United States was to sit by passively while the secularists mounted a very public campaign to get religion out of public life, especially by using the courts. Groups like the ACLU, Americans United for the Separation of Church and State, and others, have not met with an effective response from traditional religions. Indeed, some traditional religious believers have supported these

groups over the years! The arguments of my earlier chapters are an attempt
to show why I think this support is misplaced. Traditional religious believers
have also failed in general to be as countercultural as they should be, and
this has contributed to the marginalization of religion. Religions have been
more often mirroring contemporary American culture than critiquing it.
They have especially failed to promote clear rational and moral reflection
on ethical and political questions, and to combat moral relativism. As a result, religious worldviews are now significantly infected with moral relativism themselves; indeed the rhetoric of relativism, illustrated in this chapter,
is not only widely used by secularists, but by (usually liberal) religious believers as well (also as a way of intimidating those whose moral and political
views they disagree with).

I have tried to show in this chapter how the arguments of the book help
us to take a fresh look at specific issues that are frequently the subject of
contentious debate in U.S. society. I have suggested how these matters
should be handled in a democratic society once we recognize the centrality
of the concept of a worldview for understanding modern pluralism, and also
recognize that secularism is a significant worldview in itself. An appreciation
of the implications of moral relativism as a background theme of democratic
pluralism and of the logical moves involved in the rhetoric of relativism also
helps us to avoid further spurious arguments for keeping religion out of politics in modern democracies.

Epilogue

It is obvious that the subject of religion and politics is intellectually exciting, deceptively complex, frequently contentious and simply impossible to ignore!

We have seen that in modern times we must approach pluralist debates about basic issues of beliefs and values from the point of view of our respective *worldviews,* that secularism must be regarded as a worldview in itself and that this fact changes everything in our thinking about the relationship between religion and politics. We have argued that the general worldview of religious belief is a rational worldview, something we tend to downplay or forget in the United States, and that religious belief is, in fact, a more rational worldview than that of secularism.

I have criticized all of the standard arguments for excluding religious belief from politics, including the arguments that religious beliefs are only "a matter of faith," not reason; that religious beliefs are always based on superficial appeals to texts, authorities or traditions; that religious beliefs should not be forced by law on those who do not think they are true; that religious beliefs are dangerous, but secularist beliefs are benign; that the state should be neutral between worldviews and so forth. I have argued that modern democratic politics needs religious belief, not just because this is required by a truly democratic and free society, but also because religious belief can profoundly enrich public discussion.

We have seen that in the United States we need to move beyond the constitutional question to focus on the moral question that is at the heart of a democratic society, that the constitutional question logically cannot be answered until the moral question is first addressed. Consideration of the moral question also prompts us to examine the philosophical foundations of democracy itself.

I have defended the view throughout that what I have called lower-order religious beliefs—rational religious beliefs—can be introduced into public-square debates, where they can compete along with all other worldviews in the marketplace of ideas to influence public policy on a host of important matters.

I have asked the reader to think outside the box on the issue of religion and politics. Thinking this way involves giving due weight to the fact that secularism is a legitimate worldview in itself that competes with religious belief in trying to shape modern society and culture. Once this is acknowledged, it helps us realize that *all* worldviews must be considered in their relationship to the state in a modern democracy, not just religious ones. When one appreciates this point, it follows that no good reasons can be given for excluding religious arguments from politics. This is the kernel of my position.

It may be an effort for some readers to think outside the box on religion and politics, especially in U.S. society, where we have been conditioned to see religious belief as mostly a matter of faith and to regard it as nonrational at best. We have also been conditioned to view the relationship between religious belief and politics almost entirely through the lens of the constitutional question. Indeed, we are often obsessed with what the Constitution says on this subject and how it is to be interpreted, to the neglect of other serious matters. We are hampered in the United States from seeing the moral question clearly as it applies to a democratic society by these two features of our tradition.

I am asking readers to put all of this aside and to begin in earnest to look at the moral question in its own right. My hope is that when we do this we will be unable to look at the subject of religion and politics in quite the same way again.

Select Bibliography

This brief bibliography contains many of the key works referred to throughout this book. These books are concerned either in whole or in part with religion and politics, with secularism and naturalism, or with liberalism and pluralism. This list is intended primarily as a resource for readers who wish to explore further into these topics.

Audi, Robert. *Religious Commitment and Secular Reason*. Cambridge: Cambridge University Press, 2000.

Audi, Robert, and Nicholas Wolterstorff. *Religion in the Public Square*. Lanham, Md.: Rowman & Littlefield, 1997.

Canavan, Francis, S.J. *The Pluralist Game*. Lanham, Md.: Rowman & Littlefield, 1995.

Carter, Stephen L. *God's Name in Vain*. New York: Basic Books, 2000.

Craycraft, Kenneth. *The American Myth of Religious Freedom*. Dallas: Spence Publishing, 1999.

Dawkins, Richard. *The Blind Watchmaker*. New York: Norton, 1987.

Eberle, Christopher. *Religious Conviction in Liberal Politics*. New York: Cambridge University Press, 2002.

Greenawalt, Kent. *Private Consciences and Public Reasons*. New York: Oxford University Press, 1995.

———. *Religious Convictions and Political Choice*. New York: Oxford University Press, 1988.

Hamburger, Phillip. *Separation of Church and State*. Cambridge, Mass.: Harvard University Press, 2002.

Koyzis, David T. *Political Visions and Illusions: A Survey and Christian Critique of Contemporary Ideologies*. Downers Grove, Ill.: InterVarsity Press, 2003.

Kraynak, Robert. *Christian Faith and Modern Democracy*. Notre Dame, Ind.: University of Notre Dame Press, 2001.

Kurtz, Paul. *Living Without Religion*. New York: Prometheus, 1994.

Kurtz, Paul, ed. *Humanist Manifesto 2000*. New York: Prometheus, 2000.

Marshall, Paul. *God and the Constitution*. Lanham, Md.: Rowman & Littlefield, 2002.

Murray, John Courtney, S.J. *We Hold These Truths: Catholic Reflections on the American Proposition*. New York: Sheed & Ward, 1960.

Nagel, Thomas. *Equality and Partiality*. New York: Oxford University Press, 1991.

———. *The Last Word*. New York: Oxford University Press, 1997.

Naugle, David K. *Worldview: The History of a Concept*. Grand Rapids: Eerdmans, 2002.

Neuhaus, Richard John. *The Catholic Moment: The Paradox of the Church in the Modern World*. San Francisco: Harper and Row, 1987.

———. *The Naked Public Square*. Grand Rapids: Eerdmans, 1984.

Nielsen, Kai. *Naturalism and Religion*. New York: Prometheus, 2001.

Novak, Michael. *On Two Wings: Humble Faith and Common Sense at the American Founding*. San Francisco: Encounter Books, 2002.

Perry, Michael. *Religion in Politics*. New York: Oxford University Press, 1997.

Pinker, Steven. *How the Mind Works*. New York: Norton, 1997.

Rawls, John. *Political Liberalism*. Paperback ed., with a new preface. New York: Columbia University Press, 1996.

Sagan, Carl. *Cosmos*. New York: Random House, 2002.

Sandel, Michael. *Liberalism and Its Critics*. New York: New York University Press, 1984.

Sire, James W. *Naming the Elephant: Worldview as a Concept*. Downers Grove, Ill.: InterVarsity Press, 1976.

Skillen, James. *In Pursuit of Justice: Christian-Democratic Explorations*. Lanham, Md.: Rowman & Littlefield, 2004.

Smith, Christian, ed. *The Secular Revolution*. Berkeley: University of California Press, 2003.

Solomon, Robert C. *Spirituality for the Skeptic*. New York: Oxford University Press, 2002.

Weithman, Paul J. *Religion and the Obligations of Citizenship*. New York: Cambridge University Press, 2002.

Weithman, Paul J., ed. *Religion and Contemporary Liberalism*. Notre Dame, Ind.: University of Notre Dame Press, 1997.

Index